Recognizing Biography

Recognizing Biography

WILLIAM H. EPSTEIN

upp

University of Pennsylvania Press / Philadelphia

Library of Congress Cataloguing-in-Publication Data

Epstein, William H.
   Recognizing biography.

   Bibliography: p.
   Includes index.
      1. English prose literature—History and criticism.
   2. Biography (as a literary form)   I. Title.
   PR756.B56E67   1987   820'.9492   87-19770
   ISBN 0-8122-8081-4

For my parents

Contents

Acknowledgments

Parts of Chapters 1 and 3 originally appeared in *Biography: An Interdisciplinary Quarterly,* Fall 1983, as "Recognizing the Life-Text: Towards a Poetics of Biography," copyright © 1983 by the Biographical Research Center. Parts of Chapter 2 originally appeared as "Walton's *Life of Donne* and the Generic Plot of English Biography" in *Genre,* Fall 1984, copyright © 1984 by the University of Oklahoma. I should like to thank both these institutions for permission to reprint, as well as the Master and Fellows of St. John's College, Cambridge, for permission to quote from Add. Mss. 32,514–17. I also want to acknowledge the American Council of Learned Societies and Purdue Research Foundation for providing international travel grants in support of my work, and the Purdue University Center for Humanistic Studies for a Fall 1984 fellowship releasing me from classroom obligations.

I have been working on this book a long time and have been helped by many people. For supporting this project at crucial stages of its development I wish to thank: Jacob Adler, Ralph Cohen, Leon Gottfried, Carolyn Heilbrun, Dominick La Capra, Gerald Prince, Victor Raskin, Zachary Simpson, and George Simson. For reading portions of early and later drafts of the manuscript I wish to thank: Lester Cohen, Robert Folkenflik, Lawrence Lipking, Alan McKenzie, Robert Magliola, Alan Nadel, Margaret Moan Rowe, Donald Seybold, John Shawcross, and G. Richard Thompson.

In addition, I have some special debts to acknowledge. The late James Clifford introduced me to the study of biography and offered a model of scholarly enterprise and integrity. Virgil Lokke is a treasured colleague and master teacher who has gently and patiently guided my reading and understanding of critical theory. Paul Korshin has reinforced his belief in my work with actions and has been instrumental more than once in its appearance in print. The late David Novarr was an enthusiastic and learned patron of this project with whom I enjoyed an all too brief professional association. Jerome Christensen and Clayton Lein have been true friends and important intellectual influences; tolerant of my errors, careful and probing readers of more versions of this manuscript than I had any right to ask them to read, they have traced patterns of professional practice and individual character which I struggle to emulate. My wife, Mildred, and my children, Jessica and Rebecca, have provided a stable and loving environment in which I could work; they too have lived with this project a long time, indeed, for what seems like, and in two cases is, most of their lives. Finally, I want to acknowledge the constant, unwavering love and support of my parents, Benjamin M. Epstein and Elena Freedman Epstein, who have given me so much and to whom I now return a small portion of that gift with this book's dedication.

chapter 1

INTRODUCTION:

RECOGNIZING BIOGRAPHY

"Corruption of blood: the effect of an attainder upon a person
attainted, by which his blood was held to have become
tainted or 'corrupted' by his crime, so that he and his descendants lost all rights of rank and title" (*OED*).

I

In recent years, as during other periods in the past, the complex
activity of reading and analysis associated with the cognitive experi-
encing and re-experiencing of biography (an activity which I shall call
here *biographical recognition*) has intensified its efforts to distinguish
itself from literary recognition (or, more commonly, literary response)
and historical recognition (more commonly, historical understanding).[1] Despite (or perhaps because of) the post-structuralist endeavor
to deconstruct distinctions between discursive modes, biographical
recognition, which has always struggled to establish and maintain an
independent scholarly tradition, has begun to reassert itself once
again. The appearance of the journals *Biography* and *Prose Studies* in
1978, the recurrence during the last decade of convention panels,
special journal issues, and scholarly publications devoted to biography, as well as recent mass-media observations about the current
popularity of the genre, indicate that biographical recognition is
clamoring for attention.[2] Hence the moment seems appropriate for
studies which project a terminology and a protocol for biographical
recognition, which propose, as this book does, to explore the poetics
of biography from a post-modern perspective.

Any approach to the generic study of biography should try to respect traditional associations with literary response and historical
understanding while it seeks to honor biographical recognition as
itself a powerful and meaningful activity.[3] For the avidity with which
literary, historical, and biographical recognition try to consume each
other is a sign not only of their similarity but also of their difference—

of their continuing efforts to present and represent themselves as related to yet distinguishable from each other as well as other cognitive activities. This capacity to assert, simultaneously, its similarity and difference is characteristic of every genre. How biographical recognition asserts its similarity and difference is, or ought to be, the enterprise in which a post-modern poetics of biography is engaged. Thus the term "recognition" or "recognizing," which will be used throughout this study, supports various meanings. First, recognition in its most common sense is the perceptual process of classifying within conventional categories; hence recognition is the informal authority genre assumes as it collects and separates information, as it particularizes the General by fractionalizing "Literature constituted as its own Absolute (and as the Absolute of all discourse and all writing)."[4] In this sense, recognition is an activity generated by the relationship between reading and genre. Recognition is also an enabling act accompanying the transfer of authority, an act performed, for instance, by this present study, which seeks to acknowledge and authorize certain discursive practices associated with the critical reception of English biography; hence recognition is the formal authority analysis assumes as it acts within a particular context, as it 'recognizes' its own project. In this sense, recognition is an activity generated by the relationship between analysis and genre. Recognition, furthermore, is re-cognition, a (not necessarily conscious) process which, like *déjà vu*, evokes the already seen, known, or experienced; hence recognition is ambiguously formal and informal; its authority derives from the dynamics of repetition which inform the constant shifts between reading and analysis. In this sense, recognition is an activity generated by the operation of repetition that characterizes the discourse of genre.[5]

Like the processes of recognition associated with other genres, biographical recognition can be said to traverse or emplot generic space through dynamic, cognitive activities of generic encoding and decoding that I shall call *generic frames*. An already inscribed narrative scheme that is part of a reader's intertextual and contextual knowledge, a generic frame is a familiar, embedded, and complex cognitive activity associated with and distinguished from *common frames* (a term cognitive scientists use to characterize the cognitive protocols for typical, 'everyday,' cultural activities like eating out in a restaurant or shopping at a supermarket) and from other generic frames (which characterize a reader's competence in recognizing and differentiating the 'rules' of various genres).[6] Although I shall refer to the notions of biographical recognition and generic framing often in the ensuing pages, it is important to remember that I am always doing so as if these notions and the approaches to genre study that they authorize were, as the saying goes, "under erasure." The generic frames that I describe are only momentarily and provisionally privileged in and through my practice, which itself can be situated only in the mutual displacements and inadequacies of alternative articulations. Moreover, in attempting to describe how my articulation of generic framing can guide our recognition of biography, this book will (because it cannot avoid doing so) disrupt, deform, and de-authorize the rule-governed relationships (the so-called generic conventions) by and through which the 'law' of biography is and has been understood.[7] Thus, throughout this study, we shall constantly return to the vexing problem of how the framing alters the framed—an unavoidable consequence of discursive practice that constantly re-poses the question, "Why is there genre, rather than generalized Literature?"[8]

In this book I emplot four generic frames: "recognizing the life-text," "recognizing the biographical subject," "recognizing the biographer," and "recognizing the life-course." All but one of the terms invoked here is in common usage; the other, "life-text," is a concept I have developed to explore the familiar notion of 'facthood.' The discussion of each of these frames is linked to a major work in English biography by Walton, Johnson, Boswell, and Strachey, a strategy that encourages an interweaving of the theoretical and the historical. This approach induces and is induced by the assumption that the theoretical can only be recognized in specific historical contexts and the historical can only be recognized in specific theoretical contexts. It should be pointed out, however, that the mutual relationship and reciprocal displacement of the historical and theoretical are not consistently represented throughout the book. The 'weave' becomes progressively tighter as the narrative proceeds. Thus, although the chapter on Waltonian biography develops the notion of the "life-text" in a specific interpretive context (a close reading of the *Life of Donne*), the chapter that follows formally 'theorizes' the recognition of this generic frame by invoking a more or less contemporary historical situation in which Waltonian biography is hardly mentioned. The second pair of chapters, which interlinks a reading of Johnson's *Life of Savage* with an examination of the generic frame "recognizing the biographical subject," maintains a nominal separation between historical and theoretical approaches that is more or less broken down by the stress, in both chapters, on the cultural practice of 'patronage' in eighteenth-century discourse. Such distinctions disappear altogether in the last two chapters, where historical and theoretical approaches to the generic frames "recognizing the biographer" and "recognizing the life-course" are interwoven throughout with close readings of Boswell's *Life of Johnson* and Strachey's *Eminent Victorians*.

This gradual coming together (which is also, of course, a pulling apart, in that it disrupts certain conventional expectations) of the historical and theoretical into a relationship of mutual displacement describes a kind of plot to my narrative that is, I think, instructive in several ways. For one thing, it may be said to convey the progress of my thinking and the composition of this book, elusive processes that authors often feel are obscured by formal publication. Now, I realize that I cannot recover those processes either fully or partially, that their 'existence' is itself problematical, that such inarticulate practices are inadequately expressed by formal retrospective articulations. Yet, in a sense, we are always in this marginal situation, no matter where we are in our narratives, and thus this desire to 'center' myself in my own nostalgia is as likely (or unlikely) to clarify, rationalize, or justify my work as any other statement I make in this book. Moreover, this plot is, in traditional terms, dynamic and developmental, 'maturing' as it 'ages.' Hence, I could assert, my narrative traces a mode of emplotment that, though not exclusive to biographical recognition, is often associated with it. In this respect my book can be said to reproduce (to a limited extent) the form, if not the poetics, of its subject, an imitative gesture that we know is a traditional and familiar way of (more or less self-consciously) authorizing critical projects.

Although my narrative plays across an historical field—English biography from Walton to Strachey—it should not be construed as an attempt to write *the* or *a* history of that field. I do not believe the former is possible; my focus is too narrow to accomplish the latter. Rather, I have chosen certain works by four generally acknowledged major figures (as well as some contemporaneous texts about biography) in an effort to situate my post-modern poetics in specific historical and interpretive contexts. I have chosen this field and these works both because I am familiar with them and because (unlike, for instance, the same period in American biography) they have generally been thought to form a rather coherent body of widely read and mutually influential work. Johnson and Boswell read Walton and quite consciously borrowed from him; Boswell invoked Johnson's authority for his own biographical projects; Strachey was an ardent admirer of Johnson and Boswell and consistently reworked Waltonian themes and language. These are the four English biographers whom *everyone* seems to have read; if there is a 'great tradition' or 'patriarchal mainstream' of English biography, it flows through these writers. Although (as I shall suggest in the last chapter) it may be just as instructive, if not more so, to explore other channels, especially those which seem to resist or to have been systematically 'curved' away from this well-known line of authority, I have decided that this initial, exploratory venture into biographical recognition would probably benefit more by dealing with easily recognizable texts that are already enshrined in cultural discourse.

By suggesting some ways in which biographical recognition might be said to have participated in English cultural discourse, I have tried to show how generic framing can be allied with or opposed to certain national, social, economic, literary, and other projects. But, despite my occasional lapses in rhetoric (which I attribute to the deeply engrained, unavoidable critical practice of 'making claims'), I am willing to grant only a temporary and provisional privilege to the readings and relationships that this book articulates. The various generic plots I describe are neither inevitable nor irreplaceable. For instance, I just as well could have situated "recognizing the biographer" and its dominant economic metaphor of establishing credit in the context of Waltonian rather than Boswellian biography. Walton, after all, was an active and successful merchant-adventurer who lived for much of his life in a trading world dependent on credit, and who, as he wrote and rewrote his *Lives*, often invoked its mercantile language to express an increasing awareness of how the biographer can be recognized. Of course, the credit economy Walton inhabited cannot be as readily situated in the emergent industrial capitalism that, I claim, enveloped Boswell's late-eighteenth-century lifewriting. Thus the operations of economic exchange in which, I argue, the Boswellian biographer participates would have to be reformulated for the Waltonian biographer. Similarly, I could have stressed how, in Roger North's pioneering early-eighteenth-century study of "the history of private lives," the biographer was already being recognized in terms of the "kind of authority or warrant a life-writer may hope for to credit his history of the life and behaviour of any private person."[9] Indeed, a comparison of North's manuscripts reveals that "credit" replaces the word "justify" in an earlier version of this passage. Such a substitution conventionally suggests a more or less 'conscious' manipulation of language that, it could be claimed, makes North more of a transition figure in this respect than Boswell, who is inclined to take this metaphor for granted. Thus the privilege I temporarily grant Boswell and his 'new species of biography' would be revoked by an approach that situates the plot of the generic frame "recognizing the biographer" in early- rather than late-eighteenth-century cultural discourse.

The point here is that the generic plots I describe should be seen not only as situated in particular literary, social, economic, and cultural circumstances but also as discursive practices that are always already occurring in biographical recognition and thus have neither an origin nor a singular locus nor a necessary teleology. To "recognize the biographer" through a reading of Waltonian biography or North's *General Preface* would be to re-emplot not only this generic frame but, because my approach is more or less chronological and incremental, all the other frames as well. This 'instability' does not bother me; indeed, I prefer to think of biographical recognition as a perpetually 'open' discourse in which the language of inquiry is constantly shifting and the generic frames that I have emplotted are being constantly called into question. In any event, this is what is always happening in critical discourse; I could not 'close' this discussion even if I wanted to do so (the absence of a formal conclusion to this book is one way of trying to frustrate this desire). Biography (as we shall see below) has never really had a generally accepted terminology and protocol, a poetics that could be upheld and resisted. Thus I have had to adopt a kind of 'push-me/pull-you' strategy: simultaneously opening and closing, embedding and displacing, privileging and de-authorizing, forming and deforming, upholding and resisting. In a sense, that is what we are always doing in critical study, but perhaps we can say that the effort to construe a post-modern poetics of biographical recognition forces us to deploy these tactics over a terrain that has been reconnoitered somewhat less often and even more uncertainly.

II

In preparation for *From Puzzles to Portraits: problems of a literary biographer* (1970) James L. Clifford interviewed a number of distinguished

British biographers in order "to find out how aware they were of what they were doing." He discovered that "they recognized no general rules and thought very little about critical theories." His experience led him to conclude tentatively: "As one friend later remarked to me, apparently life-writing is the last major discipline uncorrupted by criticism." Of course, Clifford knew that biography had already been corrupted: in 1962 he had edited an anthology of four hundred years of selected, general criticism on biography and (as he reports in the ensuing paragraphs of *From Puzzles to Portraits*) he was later to interview "some practicing biographers who had thought deeply about these problems."[10] Furthermore, as David Novarr's recently published *The Lines of Life: theories of biography, 1880–1970* reveals, the year 1970 marked the end of nearly a century of rather vigorous activity in the study of biography in both England and America.[11] Nevertheless, the feeling persists that, as Clifford wrote that sentence, the notion of biography as a more or less 'uncorrupted' genre of reading and writing was strongly embedded in cultural discourse. Indeed, we might claim that one of the most powerful conventions of writing about biography has been the 'resistance to criticism,' an interpretive practice often expressed as a desire to oppose corruption, to maintain the 'purity' of the genre. Although it is obvious by now that this book seeks to resist that resistance, to spoil, infect, adulterate, pervert, debase, defile, bribe, and dissolve the composition, purity, integrity, fidelity, law, text, and language of biography, we might pause briefly to consider why the trope of 'corrupting purity' is so prevalent in this critical discourse, before we go on to review the scholarship with which the recognition of this genre is already tainted.

As we shall see in Chapter 5 ("Recognizing the Biographical Subject"), the notion of an 'untainted' or 'pure' biography free of infection or corruption is a familiar one in the criticism of English biography. From Roger North's *General Preface* (c. 1718–22), the most extensive English commentary on biography before Johnson and Boswell, through the work of such nineteenth- and twentieth-century observers as George Saintsbury, Edmund Gosse, Waldo Dunn, J. I. M. Stewart, and, most prominently, Harold Nicolson, this trope has played a significant role in biographical recognition. North, for instance, writes of the need for the biographer "to be of good fame, and, as to truth and honesty, untainted."[12] Saintsbury differentiates "biography pure and simple" from "applied" or "mixed" biography as a consequence of the kinds of source materials employed. Gosse posits biography "in its pure sense" so that he can (in Novarr's words) "delimit a particular biographic domain which has not been invaded by other disciplines." Dunn tends to see "pure" biography as verging toward the autobiographical; Stewart contends that the use of biography as "a vehicle for self-expression" introduces "impurity."[13] Nicolson's notion of "'pure' biography" ("written with no other purpose than that of conveying to the reader an authentic portrait of the individual whose life is being narrated") has been cited frequently over the last half century. "'Impure' biography," Nicolson warns, harbors the "'extraneous purposes' by which the purity of biography is infected"; 'pure biography,' on the other hand, is a sanitized organism threatened but never nourished by "the pests and parasites that gnaw the leaves of purity."[14]

All these critics entertain a utopian vision of biography as untainted and uninfected, a 'natural' locus of purity within and yet isolated from cultural practice. As I shall discuss in Chapter 3 ("Recognizing the Life-Text"), such a relatively naive collaboration with the 'natural' is characteristic of biographical recognition, which, in this respect at least, represents itself as one of the last strongholds of empirical knowledge. Traditionally, the desire to remain uncorrupted by criticism has been allied with what has been seen as a 'natural' tendency of the genre itself: the promotion of an ongoing sanitation project designed to cleanse and disinfect the organism. Unless criticism can avoid the charge of parasitism (with which, in English cultural discourse, it has usually been associated), it can play no significant role in this project, for, in this view, to criticize *is* to corrupt. As we know, this is a conventional indictment in Western culture, with which all modes of critical discourse stand accused and for which perhaps there is no defense but to plead guilty and serve one's sentence in the prisonhouse of language. By violating this 'law,' the critic of biography, we might say, comes under the jurisdiction of an ancient English legal principle especially appropriate to an activity of generic recognition committed to genealogical continuity—the 'corruption of blood,' "by which [a person's] blood was held to have become tainted or 'corrupted' by his crime, so that he and his descendants lost all rights of rank and title" (*OED*). In this respect, every act of biographical criticism is a crime against generic recognition, a 'corruption' that, in turn, disinherits the 'bloodline' of every subsequent act. No wonder it seems as if the genealogy of biographical recognition has to be recharted every generation.

Corrupted and corrupting, the study of biography continues to seek recognition. In briefly surveying work over the past fifteen years or so (and occasionally relating it to earlier efforts), I will not attempt to be comprehensive. Rather, by naming and instancing various approaches and texts, I merely want to trace some of the more prominent, resurgent branches in this dispossessed family of scholarship to which I am claiming affinity. I have already mentioned the journals *Biography* and *Prose Studies,* which for the first time are providing regularly recurring venues for scholarly publication in this field; to these might be added the somewhat recently established annual panels on biography, autobiography, and non-fictional prose at the meetings of such learned societies as the Modern Language Association and the American Society for Eighteenth-century Studies. Occurring more sporadically, but with increasing frequency over the last decade, are special journal issues devoted to biography and autobiography, such as those in *Sewanee Review* (1977), *Georgia Review* (1981), and *Yale Review* (1983–84),[15] and occasional conferences focusing on life-writing, such as those at the National Portrait Gallery (Smithsonian Institution), the University of Hawaii, and Texas A & M University in the late seventies and early eighties. All these conferences resulted in anthologies of articles on specific biographical texts and themes (edited by Marc Pachter [1979], Anthony M. Friedson [1981], and James F. Veninga [1983]), a mode of publication becoming increasingly more common in the last decade and not limited to conference proceedings (for example, anthologies edited by Daniel Aaron [1978], Daniel Bertaux [1981], and Jeffrey Meyers [1985]).[16]

Single-author books elaborating general approaches to biography have also appeared: recent works by Ira Bruce Nadel (1984) and Leon Edel (1984), both of which consider the possibility of a 'poetics of biography,' follow upon less specifically theoretical introductions by Robert Gittings (1978) and Alan Shelston (1977) as well as upon oft-cited earlier studies by Paul Murray Kendall (1965) and John Garraty (1957).[17] Literary biography (that is, biographies of literary figures), with which this book is primarily concerned, has always been the biographical subgenre which has received the most attention and through which general approaches to biography have most often been directed. Books on this topic by Leon Edel (1957), Richard Altick

(1965), and James L. Clifford (1970) continue to influence more recent specialists such as Dennis Petrie (1981), Peter Nagourney (1978), and Katherine Frank (1980).[18] Other traditional modes, such as classical Greek and Roman biography and classical and medieval panegyric biography, have been the subjects of learned monographs by Arnaldo Momigliano (1971), Patricia Cox (1983), and Michael Rewa (1983).[19] Histories of English biography organized in terms of periods, modes, authors, and cultural contexts have appeared occasionally in recent years: to the pioneering books by Donald Stauffer (now about fifty years old) on English biography before 1800 we can add A. O. J. Cockshut (1974) on Victorian biography, Francis R. Hart (1971) on Lockhart and Romantic biography, and Judith H. Anderson (1984) on biographical truth in Tudor-Stuart writing.[20] Of course, there have also been many studies of the work of individual biographers; I cite them throughout this book. We might also mention two biographical subgenres, psycho-biography and feminist or women's biography, in which there has been a great deal of recent scholarly activity; essays, review articles, and edited collections—too numerous to mention or epitomize here—appear constantly, suggesting that these more or less 'modern' modes continue to attract attention and to occupy important sites in the discourse of biographical recognition.

To this family tree should be added two works I mentioned previously: the anthology edited by Clifford (1962), which made available for the first time a selection of criticism over a four-hundred-year period, and Novarr's *Lines of Life* (1986), which summarizes nearly a century of English and American theorizing about biography. Both these books, as well as Donald Winslow's glossary of life-writing terms (1980),[21] bring together the kinds of materials through which a genealogy of biographical recognition can begin to be traced. Finally, there are a number of recent experimental biographies and fictional works which have adumbrated approaches to lifewriting and, in some cases, influenced critics. From a very long list one might mention Norman Mailer's *Marilyn* (1973) and *The Executioner's Song* (1979), Vladimir Nabokov's *The Real Life of Sebastian Knight* (1941—but most influential after its 1959 reprinting), Bernard Malamud's *Dubin's Lives* (1979), Julian Barnes' *Flaubert's Parrot* (1985), Richard Holmes' *Footsteps: adventures of a romantic biographer* (1985), and Steven Millhauser's *Edwin Mullhouse: the life and death of an American writer*

1943–1954 (1972),[22] as well as two older works at which I glance in the last chapter, Virginia Woolf's *Orlando* (1928) and A. J. A. Symons' *The Quest for Corvo* (1934).

This book also claims kinship with work in various critical discourses, such as literary theory (particularly genre theory, to which my project aspires to make a contribution), the philosophy of history, and the philosophy of science, as well as diverse studies in social and economic history, cognitive science, political science, and human sexuality. These relationships are cited in context throughout the ensuing narrative, although I should mention specifically here the 'corruption of blood' visited upon me by my affinity for the work of Jacques Derrida and Michel Foucault, with whom I have allied myself in nearly every chapter. The possibility that I have negotiated an 'unholy alliance,' both between these two major twentieth-century theorists and between structuralist or post-structuralist perspectives and biographical recognition, is raised, if not tested, throughout this book. Indeed, the notion of a 'post-modern poetics' of biographical recognition is itself problematical, a slippery concept which, to paraphrase Pierre Bourdieu (another contemporary theorist with whom I seek consanguinity), can only be *mis*recognized as a representational formalism displacing and inadequately articulating a discursive practice which is always changing. I discuss (mis)recognition further in Chapter 5 ("Recognizing the Biographical Subject"), where it is related specifically to generic framing as a form of 'truthful lie,' and in Chapter 7 ("Recognizing the Life-Course: Strachey's *Eminent Victorians*"), where it is associated with Einsteinian relativity and the trajectories of human bodies in cultural space-time.

At one time I planned to write this introduction as a biography (or, more appropriately, a mock-biography) delineating the 'life-course' of this project. I am still not sure why I abandoned this approach. The 'life-text' over which I would have ranged contains a familiar enough matrix of 'facts' through which, as 'biographer' and critical theorist, I could have earned credit with my readership for having established a sympathetic relationship with my '(biographical) subject.' For instance, I could have written how I studied under an important figure in the field, published a biography of an eighteenth-century British author, became interested in the theory and practice of the genre in which I was writing, investigated what had been done in genre theory and the critical study of biography, discerned an opportunity to make a contribution to scholarship, tested the waters in conference papers and journal articles, received encouragement from other specialists and readers, and, finally, after years of reading and writing and making mistakes, produced this book. Yet this little narrative, which also traces an all-too-common path through the contemporary American academic career, is, as we know, insufficient. It lacks anecdotal and other materials relating this project to the families of my birth and marriage, to my early schooling, sibling relationships, and adolescent fears and loves, to the 'passages' and 'crises' of my adulthood, to the institutional, social, economic, cultural, and other contexts in which I have been and am situated, to the belief structures which I have been inhabiting, to all those ways (infinitely regressing and expanding) by which biography and I are mutually misrecognized. Perhaps I abandoned this introductory approach because, like Tristram Shandy, I realized I could never catch up to myself. Yet Tristram revelled in that prospect and biographers are forever ignoring its implications. I suspect I would have been pleased to have done both. So why did I elude biography just when I should have been embracing it? Perhaps because I could not do otherwise, because, like everyone else, I am always misrecognizing my relationship with biography. In any event, 'how I came to write this book' is not apparently a story about biographical recognition that I wish to tell. If, as some contemporary theorists argue, knowledge comes to us already inscribed in narrative, then perhaps all we can do is tell or retell stories. The story I prefer is one in which the 'biography' of this book is recognized through the stories of generic framing emplotted in the ensuing chapters. Thus (less to my surprise than I might have thought) I discover that I too harbor a desire for a mode of 'pure biography' untainted by the possibility that the story I am telling is a vehicle of self-expression. It is, of course—but I act as if it were not. Perhaps, after all, I want to claim my inheritance and leave the bloodline of biographical recognition uncorrupted.

chapter 2

ALTERING THE LIFE-TEXT: WALTON'S *LIFE OF DONNE*

> "Being speechless, and seeing heaven by that illumination
> by which he saw it; . . . he closed his own eyes; and then
> disposed his hands and body into such a posture as re-
> quired not the least alteration by those that came to
> shroud him." (Walton's *Life of Donne*)

I

In a letter crucially situated in the narrative of Izaak Walton's *Life of Donne* (generally considered the first, influential English biography of a literary figure that is itself of literary merit)[1] the biographer induces his biographical subject to "bemoan himself": *"and yet, I would fain be or do something; . . . for, to chuse is to do; but, to be no part of any body, is as to be nothing."* [2] *"Any body,"* of course, is a characteristically complex Donnean pun suggesting his estrangement not only from himself and his family but also from what, later in this letter, he terms, variously, *"business," "occupation,"* and *"service"* (37). The letter is crucially situated for two reasons. First, it follows directly upon and delineates the consequences of Donne's early, unfulfilled efforts to be a *"part of any body"*—efforts marked by university and private study in various fields but an unwillingness to take a degree, accept a benefice, or set up in a profession, and by an interrupted and opposed courtship and marriage, which, for a time, separate him from family and friends and, despite a later reconciliation, displace him from government service. Second, the letter immediately precedes the series of events by which eventually Donne will become (as the letter laments he may never be) *"incorporated into a part of the world"* (37). The word "incorporated" (from *incorporare,* to embody) re-inscribes the key term "body," and, in its various senses, suggests that the range of Donne's estrangement includes a failure 'to combine into a uniform substance, to form an integral whole, to be admitted or received into a corporation or body politic, to be given or assume bodily shape, and to form an intimate union' (*OED*). Yet, as we shall see, Walton's narrative seeks to incorporate Donne in all these senses, indeed, to develop a language of incorporation which 'employs,' 'converts,' and 'monumentalizes' Donne through an intimate union—through a 'sympathy of souls' embodied in Donne's poetry, sermons, and letters, and then 'reanimated' in Walton's narrative.

As I have indicated, this incorporation or embodiment begins just after the crucially situated letter in which Donne bemoans he is "*no part of any body.*"[3] For the narrative then goes on to describe how Donne at last finds a patron (Sir Robert Drury), with whom he lives and with whom, despite his wife's pregnancy, Donne travels to France on a diplomatic mission. In Paris Donne has a "Vision" which, accurately as it turns out, depicts his wife's delivery of "a dead child" (40).[4] The "Vision" leads to the narrative's discussion of similar stories of visions and miracles, all of which (like, for instance, that shared by St. Augustine and his mother) are linked implicitly or explicitly to conversion experiences and to the notion of "a *sympathy* of *souls*"(41). This discussion is followed by the first of Donne's poems to be inserted in the narrative—"A Valediction, forbidding to Mourn," which is introduced as "Verses given by Mr. *Donne* to his wife at the time that he then parted from her" (42), and which, in its "twin-compasses" image, offers metaphysical poetry's most famous depiction of the familiar notion of the sympathy of souls. This poem (which, if it is not the first poem by a biographical subject to be re-inscribed in English literary biography, is at least the first to be treated as revealing its author's life and consciousness)[5] is followed immediately by the sentence: "I return from my account of the *Vision,* to tell the Reader, that both before Mr. *Donne's* going into *France,* at his being there, and after his return many of the Nobility, and others that were powerful at Court, were watchful and solicitous to the *King* for some Secular imployment for him." But the King, "pleas'd" with Donne's "many deep discourses of general learning" and the book (*Pseudo-Martyr*) which the narrative contends grew out of their conversations, "gave a positive denial to all requests" for "some secular employment" and instead "perswaded Mr. *Donne* to enter into the Ministry" (44–45). As earlier, when he was offered a benefice by the Dean of Gloucester, Donne now tries to resist ecclesiastical preferment, pleading his "unfitness" for "that sacred calling." But, after a three-year period of study and spiritual wrestling compared to that of St. Paul, St. Augustine, Jacob, Moses, and David, he defers to God and the

King and is moved "to serve at the Altar" (46–47). The narrative continues:

> Now the *English Church* had gain'd a second St. *Austine* [*sic*], for, I think, none was so like him before his Conversion. . . . And now all his studies which had been occasionally diffused, were all concentred in Divinity. Now he had a new calling, new thoughts, and a new imployment for his wit and eloquence: . . . and all the faculties of his own soul, were ingaged in the Conversion of others. . . . and now, such a change was wrought in him, that he could say with *David*. . . . *that when he required a temporal, God gave him a spiritual blessing.* And that, *he was now gladder to be a door-keeper in the house of God, then* [*sic*] *he could be to injoy the noblest of all temporal imployments.* (47–48)

Here, then, is a significant passage in Walton's *Donne*. "*No part of any body,*" not yet "*incorporated into a part of the world,*" Donne has a "Vision" which is compared to a conversion experience governed by a "*sympathy of souls*"—a visionary, sympathetic conversion which the narrative then depicts as recorded in one of Donne's poems, and later reifies in the King's persuading Donne to reconsider his desire for secular employment and re-examine his fitness for sacred calling. By the end of this passage Donne is, figuratively if not literally, a convert, incorporated by the narrative into both the ministry of English religion and the visionary company of various biblical and religious figures who, like Donne, experienced a conversion from a life of passionate, sensuous diffusion to one of settled, spiritual service.[6] The language of this passage and of the opening section of the narrative which surrounds it is characterized by the frequent repetition of such terms (and their cognates) as employment, office, undertaking, occupation, service, calling, sympathy, affection, fitness, and conversion. This language, and the language-structures with which it is related, initiate what we shall come to call a plot of 'alteration.' We shall begin our formal description of this plot with a brief exploration of the term "employment."

Walton's biography habitually deploys various senses of this term. For instance, early in the narrative, the Lord Chancellor engages Donne "to be his Chief Secretary; supposing and intending it to be an Introduction to some more weighty Employment in the State" (27)—employment as 'an official position in public service.' After his unfortunate courtship, Donne loses his place and is described as "out of all employment that might yield a support for himself and his wife" (30–31), that is, Donne now lacks a specific 'business, occupation, trade, or profession.' When, after his "conversion," he finds "a new imployment for his wit and eloquence" (48), the term is used in the more general senses of 'the action of being at work' or 'the purpose to which a thing is devoted,' the same senses and nearly identical wording invoked by Charles Cotton in a dedicatory poem preceding the narrative (11). Later, when "by a special command from his Majesty Dr. *Donne* was appointed to assist and attend that employment [an ambassadorial mission] to the Princes of the [Germanic] Union" (53), he serves as a public official sent on 'a special errand or commission.' These are just a few of the more than twenty times the term is used in the narrative to describe events or features of Donne's life. It is also used to describe the narrative itself. For instance, in the introduction Walton explains how Sir Henry Wotton, who intended to write a life of Donne to be published with Donne's sermons, asked Walton to collect materials for this project and how "*I did most gladly undertake the employment*" (21), as if he were performing 'a special errand in the service of a private person.' Later, the Waltonian biographer announces a topic (the Dean of Gloucester's offer of a benefice) "which shall be the next employment of my Pen" (31), a use invoking divers senses of the term, of which perhaps the most interesting is employment as 'an implement.'

Similar terms, like undertaking, office, occupation, service, and calling, occur almost as often and in similar and even the same contexts ("*I did most gladly undertake the employment*" [21], "Now he had a new calling, new thoughts, and a new imployment for his wit and eloquence" [48]), and are also used to refer both to Donne's life and to Walton's narrative of it. One result of the 'entwining, enclosing, or encircling' (another sense of employment) of all these terms and their various nuances is that the biographical narrative comes to describe the 'implication or signification' (yet another connotation of the term) of its own employment: that is, in Walton's *Donne* biography itself becomes, variously and simultaneously, a special errand or commission performed in the service of the biographical subject; a trade, profession, or (semi-)official position serving the public and the individual; an implement devoted to the purpose of enclosing and signifying a life. In all these ways, Walton's narrative implies that biography is, like Donne's life, a conversion (a turning or returning) from a secular employment to a sacred calling, a conversion, moreover, undertaken through the offices of a sympathy of souls.

The introduction to the *Life of Donne* establishes this pattern through the language we have been tracing.

> *If that great Master of Language and Art, Sir* Henry Wotton, *the late Provost of Eaton* Colledge, *had liv'd to see the Publication of these Sermons* [to which Walton's *Life of Donne* was originally prefixed] *he had presented the World with the* Authors Life *exactly written; And, 'twas pity he did not; for it was a work worthy his undertaking, and he fit to undertake it: betwixt whom, and the Author, there was so mutual a knowledge, and such a friendship contracted in their Youth, as nothing but death could force a separation. And, though their bodies were divided, their affections were not: for that learned Knight's love followed his Friends fame beyond death and the forgetful grave; which he testified by intreating me, whom he acquainted with his design, to inquire of some particulars that concern'd it, not doubting but my knowledge of the Author, and love to his memory, might make my diligence useful: I did most gladly undertake the employment, and continued it with great content 'till I had made my Collection ready to be augmented and compleated by his matchless Pen: but then, Death prevented his intentions.*

Hence, the narrative continues: "*I shall now be demanded as once* Pompey's *poor bondman was,* . . . who art thou that alone hast the honour to bury the body of *Pompey* the great? *so,* who am I that do thus officiously set the Authors memory on fire? . . . *I who profess my self artless.* . . . *the poorest, the meanest of all his friends, in the midst of this officious duty*" (20–21).

This dense, carefully wrought prose presents the biographer as an artless, accidental undertaker (that is, one who assists, takes up a challenge, carries out work for another, attempts an enterprise, engages in serious study, prepares a literary work, acts as surety for another, functions as a baptismal sponsor, or arranges funerals),[7] who is forced by the untimely death of an established scholar and writer, with whom the biographical subject enjoyed an inseparable affection, to convert (the narrative's actual term in this context is "transport") an "*employment*" to collect materials into an "*officious duty*" to memorialize the biographical subject. The person who is "*fit to undertake . . . the* Authors Life" is one whose competence, worthiness, propriety, correspondence, and readiness (all various *OED* senses of "fitness") can be employed. But his own death has prevented Wotton, as

Donne's death could not, from pursuing his design. The employment becomes now a special errand, an encircling instrument occupied in the service of both Donne and Wotton, an undertaking which not only carries out Wotton's design by taking up the challenge of engaging in serious study and preparing a literary work but also acts as surety for that work by functioning (as biography usually does) as the baptismal sponsor and funeral arranger of Donne's represented life. This undertaking derives its fitness from Donne's *"glorious spirit"* (21), from Wotton's *"matchless Pen,"* and from the correspondence ("the quality of fitting *exactly"*—*OED:* "fitness"), the inseparable affection, the sympathy of souls, which, according to the introduction, characterizes Donne and Wotton's relationship.

Indeed, the wording and narrative structure of the introduction entwines and implies the wording of the later "Vision" section, in which the concept of the sympathy of souls emerges as the governing affective principle of the conversion experience. In both, a secular employment (Donne's accompanying Drury's ambassadorial mission to Paris, Walton's undertaking Wotton's biographical enterprise) is characterized by "an unwilling-willingness" (39) to perform it;[8] and, in both, the physical separation (Donne's from his wife, Wotton's from Donne, and Walton's from both Donne and Wotton) which follows upon that employment is reduced or re-encompassed by a mutual spiritual affection. This sympathy of souls which *"indure not yet / A breach, but an expansion"* (the "Valediction," as in Walton, 43) causes those who were secularly employed and physically separated to be *"transported"* (21) or "alter'd" (39–40) by a visionary, miraculous conversion. Donne is converted into a minister, a poetic divine whose "studies . . . were all concentred in Divinity," whose "earthly affections were changed into divine love," whose "wit and eloquence" found "a new calling, new thoughts, and a new imployment" (48). Walton too is converted: he becomes a biographer, a divinely inspired language-user who finds "a new imployment" for his *"artless Pencil"* (21) through his "unwilling-willingness" to turn about (*con* plus *vertere*) Donne and Wotton in the enterprise of memorializing Donne's life and work. This conversion is not merely secular, not a mere alteration in employments—but spiritual, a visionary, miraculous experience governed by the sympathy of souls.

Various seventeenth-century senses of the term imply the complex significance of both Donne's and Walton's "conversion." The narrative

depicts both of them as "turning in position, direction, and destina-
tion," as "changing in character, nature, form, or function," and as
"changing by substitution of an equivalent in purport or value"
(*OED*). Indeed, the narrative habitually implies two of the more
specialized senses of conversion. In the medieval church, the familiar connotation of "a bringing over to a special religious faith, profession, or party" signified particularly "a change from the secular to
the religious life" (*OED*). Contextualized with another specialized
sense of the term ("a translation into another language [or into a
different literary form]")—a use of this term employed, as the *OED*
notes, in Walton's *Compleat Angler*—the sense of "conversion" as a
change from the secular to the religious describes not only how the
narrative depicts Donne's redirecting of his life and language but also
how the narrative converts its own secular employment into a sacred
calling, how it translates the language and language-structures of
Donne's poetry and sermons, of medieval hagiography, and of seventeenth-century ecclesiastical biography into a somewhat different literary form that will come to exert a powerful influence on the
subsequent development of English biography.[9]

Significantly, the intimate relationship in Walton's work between
these two notions of conversion can be traced also to the last stanza of
his elegy on Donne. First printed in the 1633 edition of Donne's
Poems, this elegy has been linked to Walton's presumed editing of the
1635 edition of the *Poems;* moreover, both the elegy and the editing
have been approached as a kind of proto-biography upon which Walton drew in putting together the hastily composed "prefatory memoir" that became the 1640 first edition of the *Life of Donne.*[10] In the
1675 edition, the final one during Walton's lifetime, the elegy is the
last of the various discursive materials which surround the narrative
(the others include Walton's dedication, prefatory epistle, and introduction, as well as a poem, a letter, an epitaph, and an elegy
contributed by acquaintances of Donne and Walton). In the elegy's
concluding stanza the poet declares "*I am his Convert,*" and grieves
that, in "*this* Elegy. / *Which, as a Free-will offering, I here give* / Fame
and the World . . . / *I want abilities, fit to set forth,* / A Monument, *as
matchless as his worth*" (89). Here, in this elegiac proto-biography
which encloses the narrative by preceding it in time and following it
in space, conversion assumes the status of a spiritual and literary
transformation occasioned and authorized by the biographical sub-

ject. Furthermore, here, as in the narrative, the elegist/biographer presents himself as unfit to undertake his employment or set forth his monument, unless, as the elegy's first stanza suggests, he is inspired by *"that man where Language chose to stay / And shew her utmost power"* (87). Subordinate to his subject, who acts as his spiritual and literary inspiration, the biographer implies that the narrative's collation and translation of traditional life-writing forms derive from the sympathetic, incorporating employment he undertakes as his subject's convert. Simultaneously the biographer is undertaking another related effort to establish his credentials as an intimate friend of Donne and his circle. Through this effort, which he pursues both in the surrounding discursive materials and in the opening section of the narrative, the biographer is trying to situate his biography within an ecclesiastical hierarchy of men of letters, an intellectual enclave of devotional poets or poetic divines, who will function as verifiers of both the 'factual' integrity of the life-course presented and the spiritual and literary worthiness of the biographer who presents it.[11] Hence it is as Donne's convert and this enclave's intimate that Walton assumes the authority to establish the symbolic structure with which he incorporates the plot of his mode of secularized/spiritualized biography. This strategy serves well the two interrelated notions of conversion upon and about which Waltonian and much subsequent English biography turn. But, as we shall see, the effort, and the failure, to sustain this strategy endanger both the middle section of Walton's narrative and this emerging plot of generic recognition.

II

After Donne's conversion from secular employment to sacred calling, the narrative turns to the process and occasions by which he becomes an ordained priest and then "A Preacher in earnest" (49)—indeed, by which he becomes one of the most eloquent and effective Anglican preachers of his time.[12] As Donne approaches the altar and administers the sacrament, the ritual ceremony that reaffirms the holy covenant between man and God, so too the biographical narrative becomes an altar at which the biographer reaffirms the earthly covenant, the sympathy of souls, that links him and his biographical subject. As we have seen, this priestly reaffirmation is a sacramental rite that this narrative frequently performs. Yet in following Donne from priest to preacher, from altar to pulpit, the narrative must also make a different, if complementary, gesture. For, as Donne assumes the pulpit and (through his rapturous delivery of the pious language of a transplanted poetic wit) comes to symbolize the "excellent and powerful Preaching" of the "whole Clergy of this Nation" (54, 56), so too the biographical narrative becomes a pulpit from which the biographer preaches a sermon. The text of this sermon is the biographical subject's life, which as been 'altered' at the 'altar' (the two words share a Latin root and a variety of medieval spellings, an etymological and orthographic congruence that enriches, if not anticipates, their repeated use in Walton's and other seventeenth-century narratives) of Donne's language from a "life" (that is, an individual existence in concrete time and space) to a "text" (that is, a generically recognizable narrative of such an existence, the kind of narrative which, until the term 'biography' superseded it in the course of the eighteenth century, was conventionally designated a 'life'). This alteration is, as we know, a crucial discursive transformation in biographical recognition—a fateful shift from life to text, from the natural to the narratable, which must alter the relationship between biographer and biographical subject. As we shall see, placing this conversion at the altar is the symbolic strategy with which Waltonian biography ordains and nearly interdicts English life-writing. For it is through the altar of Donne's devotional and poetic language that Walton's narrative discovers a key which permits the life-writer to unlock the traditional, hierarchical enclave (from *clavis,* key) enclosing him, and yet which, in opening up that enclave to alien influences, endangers the previously protected discursive relationships between life and text, biographical subject and biographer.

Although this interplay of sacrament and sermon appears throughout the biography, it is most prominent and most significant in the middle section, which traces Donne's life from his ordination to his rising up out of his death-bed in order to preach *"his own Funeral Sermon"* (74). At the beginning of this section the biographical narrative can comfortably locate itself at the altar, where the ceremony of holy communion recalls and sacramentalizes the earthly covenant, the sympathy of souls, which unites the Waltonian biographer and biographical subject. But by the end of this section Donne and this narrative of his life are situated almost exclusively in the pulpit, the place in which Donne and his biographer are determined to "take my death" (74). In this shift from altar to pulpit, sacrament to sermon, the narrative confronts Donne's and its own death, and discovers a way of preserving the endangered relationship between life and text that characterizes biographical recognition.

This crucial middle section begins with Donne's moving from altar to altar and pulpit to pulpit as he and the narrative explore the spiritual topography of his new calling. At first "his modesty in this imployment" prompts Donne "to preach privately in some village, not far from *London,*" but the King sends for him and he begins "preaching the Word so, as shewed his own heart was possest with those very thoughts and joys that he laboured to distill into others: . . . and all this with a most particular grace and an inexpressible addition of comeliness" (48–49). Concerned lest those who "have not heard" Donne may conclude "that my affection to my Friend, hath transported me to an immoderate Commendation of his Preaching" (49), Walton brings various "witnesses" to testify to the spiritual power and grace of Donne's sermonizing. These witnesses include the King, who makes Donne one of his Chaplains in Ordinary, recommends him for a Cambridge D.D., and appoints him Dean of St. Paul's; the Queen of Bohemia, who "was much joyed to see him in a Canonical habit, and more glad to be an ear-witness of his excellent and powerful preaching" (54); "the grave Benchers of *Lincolns Inne,*" formerly Donne's unincorporated acquaintances, now "his beloved brethren," who see and hear "a *Saul* . . . become a *Paul,* and preach salvation" (52–53); and, from among his numerous auditors, "a Gentleman of worth . . . , a frequent hearer of his Sermons," whose elegy on Donne notes "—*Each Altar had his fire* / . . . wit, / *He did not banish, but transplanted it;* / *Taught it both time and place, and brought it home* / *To* Piety, *which it doth best become*" (49). Here, as earlier, the narrative re-presents Donne in the language of conversion: for it is not merely his eloquent delivery but also his example which impresses and moves his auditors.[13] A conspicuous sensualist has become a famous minister, and the narrative reveals, as Cotton's dedicatory poem pointedly remarks (11), not only how this conversion occurred but the impact it continued to have on Donne's auditors and admirers:

> . . . *after his youthful swing,*
> *To serve at his Gods Altar here you bring:*
> *Where, an once-wanton-Muse, doth Anthems sing.*

And, though by Gods most powerful grace alone,
His heart was setled in Religion:
Yet, 'twas by you we know how it was done.

As Cotton's verses (and their nearly obligatory pun on Donne's name) suggest, the narrative brings not only Donne but itself (and through itself, life-writing) *"to serve at his Gods Altar."* For the altar is the sacred cultural locale in which Walton's secularized/spiritualized biography of sympathetic employment will initially situate itself.

Like Donne, the Waltonian biographer discovers that his narrative, *"this well-meant sacrifice to his* [biographical subject's] *memory"* (22), is fitly employed only when it comes "to serve at the Altar" (a phrase repeated often in both the account of Donne's life and its surrounding materials), where it can receive the sacrament that ritualistically reaffirms and reconceives the sympathetic bond between biographer and biographical subject as a holy covenant. Indeed, at about this point—after it has established the general pattern of Donne's ecclesiastical career and described the death of Donne's wife, following which both the biographical subject and the narrative emerge from the dark night of the soul and make "new ingagements to God" (52)[14]—the narrative explicitly introduces the notion of a written text as an altar. Donne's recovery from "a dangerous sickness" (57) is marked by the publication of "his most excellent Book of *Devotions. . . .* a book, that may not unfitly be called a *Sacred picture of Spiritual Extasies,* occasioned and appliable to the emergencies of that sickness; which book, being a composition of *Meditations, Disquisitions and Prayers,* he writ on his sick-bed; herein imitating the Holy Patriarchs, who were wont to build their Altars in that place, where they had received their blessings" (59).[15] Here a written text emerges as an altar, as a sacramentalized locus of language which reaffirms God's Word. Here too, as it characteristically appropriates the language of its biographical subject, the narrative is converted into a "Book of *Devotions. . . .* that may not unfitly be called a *Sacred picture of Spiritual Extasies."* The author of this "Book," the biographer, builds his altar in that place (the language of spiritual ecstacy explored so profoundly in Donne's devotional writing) wherein he has received his blessing. Indeed, by this point, Donne's language and the language of this narrative of his life seem to have become almost thoroughly contextualized. Donne's 'life' and this 'text' of his life seem to be disappearing into one another. Altered by the altar of his language, Donne has been converted by his own convert into a locus of discursive activity in which biographer and biographical subject are now virtually indistinguishable.

And it is precisely at this point that the narrative skips rapidly over some nine years in Donne's life to present its biographical subject's falling into the lingering illness which leads to his death. This maneuver may seem premature (indeed, at least one-third of the narrative and many previously unmentioned details of Donne's life are still to come), but, in the sense that Walton's narrative has brought Donne to the brink of death by de-scribing and dis-embodying him in the language of his own language, this premature death in and of discourse is appropriate. The narrative, like Donne, is becoming undone.

A remarkable and witty strategy both signals the death of the narrative and tries, simultaneously, to re-embody and reanimate it, to initiate a procedure by which life converted into text can become text reconverted into life. For suddenly the narrative breaks into and away from its diachronic account of Donne's nearly exhausted life-course. In a brief, one-paragraph, first-person address to the reader (60) the biographer introduces an alternative narrative strategy—a synchronic account of Donne as devotional poet, public figure, "impartial father," "happy reconciler," and "lover of his friends" and family (68, 71). The narrative as we know it has been displaced. The counter-narrative dislodging it tries to reanimate Donne both by putting him in the context of a new rhetorical structure and by treating his final illness not as a retrospectively described incident that portends Donne's and the narrative's death but as if this and the other incidents of Donne's life were somehow being lived or relived simultaneously in and with the narrative:

> Reader, this sickness continued long, not only weakening but wearying him so much, that my desire is, he may now take some rest: and that before I speak of his death, thou wilt not think it an impertinent digression to look back with me, upon some observations of his life, which, whilst a gentle slumber gives rest to his spirits, may, I hope, not unfitly exercise thy consideration.

As Donne gently slumbers and awaits his death, so the narrative's diachronic account of Donne's life rests momentarily in its inexorable movement toward its own exhaustion. Activated now is a digressive, synchronic account that seeks to reanimate this life-converted-into-text (this 'life-text') by deferring, if not denying, the dis-embodiment or disengagement of the sympathetic bond between biographer and biographical subject. Although this effort cannot succeed (eventually the digression must give way again to the diachronic narrative), it establishes the possibility of an ongoing alteration in which the mutual displacement of alternative narrative strategies constantly reanimates the life-text. This is a discursive tactic Walton uses yet again in this narrative and repeatedly employs in his other *Lives*. He forsakes it only when he can and must supersede it: as his subject's life and his narrative of that life draw to an end, his strategy of deferral is displaced by an even more 'miraculous' tactic—a transcendent reanimation, a divine alteration beyond discourse.[16]

The story of Donne's friendship with George Herbert, the central passage of this first synchronic alteration, typifies its basic concerns and indicates that, like the diachronic account which it is momentarily dislodging, this digression re-inscribes the language of sympathetic employment. Like Donne, Herbert is a divine poet, from whose book of devotional poems, *The Temple* (1633), "the Reader may attain habits of *Peace* and *Piety,* and all the gifts of the *Holy Ghost* and *Heaven:* and may by still reading, still keep those sacred fires burning upon the Altar of so pure a heart" (64). Appropriately, this language evokes that of *The Temple,* particularly "The Altar," the well-known poem shaped like an altar, "Made of a heart, and cemented with teares."[17] Like Herbert, the narrative has made an altar of its language and its heart, an altar upon which the "great and glorious flames" sparked when the introduction "officiously set the Authors memory on fire" (21) can continue to burn as the "sacred fires" of Donne's pious language re-inscribed in the narrative. Moreover (like Donne and Wotton, Donne and his wife, and Donne and his biographer), Donne and Herbert share "a long and dear friendship, made up by such a Sympathy of inclinations, that they coveted and joyed to be in each others Company" (64). This is the kind of sympathetic relationship we have traced earlier in the narrative, an attachment founded in mutual affective and spiritual "inclinations" and "still maintained by many sacred indearments" (64), which are typified here by the reprinting of poems Donne and Herbert exchange concerning Christ's Cross as an anchor.[18] Hence the synchronic account continues to explore the spiritual langauge that embodies the diachronic account:

the Donne re-presented here is more or less the same Donne who rests near death in the sentences immediately preceding this digression. This effort to defer this death and to reanimate him through an alternative narrative strategy is *merely* strategic: the only significant change Donne can now undergo is death, which Walton will present as a permanent conversion beyond language and the temporary discursive variety it induces.

Thus, when the diachronic account resumes with the sentence "*But I return from my long digression,*" it is still confronted, as it immediately confronts Donne, with the problem of responding to a premature "'report of my death,'" a report mixed with "'an unfriendly, and God knows an ill-grounded interpretation'" that "'I was not so ill as I pretended, but withdrew my self to live at ease, discharged of preaching.'" These are charges which the narrative, like Donne, is anxious to deny (both about Donne and itself). Donne's response could also serve as the narrative's: "'It hath been my desire, and God may be pleased to grant it, that I might dye in the Pulpit; if not that, yet that I might take my death in the Pulpit, that is, dye the sooner by occasion of those labours'" (73–74). Accordingly, Donne rises from his sickbed to undertake "*his last employment,*" appearing once more at the pulpit, his "Text [so] prophetically chosen" that many of his auditors "thought . . . that Dr. Donne *had preach't his own Funeral Sermon*" (75). As Donne struggles up from his deathbed to re-establish his "*holy ambition to perform that sacred work*" of preaching at the pulpit, so the recently resumed diachronic account is now "prepared" to perform "that imployment" for which it too has "long thirsted" (74–75) and to which it is now committed—the preaching of Donne's and its own funeral sermon.

This employment, which occupies the rest of the narrative, begins with the response to the premature report of Donne's death and with Donne's rising to preach his final sermon. It continues with a statement Donne makes "the next day after his Sermon" (75), a statement which reviews the language and concerns of his (and the narrative's) past and prefigures his (and its) future: "within a few days *I also shall go hence, and be no more seen.* And my preparation for this change is become my nightly meditation upon my bed. . . . and looking back upon my life past, I now plainly see it was his hand prevented me from all temporal employment; and that it was his Will I should never settle nor thrive till I entered into the Ministry. . . . I know he looks not upon me now as I am of my self, but as I am in my Saviour . . . *I am therefore full of unexpressible joy, and shall dye in peace"* (76–77). As we have seen, this conversion "from all temporal employment" to the sacred calling of "the Ministry" emplots the language and strategy of alteration with which the narrative has tried to reanimate Donne's life-text. Now, as the narrative prepares for its 'extinction,' for the 'quenching' (*extinguere*) of its flames which will *"be no more seen,"* it prepares for the "change" which will alter life-made-text into text-made-life, for the miraculous, visionary conversion through which Donne and the narrative will be seen not "as I am of my self, but as I am in my Saviour." This is the change that will rescue from the flames both the narrative and the altered discursive relationships which it envisions for this emerging plot of generic recognition.

Significantly, this change is initiated not in the altar, the sacramental language of which is ritualistically always the same (that is, unalterable), but in the pulpit, where reading and (especially) commenting on holy text induce discursive variety. It is not as priest but as preacher that Donne displays his "most particular grace" (49), his astonishing capacity to be *"that man where Language chose to stay / And shew her utmost power"*(87). In the pulpit, as in the biographical narrative, language can convert life-made-text into text-made-life, can transform human death into biographical life and biographical death into a discursive existence continuously renewed. Hence it is in the pulpit, where holy text is altered, constantly and variously contextualized, that the narrative locates itself as it confronts its biographical subject's and its own death. In preaching its own funeral sermon, the narrative seeks and finds a way to honor the complementary functions of Donne's sacred calling and yet to convert itself and English biography once again.

III

This final change, this last conversion in and of the narrative, is brought about through a maneuver characteristic of the sacramentalizing culture in which the narrative situates its biographical subject and of the secularized/spiritualized form of life-writing with which Walton's *Life of Donne* emplots English biography. Perhaps the best way of describing this maneuver is to term it a monumentalizing—a converting of an individual existence, biographical subject, or biographical narrative into a monument. For this is indeed the activity in which the narrative is next employed, as it describes how Donne "easily yielded at this very time to have a Monument made for him," a "white Marble" likeness modeled after a drawing of Donne in his funeral shroud, an unusual pose upon which the dying subject insisted. Later, the monument was placed in St. Paul's (probably facing the altar) and to it was "affixed" a Latin epitaph which, the narrative asserts, was composed by Donne himself (78). The notion of the biographical narrative as itself a monument has already been introduced by Cotton's dedicatory poem (9):

Where one, has fortunately found a place,
More faithful to him, than his Marble was:
Which eating age, nor fire, shall e're deface.

A Monument! that, as it has, shall last
And prove a Monument to that defac't:
It self, but with the world, not to be rac'd.

Walton's *Life of Donne* emerges in Cotton's poem as a monument analogous to the marble statue at St. Paul's, but "more faithful" because, unlike that other public monument to Donne's memory (which, as Cotton's verses and a note attached to them suggest, was damaged by "the late dreadful fire" [9]),[19] this narrative will escape immolation as (to quote Walton's introduction again) it contrives to "thus officiously set the Authors memory on fire" (21).

The biographical narrative as a monument to the biographical subject's memory is a familiar image that Walton's narrative (itself enclosed by Cotton's dedicatory and Walton's elegiac invocations of this image) helped to incorporate into English biography. The various intertwined senses of the terms "monument" and "memory" suggest how appropriate the image is to biography. Besides "a structure of stone or other lasting material erected in memory of the dead, either over the grave or in some part of a sacred edifice," the term "monument" (derived from a Latin word meaning "something that remains, a memorial") also signified to the mid-seventeenth century "a sepulchre," "a written document" or "record" or a "piece of information given in writing," and "a token (of some fact)" or a "mark . . . serving to identify." Among the many senses of "memory" are the now obsolete denotations current in Walton's time, both of which are still retained in the term "memorial": "a memorial tomb, shrine, chapel, or the like; a monument"; and "a memorial writing; a historical account; a record of a person or an event; a history" (*OED*). Hence the biographical narrative as monument/memory/memorial is a written document which records, identifies, enshrines, and entombs—a textualized token of fact which functions as the sacred, monumentalized structure of perpetuated memory. This is the final employment of Walton's *Life of Donne:* the undertaking which will restore the endangered relationship between biographer and biographical subject; the undertaking which will make Donne live again as it converts life-made-text into text-made-life; the undertaking through which the narrative (like Donne's monument) will seem (the narrative is quoting Wotton) "*to breath faintly; and, Posterity shall look upon it as a kind of artificial miracle*" (83).[20]

The narrative's ultimate effort to confront its own and Donne's death by miraculously converting itself into a monumentalized memorial that reanimates its biographical subject is undertaken through the dense language of employment and conversion we have been tracing. This 'undertaking' begins, appropriately enough, at "the gates of death and the grave," as the biographer once again informs his reader that Donne will "rest," this time for a brief synchronic account of various "Pictures" of Donne "in several habits, at several ages, and in several postures" (79). The first "Picture" is of Donne as a fashionable youth, whose "Motto then was, *How much shall I be chang'd, / Before I am chang'd*," a representation which the narrative compares with "his now dying Picture" by invoking the word "change" seven times in the next paragraph. This comparison concludes with the narrative's remarking how Donne "would as often say, *His great and most blessed change was from a temporal, to a spiritual imployment*," "the beginning" of which was "his first entring into *sacred Orders;* and serving his most merciful God at his Altar" (79–80).[21] Here again, in the language of change, of the altering altar, the narrative reviews its initial conversion from temporal to spiritual employment. Then, "after the drawing this Picture," the narrative represents Donne as he "retired himself to his bed-chamber" and "lay fifteen days earnestly expecting his hourly change," that is, of course, "change" as his and the narrative's final conversion in and as death. With the pun on his name anticipated by Cotton's dedicatory poem, Donne ends his life of language ("closed many periods of his faint breath") "by saying often, *Thy Kingdom come, Thy Will be done*" (80–81). Now "speechless," he envisions heaven, "close[s] his eyes; and then dispose[s] his hands and body into such a posture as required not the least alteration by those that came to shroud him."

Hence, in an unalterable posture, ends "the Life" which the next sentence epitomizes as "Thus *variable,* thus *vertuous.*" Donne will change no more. "His speech, . . . his ready and faithful servant," has "become useless to him that now conversed with God on earth, as Angels are said to do in heaven, *only by thoughts and looks,*" but it "left him not till the last minute of his life" (81–82). Unable to converse except with God, Donne abandons or is abandoned by the language of his life; 'conversing' with God, he will be finally 'converted' (like 'alter' and 'altar,' the two words share a Latin root) beyond the language that was and is still (in this narrative) his life (or the text of his life) into "a posture as required not the least alteration." This desire to convert beyond conversing, to become "speechless, and [see] heaven by that illumination by which he saw it" (81), to be employed as the "ready and faithful servant" (a re-inscription of the introduction's "Pompey's *poor bondman*") who erects an unalterable monument that closes the many periods by which the biographer attempts to memorialize the biographical subject, is the sympathetic employment which this and, indeed, most biographical narratives undertake. Most biographies implicitly or explicitly claim that they can change life into text and then back into life again: that biography is a preserving monument which escapes the flames by which it sets the biographical subject's memory on fire; that biography is a converting vision which illuminates forever the fitness of the relationship between biographer and biographical subject; that biography is *a kind of artificial miracle* that will enable all biographical narratives to claim of the *small quantity of . . . dust* (which their monumentalized biographical subject has become) what Walton's narrative claims in its last sentence—*But I shall see it reanimated* (84).

Thus the narrative ends with "A Valediction, forbidding to Mourn," with a leave-taking, a farewell, which denies or at least challenges its own and Donne's disembodiment. In a characteristic gesture, it returns to and turns about Donne's language, particularly the language of the sermons, which, in the early editions, followed the biographical narrative.[22] For instance, Donne's final sermon (*"his own Funeral Sermon"*) contains a passage ("by *recompacting* this *dust* into the *same body,* and *reanimating* the *same body* with the *same soule*") which inscribes the relatively rare seventeenth-century word "reanimate" in a verbal and conceptual context similar to the end of Walton's narrative.[23] Hence, like the entire narrative, the final re-inscribed sentence (*"But I shall see it reanimated"*) contextualizes the sympathy of souls by employing the language of the biographical subject as the language of the biographer. Moreover, its privilege of place, its valedictory locale, implies yet another alteration entwined in its language. For its last word, *"reanimated,"* suggests that the textualizing and spiritualizing conversion we have been tracing in the narrative's language of "incorporation" has or is occurring. *Corpus* is converted or reanimated into *anima:* that is, body returns to soul, textual embodiment returns to living substance (or essence).[24] Valediction, a speaking farewell, becomes interdiction, not only in the sense of the medieval church (debarring a person from ecclesiastical functions and privileges, as the biographer has done by appropriating his subject's devotional language and spiritual duties) but also in the sense or state in which the narrative represents Donne on his deathbed—that is, an inter-diction, a speechless, blessed condition, a conversation without words, a speaking between man and God *"only by thoughts and looks"* as the soul departs the body and ascends to heaven. In this interdiction, this sacred, wordless locale between body and soul, life and text, man and God, biographical subject and biographer, Walton's *Life of Donne* ultimately situates biography.[25]

IV

As I have suggested, the *Life of Donne* delineates some of the symbolic patterns and fundamental issues that characterize English biography after Walton. For instance, its appropriation of hagiography and ecclesiastical biography emphasizes in these traditional forms of English life-writing a dynamic relationship between secular employment and sacred work that English biography probes throughout the succeeding centuries—as, for example, in Lytton Strachey's *Eminent Victorians,* which, as we shall see, ironically de-authorizes the 'ministry of work' and the 'work of ministry' with which Waltonian biography ordains the traditional English life-course. Moreover, the *Life of Donne* implies that English biography will continue to alter in and between the employment of various secular and sacred structures of authority, a prosopographical approach which describes biography as undertaken or underwritten by state, church, family, academy, and other cultural institutions. This approach is memorialized most conspicuously in such collections as Johnson's *Lives of the Poets,* the *Dictionary of National Biography,* and the many other biographical dictionaries, compilations, registers, and records frequently and continuously sponsored by these institutions. Furthermore, Walton's *Life of Donne* suggests that the narrative situation of English biography will continue to endorse a constantly shifting relationship between biographer and biographical subject, a relationship marked either by the blessed, wordless condition of valediction becoming interdiction, where the biographical subject is treated with a reverence which Boswell (describing his reading of Waltonian biography) labelled "unction," [26] or by interdiction becoming malediction, where the word as curse or slander is the instrument of damnation and, as in 'debunking' biography, suggests an alternative vision of the relationship between biographer and biographical subject. In these and many other ways that we shall note in subsequent chapters Walton's *Life of Donne* inscribes and describes English biography as it has come to be written and read over the last three hundred years. [27]

Perhaps the most significant contribution to generic recognition undertaken by Walton's *Life of Donne,* however, is its effort to present biography as altering in its employment between life and text. As we have seen, the *Life of Donne* incorporates into English biography a plot of alteration which implies that biographical narrative can summarily authorize the sympathetic, visionary conversion of life into text and then reconvert the miraculously preserved monument of that life-made-text into a reanimated text-made-life. This is a 'law' or 'principle' of alteration which, as we shall see in the next chapter, adduces the plot of the generic frame "recognizing the life-text."

Thus we shall end this chapter with a brief preview of the concerns and argument of Chapter 3, which offers a formal theoretical framework for recognizing how the familiar biographical commitment to 'facthood' emerges from varying relationships between and among the natural, the cultural, and the narratable, that is, the ways in which biographical recognition habitually oversees the conversion of life into text and text into life. This looking forward begins with a glance backward at a word to which this chapter has already devoted much attention. The Latin root of "employment" is *implicare,* to fold, which, as we shall discover in the next chapter, is a fit term to describe how biographical recognition conventionally tries to unobtrusively fold life (the 'pre-text') into text by establishing an ontological space between the natural and the narratable where the cultural 'facts' of institutional documentation are treated as remnants of the natural events of a concrete life.[28] In this ontological space of life-made-text, this cultural life-text which is both life and text simultaneously, a 'fact' becomes a remnant, a discursive trace or track of a natural occurrence in the concrete world that can be employed, implied, folded into the narrative, where it becomes an unalterable monument of and to the life of the biographical subject—a traditional strategy which, as we have seen, Waltonian biography deploys and authorizes.

What this conventional maneuver conceals is that this folding may be no more (or less) than an epistemological operation of discursive conversion, through which the activity of living can be treated as the activity of encoding and then re-encoded in and by the life-text (which is itself re-encoded in and by the narrative). To employ the fold in this way is to deny any vestigial, natural connection between 'facts' and events; rather, to do so is to imply that a fact is a trace within discourse of discourse, a culturally motivated, value-laden sign that, simultaneously, encodes and re-encodes a self-referential process which has been called "unlimited semiosis."[29] Employed or folded in this way, the life-text resists the monumental as it alters continuously in and between various discursive contexts. Employed or folded in this way, the life-text avoids the monumentalizing of the memorial, the entombment in a written statement of facts, which characterizes and threatens the life and death of all biographical subjects, all biographical narratives. As we have seen, Walton's *Life of Donne* confronts this unavoidable situation as it alters between various approaches to the textualizing and contextualizing of Donne's life and to the threat of its and Donne's death. Yet it always seeks to convert (to turn about, not turn away from) this constantly altering law of conversion which governs the generic frame "recognizing the life-text." That it does so, that it (re-)inscribes this alteration between the ontological and epistemological operations of monumental employment as it seeks the blessed inter-diction beyond human language, is yet another witness to the secular power and spiritual grace with which Walton's *Life of Donne* incorporates English biography.

chapter 3

RECOGNIZING THE LIFE-TEXT

"Every text participates in one or several genres, there is
no genreless text; there is always a genre and genres, yet
such participation never amounts to belonging." (Jacques
Derrida)

I

The previous chapter's exploration of Walton's *Donne* suggests that
biographical recognition employs and endorses an ongoing alteration
between life and text that plays across a field designated by the relationships between and among the natural, the cultural, and the narratable. In this chapter we shall emplot these relationships as the
generic frame "recognizing the life-text," a narrative scheme of biographical recognition some features of which are suggested by the
diagram below. The diagram can be read both vertically and horizon-
tally.

('natural')	event	life
('cultural')	fact	life-text
('narratable')	statement	narrative

Although prompted in part by the seventeenth-century discourse of
Waltonian biography, our discussion of this generic frame will be
situated primarily in a late-twentieth-century context marked, as we
shall see, by two contesting sets of assumptions, assumptions that,
one could argue, have always played across this field in one way or
another. By locating this discussion and this contest in a more or less
contemporary environment, I hope to benefit from my readership's
familiarity with the ways in which the complex and vexing issues
broached here are presently being debated. Of course, I am more than
a little aware that familiarity can breed contempt, but this is a risk I
will have to take.

We begin our exploration of the generic frame "recognizing the
life-text" with a consideration of the term "event." Biographical rec-

ognition treats an "event" as non-discursive, that is, as resistant to semiotic encoding. Now, we could make the case that no "event" is or ought to be so privileged—that, as Umberto Eco would have it, culture "proposes to its members an uninterrupted chain of cultural units," and "that a given cultural unit never obliges one to replace it by means of something which is not a semiotic entity."[1] Hence even a biographical "event" like birth could be considered not as a concrete happening but as a discursive occurrence, as a sign within a network of signification that reticulates the discursive conventions of biological reproduction, genealogical consanguinity, religious sanctification, and linguistic competence (among others). This self-referential process of cultural discourse, which Eco labels "unlimited semiosis," denies the autonomy of any sign or referent: "every attempt to establish the referent of a sign forces us to define the referent in terms of an abstract entity which moreover is only a cultural convention."[2] Yet we generally act as if "unlimited semiosis" did *not* characterize our recognition of a biographical "event." Rather, we usually recognize an "event" within limited contexts which allow us to proceed as if we were interpreting it 'naturally.'

This practice is very familiar. Most scientists, for example, try to establish fixed, experimental conditions governing their observations, conditions that limit their field of inquiry yet enable them to perform 'meaningful' experiments. Moreover, they treat the results of such experiments not only as significant within the pre-established context but also as descriptive of the 'natural' world. Now, this second way of using the experiment is, like the first, a convention of scientific inquiry, but, because it tries to fix the referent, to interrupt the process of semiosis by privileging certain events as 'natural,' this second use appropriates for scientific inquiry a special relationship to the non-discursive. The character of this relationship has been challenged and explored often during the twentieth century: the theoretical work of Einstein, Popper, Kuhn, Feyerabend, Polanyi, and others suggests that the relationships between and among the 'natural,' the 'cultural,' and the 'narratable' are as difficult to sort out in the philosophy of science as they are in the philosophy of history and the study of literature. As Thomas Kuhn has written: "A scientific theory is usually felt to be better than its predecessors not only in the sense that it is a better instrument for discovering and solving puzzles but also because it is somehow a better representative of what nature is really like. One often hears that successive theories grow ever closer to, or approximate more and more closely to, the truth. Apparently generalizations like that refer not to the puzzle-solutions and the concrete predictions derived from a theory but rather to its ontology, to the match, that is, between the entities with which the theory populates nature and what is 'really there'. . . . There is, I think, no theory-independent way to reconstruct phrases like 'really there'; the notion of a match between the ontology of a theory and its 'real' counterpart in nature now seems to me illusive in principle."[3]

Kuhn is expressing here, as Elizabeth Bruss has recently noted, a contemporary "decline of faith" in "unmediated empirical observation," which has produced, for the natural and social sciences as well as for historical understanding and literary study, a "crisis of epistemology" characterized by a "challenge to the dominion of a model of knowledge based almost exclusively on perception."[4] Hence Kuhn's observation is but one of many similar challenges to the ontological status of "events," especially those for which an innocent, unexamined 'reality,' 'naturalness,' or 'referentiality' is invoked. Indeed, it no longer seems possible to treat a biographical "event" as a 'natural' occurrence in the concrete world; rather, the contemporary theoretical crisis suggests, we must treat a biographical "event" as an epistemological operation to which ontological status is frequently, if inappropriately, granted, as a transient, discursive moment in a constantly receding and endlessly replicating semiotic wonderland. That we may feel more or less comfortable with this situation is, I suppose, one of those many little gauges by which we measure our proximity to or distance from contemporary theoretical debate. But the decline of faith in the unmediated, ontological status of "events" is now a powerful factor which must influence, if not guide, all but the most innocent, unexamined approach to biographical recognition. As I remarked in Chapter 1, this is one of the ways in which our attempt to frame biographical recognition disrupts and deforms that which it is trying to frame.

Our contemporary decline of faith in the ontological innocence of "events" also affects our recognition of the 'natural' discreteness of "events." We can no longer naively assume that "events" have beginnings and endings, that they are distinct entities which can be separated from the flux or mass which, nominally, structures or is structured by a "life." The problem here, of course, is in describing the conventions which govern discreteness. From one perspective—that of the mathematical limit—the number of such "events" is potentially infinite, for the distance between any two points or "events" can always be conceived as smaller. Hence distinctions between "events" break down as the notion of "event" encompasses smaller and smaller units. The biographical subject's space-time configurations can be fractionalized infinitely or at least to the point that any ordinary sense of discreteness is useless. Nevertheless, biographical recognition has and no doubt will continue to privilege a certain degree of discreteness—that degree which has been called the "natural attitude," that which appears so familiar, so taken-for-granted, so 'natural' that it seems to require no explanation.[5] I am referring here to a broad scope of actions, feelings, and conditions: what it is like to breathe or feel pain, to walk across the room or get wet, to remember or forget. Of course, research in various fields has suggested that these and similar sensations are not as 'natural' as they seem. Many (by now familiar) experiments and studies imply that our sense perceptions are governed by linguistic, cultural, psychological, and other contexts (including that of the experiment itself). Indeed, the history, theory, and practice of most scientific research is devoted, more or less self-consciously, to distinguishing between sensation and what Paul Feyerabend terms "natural interpretations"—"those 'mental operations which follow so closely upon the senses,' and which are so firmly connected with their reactions that a separation is difficult to achieve."[6]

Nevertheless, biographical recognition has tended to ignore such fine distinctions, to function as if caveats about the conventionality of the 'natural attitude' had never been uttered. Rather, it has generally privileged the 'natural attitude' as the degree of discreteness that governs the generic relationship between "event" and "life." Thus biographical recognition has usually treated "events" as naturally discrete occurrences which are congruent with the space-time configurations of the biographical subject, delimited by the subject's birth and death, and constituent of a "life." Now, a more radical contemporary approach to biographical recognition might wish to treat a "life" as 'culturally' and not 'naturally' constituted, as a structuring operation within cultural discourse through which an "event" (construed as a cultural sign) is separated from most other "events" and yet collected with some such "events." In this approach a "life" is considered "naturalized" not 'natural'—a shift in terminology that emphasizes, as Roland Barthes has suggested, how conventions which have been intensely or protractedly inscribed in our experience come to appear 'natural.'[7] But biographical recognition has been and, for the most part, still is reluctant to abandon the 'natural attitude,' for, here as elsewhere, we discover that epistemological naivete is a distinctive feature of biographical recognition, a feature which is, moreover, freighted with ontological significance. Indeed, to continue to assert the naivete of the "event"/"life" relationship, especially in the present theoretical climate, might be construed as declaring faith in "a prereflective stratum of living which is, if anything, more authentic than conceptual behavior."[8] In the sense that this or a similar justification can be said to inform the "event"/"life" relationship, biographical recognition would seem to encourage (more or less self-consciously) a relatively naive collaboration with the 'natural' that locates it outside (or to the side) of contemporary theoretical discourse and maintains it as one of the last strongholds of empirical knowledge.

II

The "event" is also in a relationship with the "fact." Biographical recognition can describe a "fact" in two ways. Most commonly, a "fact" has been treated as a trace of an "event," as an imprint or vestige within discourse of someone or something once present which is treated as a slight remnant of that person or object. In order to explain the special status with which cultural documentation invests a "fact," this approach appeals to the vestigial, 'natural' connection between "events" and "facts." More radically, a "fact" could be treated as a trace within discourse of discourse, as a culturally motivated, value-laden sign which, simultaneously, encodes and re-encodes the self-referential process of unlimited semiosis. In this approach the special status with which cultural documentation invests a "fact" is explained by calling attention to the possibility that culture can privilege its own documentation by treating cultural re-encoding as if it were 'natural' encoding. The second approach is then a kind of meta-commentary on the first approach: in its insistence on the recognition of a biographical "fact" as an epistemological operation, it denies even the remnant of a match between ontology and nature.[9] I shall return later to the implications of these different approaches. For now it is sufficient to stress that, regardless of their difference, both descriptions allow biographical recognition to treat "facts" as enmeshed in a network of cultural signification constituted by the documentation of church, state, family, commerce, history, tradition, and other cultural institutions. I refer here not only to the discourse of parish registers, rate books, legal proceedings, property records, and family Bibles, but also to that of myths, legends, anecdotes, icons, and objects.

Unlike "events," "facts" do not separate and collect as a function of the 'natural attitude.' Rather, they are recognized as discrete cultural entities in and through which is constituted what I have been calling the "life-text." For, as pointed out above, biographical recognition entails the crucial assumption that "life" can be construed as a process of discursive encoding either in the sense that biographical subjects encode their lives in the activity of living or (more radically) that the activity of living is or can become the activity of encoding or re-encoding. In either sense, the result of such encoding is the "life-text," which, like "facts," occupies that generic space in which the non-discursive can be transformed into the discursive, in which "life" can be made into or construed as Text. Like Jonathan Culler's "general cultural text," the "life-text" can be described as being constituted in and by "shared knowledge which would be recognized by participants as part of culture," or through "cultural categories which may over-simplify but which at least make the world initially intelligible and consequently serve as a target language." Moreover, to quote Culler quoting Stephen Heath, both the "general cultural text" and the "life-text" "control what has been called the 'threshold of functional relevance, that which divides the narratable from the non-narratable'"[10]—a crucial division to which I shall return later. Hence governing the separation and collection of "facts" is what we might call the 'cultural attitude,' that is, that degree of discreteness conventionally associated with the introduction of a 'natural' "event" into the 'cultural' Text.

As an example of the cultural relativity with which biographical recognition distinguishes a "fact" let us explore a famous instance of a typical "fact." The baptismal entry in the parish register reads: "26 Gulielmus, filius Johannes Shakspere."[11] Our knowledge of the conventions of reading parish registers readily supplies some important information: the number is the day of the month, which other entries

in the register inform us is April 1564; the language is church Latin;
the type of entry is a baptism; the name to the left of the comma is
that of the baptized; the phrase to the right of the comma locates the
baptized within a specific genealogical context. But there are other
general and specific, tacit and salient cultural conventions involved
here. For instance, historical discourse informs us that, in 1564, the
notion of publicly recording such information was innovative, recently introduced by the newly established Church and Crown as a
means of signifying and affirming their authority and as a way of
counting and locating the population. In this respect, the recording
of an "event" in a parish register emerges as a significant if silent
gesture towards a convention (that is, if we can join two senses of the
term, a gathering together which becomes, by general agreement, a
fixed usage) of an individual with an acquisitive, anxious structure of
socio-political authority. Read in this way the parish-register entry
conventionalizes and contextualizes (weaves or joins together in a discursive network of self-authenticating surroundings) both the individual and the authority structure: each seeks textual assurance from
the other, each finds in the language of the entry a means of being
and becoming which is otherwise difficult to establish and sustain.
Indeed, historical discourse suggests that, before this period in English history, ordinary individuals were far less likely to enter cultural
discourse. The parish register becomes then a new opportunity for
textualization. Without this and similar contextualizing gestures
'facthood' might have assumed a very different character and manifestation in English culture and biography.

Moreover, we might make another point about the conventions
governing the introduction of a 'natural' "event" into the 'cultural'
Text. Note the "facts" recorded in the register—baptisms, marriages,
burials. The Church, acting on its own behalf and in concert with the
State, is seeking to valorize those "events" to which it attaches special
theological and political significance. In the process it is generating
the basic outline of the "life-text" as well as some of the crucial "facts"
which constitute or are constituted by the "life-text." The result,
intended or not, is the contextualization of biographical recognition
with the cultural conventions of the parish register. Of course, the
discursive practices of other cognitive activities also participate in
structuring the parish registers, but biographical recognition is an
important contributor. Furthermore, the "life-text" is altered to some

extent by the parish registers. The registers make available more "facts" and establish the beginnings and endings of more "life-texts." The registers also re-affirm the essential relationship of "facts" and "life-text" and thus contribute to the stability of the genre as they help to broaden its scope. Finally, the registers accompany yet another intrusion of the Church and State into biographical recognition; like classical prosopography and medieval hagiography, they validate biography as an ally of the dominant socio-political authority and appropriate for biography a valuable source of textualization.

How does this analysis affect Shakespearean biography? Consider the shape of Shakespeare's "life-text" in the absence of such culturally authorized "facts" as parish-register entries. If the name 'Shakespeare' (in its various spellings) cannot function except as signifying authorship (and a much disputed function at that), then 'Shakespeare' is a sign which can be filled only with the imputed authorship of literary texts.[12] It cannot be filled with other discursive activities conventionally associated with biographical subjects. The inability to treat 'Shakespeare' as poly-functional, that is, as engaged in more than one discursive activity, is a fatal, silencing disruption of biographical recognition. On the other hand, the availability of culturally authorized "facts" permits the recognition of poly-functional biographical subjects *only* in terms of their engagement in sanctioned discursive activities. This is how cultural institutions appropriate the 'natural' and make it an instrument of what Barthes calls their "mythology." A "fact" then becomes, as Barthes suggests, a second-order sign in and through which culture asserts its 'natural' authority.[13] And biographical recognition serves as one way of reinforcing that cultural myth. It suggests that we cannot know Shakespeare as a biographical subject unless we regard parish-register entries and other culturally authorized "facts" as if they are somehow 'natural.'

The parish-register example reinforces my point: biographical recognition has generally interpreted the relationship between "facts" and "life-text" in terms of the 'cultural attitude,' which provides a means and an environment in and through which the 'natural' (or the Text of the 'natural') can be treated as the 'cultural' (or the Text of the 'cultural'). The parenthetical remarks above suggest, once again, how biographical recognition has privileged certain operations: textualization is validated in the generic space constituted by the 'cultural' relationship between "facts" and "life-text," but denied to the

'natural' relationship of "events" and "life." Indeed, biographical recognition has ritualistically denied that the activity of living can be
construed as the activity of encoding. Rather, it has reserved a 'natural' generic space, a pre-Text, which, as the term implies, describes
not only the state before textualization but also an "excuse," a "covering," and a "cloaking." [14]

The implications of such a (common) generic structure are significant. Textualizing the 'natural' inevitably involves a loss, a falling
away from some posited ontological state of wholeness and order.
Hence textualization augurs an increase in entropy: as the potential,
available information decreases, disorder threatens. But this threat is
arrested by the submission of the chaotic to the coded. The 'natural'
information which has been lost is replaced by 'cultural' information
that tries to prevent loss by privileging certain discursive traces
(understood here in the sense of vestiges or remnants). These traces
are treated as marking inflexible channels of communication through
which information passes essentially unchanged. The language of
these traces—or, as they are subsequently styled, these "facts"—becomes "artificial," for, like scientific language, it is not generally
treated as a "source of poetic information." Moreover, as Jurij Lotman
has argued, "formal constraints placed on the flexibility of a language
. . . diminish entropy" because they deny "variety in the expression
of the same content." [15] This inflexibility is the habit (the sacred costume and characteristic tendency) of the pre-Text: it covers or cloaks
the movement towards disorder by stabilizing the 'cultural' information. This operation has the force of both conservation and preservation: that is, the "fact" is treated as an "event" which is being guarded
under official auspices, as well as a vestige or remnant of a 'natural'
event requiring protection from decay. Thus the remnant is preserved
through conservation, through its being granted a special status
within culture, which assumes guardianship of the remnant by enmeshing it within dominant socio-political authority structures. The
"fact" as remnant becomes then a kind of ward or prisoner of cultural
discourse, confined within its institutions and denied the freedom and
opportunity to change meaning except as a rehabilitation project
within institutional guidelines. Or, to pursue a cognate metaphor,
the "fact" as remnant becomes an object conserved within the museum of cultural discourse, inhibited and exhibited by institutions
which seek to preserve and cure it. As Edwin P. Hood writes in *The*

Uses of Biography (1852): "*Biography forms the Museum of Life.* Well-written lives are as well-preserved mental fossils, and they subserve for us the purpose of a collection of interesting petrefactions; they illustrate the science of life; they are the inductions of moral anatomy."[16]

The inflexibility of the "fact" as the conserving/preserving habit of a 'natural' pre-Text arises also in the familiar discussion of the relationship between 'facthood' and 'truth.' Because I have treated "facts" as discursive traces sanctioned by the 'cultural attitude,' which governs the separation and collection of these "facts" both from "events" *qua* "events" and from all other discursive traces, in a sense we have already circumvented the traditional debate. For to argue as I have done is to assert the cultural relativity of 'facthood' and hence deny that biographical "fact" has any special claim to the truth other than that granted to it by biographical recognition (a truth which, we might also claim, is itself a powerful enough assumption). Yet such assertions and denials are uncommon in the discourse of biographical poetics, where biography (regardless of whether it is described as "scientific" or "artistic") is still generally considered true to something 'natural' in the world, although usually this truth claim entails (as we shall see) an innocent 'naturalness' and posits "a sort of native and mysterious parenthood between things or between images and portrayed things."[17]

We can explore this situation by looking briefly at a suggestive statement by Paul Murray Kendall in a book on the practice of writing biography—"fact is a cold stone, an inarticulate thing, dumb until something happens to it." Now, at this point in his narrative, Kendall is acknowledging the privileged status of 'facthood' in the discourse of biographical research, not analyzing it as a practice of biographical recognition. But the statement is revealing nevertheless. For the metaphors Kendall employs give to 'facthood' a 'monumentality'—a coldness, hardness, and silence ordinarily associated with concrete objects in the physical world. Kendall's "fact" is a "thing," in particular, a kind of inscribed stone, which (he also comments), "placed in magnetic juxtaposition with other facts, . . . begins to glow, to give off that radiance we call meaning." There is an imagistic plot here: the cold stone glows, that is, means, only when it is part of a magnetic field constituted by the juxtaposition of other cold stones. This imagery both suggests and invokes the Newtonian/

Lockean concept of "attraction" or "association": "particles," "ideas,"
"facts" seek each other out, have an 'existence' of their own. The
project of the scientist, philosopher, or biographer is to attempt "the
simulation in words"—and now we return strictly to biography—"of
a man's life, from what is known about that life, from the paper trail,
the enigmatic footprint."[18] Notice in these closing phrases the use of
yet other metaphors to describe 'facthood'; notice also that, although
cold stones, paper trails, and footprints evoke somewhat different
systems of cultural discourse, each refers to 'natural' objects in a kind
of hardened landscape through which a biographer passes, shuffling
through documents, looking or listening for the radiance or the voice
of the insensate or the inarticulate. Indeed, the use of the term "footprint" returns us to the "fact" as a vestige or imprint of an "event," to
the discursive trace as a track of a 'natural' occurrence in the concrete
world, to the relatively naive collaboration between the 'natural'
and the 'cultural' that biographical recognition has generally encouraged.

Obviously, monumentality serves the same purpose as inflexibility:
both try to fix the "fact" by arresting entropy and by associating the
concreteness of the "fact" as a discrete, discursive trace with the concreteness of the "event" to which it supposedly refers as a discrete,
'natural' occurrence. In semiotic terms, biographical recognition
treats "facts" as "motivated," although different semioticians understand this term differently. For Ferdinand de Saussure, for example,
"motivation" signifies, somewhat vaguely, the general drift towards
order and regularity; for Barthes, this drift is based, somewhat more
strictly, on an analogical relationship between signified and signifier;
for Eco, this relationship is characterized, quite precisely, as one in
which "a constant proportionality between two series of entities" is
initiated and sustained by the pre-determination of culturally assigned values.[19] Out of these somewhat different approaches emerges
a movement away from "motivation" as an operation pointing to the
'natural' and towards it as an operation governed by the 'cultural.'
The relationship between signified and signifier, like that between
"event" and "fact," shifts from one in which entropy is arrested by a
'natural' movement towards regularity and order to one in which
entropy is merely slowed (or perhaps acknowledged as itself taken-
for-granted) by a 'cultural' movement towards proportionality and
value.

This shift is the crucial point or moment in "recognizing the life-text"—and a point or moment is all it is. Between the 'natural' relationship of "event" and "life" and the 'narratable' relationship of "statement" and "narrative" there is time or space for nothing but an operation of transformation, a pointed, momentous 'alteration' (the Waltonian term for this operation) in the relationship between signified and signifier. This is the point or moment when pre-Text is becoming Text, when the cover is being thrown off (as it is put on), when the 'natural' is being subsumed by (as it submits to) the 'narratable.' This is what Jacques Derrida calls "the hinge [*brisure*]," the "discontinuity" which "marks the impossibility that a sign, the unity of a signifier and a signified, be produced within the plentitude of a present and an absolute presence."[20] Or, as the philosopher of history Louis Mink has written: "there is something incompatible about our concept of 'event' and our concept of 'narrative'. . . . 'Events' (or more precisely, descriptions of events) are not the raw material out of which narratives are constructed. . . . The locus of incompatibility is the presupposition that the structure of a historical narrative, as well as its individual statements taken separately, claims truth as representative of past actuality."[21]

This discontinuity or incompatibility in biographical recognition is hinged by or hinges on the generic space constituted in and by the relationship between "fact" and "life-text," where the operation of transforming the 'natural' into the 'cultural' and the 'cultural' into the 'narratable' takes place. Both Mink and Hayden White have pointed out that there is a radical break between narrative and what is generally called "historical understanding." "Our experience of life does not itself necessarily have the form of narrative, except as we give it that form by making it the subject of stories." "Considered as a system of signs, the historical narrative points in two directions simultaneously: toward the events described in the narrative and toward the story type or mythos that the historian has chosen to serve as the icon of the structure of the events."[22] Although biography is not merely a branch of history (as has often been asserted) but, as this book claims, is also recognized as a distinct cognitive activity in a relationship with historical and other processes of recognition, nevertheless it shares with history a generic space that hinges the 'natural' and the 'narratable,' a space where, to paraphrase Derrida again, the pre-Text is "folded" into the Text.[23]

Moreover, like history, biography generally denies or refuses to acknowledge that such a hinging or folding operation is crucial in its recognition. Indeed, one way to call attention to the prominence and power of this operation would be to recognize biography, in Eco's terms, as a culturally motivated, analogical series of value-laden signs. Biographical recognition would become then an activity devoted to authorizing transformations between various processes of discursive encoding, that is, to recognizing how the activity of living as the activity of encoding is re-encoded in and by the "life-text" which is re-encoded in and by narrative. But, as we have seen, biographical recognition seeks to cloak these transformations by implying that the pre-Text folds into the Text 'naturally,' that discontinuity or incompatibility is an unnatural, momentary hesitation in the general drift towards regularity and order. Hence a biographical "fact" is usually treated as monumental or inflexible, as a cold, hard, silent thing. It does not hinge, fold, transform, or re-encode. It exists. Although contemporary theoretical discourse suggests that there is no ontological space between the 'natural' and the 'narratable,' that the "fact"/ "life-text" relationship is an epistemological operation of transformation, biographical recognition does not privilege this operation. Rather, it cloaks this transformation in naive naturalness as it rests self-assuredly in the folds of silent, generic space.

III

Before going any further I should indicate what I mean by "statement" and "narrative." Because I will be using these terms essentially as they are understood in recent narratological studies, I will place them in this familiar context before returning to a discussion of their relationship with "fact" and "life-text." According to Seymour Chatman, "narrative" is an "independently meaningful" structure that "conveys a meaning in and of itself, separately from the story it tells." Moreover, a narrative implies "a communication" between "a sender and a receiver" which is "experienced through a performance or through a text" that seeks or receives "an interpretation." Narrative discourse is the "expression" of the "story" or "content," "an abstract class, containing only those features that are common to all actually manifested narratives." More precisely, "narrative discourse consists of a connected sequence of narrative *statements*," which are "independent of the particular expressive medium," "may be manifested by questions or commands as well as by declarative constructions in natural language," and convey actions or happenings "not as actual words in . . . any natural language . . . , but as . . . abstract expressional categories" in the meta-language of narratology. Hence by "statement" and "narrative" narratologists do not mean the actual words on the pages of a biography but rather, as Chatman and Gerald Prince have asserted, categories or components of a theoretical meta-language that purports to describe the principles or conventions of order and selection, discreteness and specificity, assurance and wholeness, temporality and spatiality, chronology and teleology, pointedness and pointlessness, et al., by and through which can be recognized the 'narrativity' of specific biographical texts.[24]

This description reinforces our sense that narrative is a powerful instrument in and through which all discursive traces, including "facts," are recognized. Furthermore, it reveals the kind of operation that is necessary in order to establish the 'existence' of a "fact" prior to or separate from its appearance and locus in narrative. Because narrative issues in and governs our recognition of "facts" simultaneously with their manifestation as discursive traces, 'facthood' cannot be distinguished from 'narrativity' unless and until (a) it is treated as the hinge between the 'natural' and the 'narratable'—an approach which, as we have seen, is 'unbecoming' to biographical recognition, or (b) it is accorded a kind of hardened presence in the physical world—a maneuver which, as we know, is 'habitual' in the discursive practice of the genre.

We can illustrate this maneuver of hardened privileging by returning to the "life-text" of William Shakespeare, much of which is constituted in and by discursive traces which are conventionally styled legendary or traditional. I refer here to certain hardened discursive traces, which, through frequent repetition outside the context of appropriate institutional documentation, have assumed a privileged status in Shakespeare's "life-text" analogous to and, in most respects, indistinguishable from 'facthood.' The so-called 'deer-poaching' incident is a good example. It is textualized, in 'story' form and without documentation, in a late-seventeenth-century memorandum of an obscure Oxford clergyman, in the biographical preface to the 1709 edition of Shakespeare's *Works,* in a ballad collected and published in the eighteenth century, and in various eighteenth- and nineteenth-

century miscellanies containing local Stratford legends and traditions.[25] Throughout its many manifestations the incident undergoes
changes in locale, circumstances, participants, and consequences, yet
it continues to appear in Shakespearean biography and to occupy a
more or less firm position in Shakespeare's "life-text." Shakespearean
authorities are reluctant to give it up—not only because it is a lively
story presenting Shakespeare as a young, impulsive, imperfect personality but also because it helps flesh out the crucial "lost years"
between his boyhood in Stratford and his manhood in London. Even
Samuel Schoenbaum, the most demanding, respected, and recent of
Shakespeare's 'documentary' biographers, is hesitant to discount it.
In one of his books he summarizes his section on the incident with
this sentence: "In modern times most (but not all) responsible scholars
would reject the entire episode as traditionary romance." In another
his summary mentions those "prominent authorities" who "believe
there may be some truth to the tradition," quotes the comment that
"'the deer-stealing legend has by now a hold on popular affection that
no argument can weaken,'" suggests that the "legends" surrounding
the incident "embroider, however fancifully, a genuine escapade," and
omits entirely the powerful deprecatory phrase—"traditionary romance"—which ends the deer-poaching section in the earlier book.[26]

   This is what I mean by a hardened discursive trace—of which
Shakespearean and indeed most biography provides us with many
examples. Clearly, because it lacks appropriate institutional documentation, such a trace is not a "fact," yet generally it is treated as if
it were one or could become one. What has happened to the monumentality, the inflexibility, of the "fact"? Apparently, it has disap-
peared in one of the folds of the "life-text." The desire to grant this
discursive trace privileged status is so powerful that it uncovers itself
and reveals the weaving and cloaking necessary to sustain the distinctions between pre-Text, Text, and narrative, between the 'natural,'
the 'cultural,' and the 'narratable.' What also becomes readily apparent is that biographical recognition is itself a powerful institutional-
izing instrument which can, summarily, authorize 'facthood' or a
privileged status analogous to 'facthood' and (in the crucial respect
that it emerges as a sign initiated and sustained by the pre-
determination of culturally assigned values) indistinguishable from
'facthood.' Of course, this is not the only kind of uncovering to which
"facts" are subjected. Many "facts" disintegrate as they become en-

meshed more intricately in discourse: forgeries, misreadings, misspellings, misattributions, indeed, mistakes of all types threaten the privileged status of 'facthood' as they reveal the extent to which biographical recognition and the discursive practices of other cultural and generic institutions are responsible for the 'natural' monumentality of the "fact."

IV

The hinging or folding of the generic space constituted in and by the relationship between "facts" and "life-text" is the crucial operation in the biographical recognition of the relationships between and among the 'natural,' the 'cultural,' and the 'narratable.' Hence this chapter's title: "Recognizing the Life-Text." From Plutarch, who privileged all kinds of discursive traces, to Boswell, who grandiosely displayed his sources (of which the most prominently displayed and most summarily privileged was his own discourse in, of, and with the world), to Virginia Woolf, whose *Orlando* ironically challenges the discursive project of biographical recognition itself, the covering and uncovering of "life" as Text has most intimately and saliently informed the poetics of biography. The diagram below, which summarizes James Clifford's oft-cited categorization of "types of biography,"[27] is a tacit acknowledgement of the power of this operation.

Type	*Description*
life-records	objective (selection of facts)
scholarly-historical	objective, chronological
artistic-scholarly	creative, non-distorting
[ironic]	[creative, distorting]
narrative	subjective, non-fictional
novelistic	subjective, fictional
[ironic]	[creative, distorting]

Although it is not part of Clifford's 'arm-chair' approach systematically to define and distinguish 'objectivity' and 'subjectivity,' or, indeed, any of his major terms, it is clear that this typology rests on a (generally accepted) notion of the critical importance of the way in which the "life-text" constitutes and is constituted by "facts." Thus we might approach Clifford's categorization as one way of construing the generic frame "recognizing the life-text." In this context it is interesting to note that, although Clifford's diagram is ostensibly emplotted in terms of a movement from 'pure' objectivity (which Clifford acknowledges as "impossible") to 'pure' subjectivity, it could also be seen as moving inward towards its center, where neither recording nor novelizing—the extreme operations which reveal the transforming of "events" and discursive traces into "facts"—can dominate.

Indeed, Clifford's uncertainty where to place the ironic type exposes the problematics of his design. Clifford observes that Stracheyan biography (the exemplar of the ironic type) is "neither fiction nor objective," yet is "creative and based on genuine evidence." Placing it on the outside, beneath the novelistic type, is a tacit acknowledgement that irony invariably calls attention to the discursivity of discourse and, consequently, to any of its salient features (like "facts") as 'made things,' products or by-products of imagination, genre, culture, etc. But placing the ironic type on the inside, as "a special subdivision of the third type, 'artistic-scholarly' biography," silently testifies that irony inevitably participates in what it satirizes, and so, in that regard, it puts on the habit it seeks to remove. Perceived in this way, with the ironic type as a meta-type occupying the middle, the diagram itself can be seen as a kind of hinge or as hinging the 'natural' and the 'narratable' (suggested here by the familiar terms objective and subjective, non-fictional and fictional, non-distorting and distorting). The closer we come to the meta-type and to the operation which unobtrusively folds the pre-Text into the Text, the farther away we are from the edges of the diagram, where the textuality of the 'natural' and the 'naturalness' of the Textual are most apparent and most problematical.

For, at the frontiers of this generic space, biographical recognition is no longer the dominant differentiating activity: the relationships between the 'natural,' the 'cultural,' and the 'narratable' which it has habituated begin to weaken as the recognition activities of other genres begin to strengthen. Derrida considers this situation characteristic of the activity of generic encoding. The "law of genre"— "Every text participates in one or several genres, there is no genreless text; there is always a genre and genres, yet such participation never amounts to belonging"—is "mad" because a genre cannot close itself: it "enfolds within itself the condition for the possibility and the impossibility of taxonomy," it "begins by finishing and never finishes beginning apart from itself," it "stays at the edgeless boundary of itself."[28] Hovering always above these boundaries is the net of signification, threatening to enmesh all difference in the discourse of the Generalized. Derrida is raising here what cognitive scientists and others call the "frame problem"—"an abstract *epistemological* problem" which stresses how any particular cognitive activity alters the world and must then be revised in terms of that alteration.[29] Put in another way, the descriptive performance of any generic frame alters generic recognition to some extent (however small and obscure), an alteration that promotes a revision (however minor) in the frame. Here is the beginning by finishing, the edgeless bounding, which Derrida finds in the "law of genre." Like all other cognitive activities, generic recognition (in general) and biographical recognition (in particular) enfold within themselves the possibility and impossibility of their own descriptions. Thus to ask the question "Why is there genre, rather than generalized Literature?" is like asking the godhead its name— the answer will inevitably regenerate the question in another form. It is more interesting to ask why we want to know and what we want to do with the answer.

chapter 4

PATRONIZING THE BIOGRAPHICAL SUBJECT:
JOHNSON'S *LIFE OF SAVAGE*

"[I]t was therefore impossible to pay him any Distinction,
without the entire Subversion of all Oeconomy, a Kind of
Establishment which, wherever he went, he always appeared ambitious to overthrow." (Johnson's *Life of Savage*)

I

"The modern Western state," asserts Michel Foucault, "integrated in
a new political shape, an old power technique which originated in
Christian institutions." Because Christianity "postulates in principle
that certain individuals can, by their religious quality, serve others
not as princes, magistrates, prophets, fortune-tellers, benefactors,
educationalists, and so on, but as pastors," Christianity "proposed and
spread . . . a very special form of power," which Foucault calls "pastoral power." As its "ultimate aim is to assure individual salvation in
the next world," pastoral power "does not look after just the whole
community, but each individual in particular, during his entire life."
Hence it "cannot be exercised without knowing the inside of people's
minds, without exploring their souls, without making them reveal
their innermost secrets." Moreover, Foucault insists, "a new distribution, a new organization of this kind of individualizing power" began
in and around the eighteenth century, when the "ecclesiastical institutionalization" of pastoral power "lost its vitality" and "suddenly
spread out into the whole social body," where "it found support in a
multitude of institutions" that were integrated into and dominated
by the 'state,' which emerges now "as a modern matrix of individualization, or a new form of pastoral power." Medicine, psychiatry,
education, the family, the police, and other public and private institutions became the means by which pastoral power changed "its objective," by which "a series of 'worldly' aims," promising salvation "in
this world" rather than the next, "took the place of the religious aims
of the traditional pastorate."[1]

Throughout its development English biography can be shown to be one of those "individualizing 'tactics'" through which, Foucault claims, pastoral power became "coextensive and continuous with life" and "linked with a production of truth—the truth of the individual himself."[2] In its most common early form—saints' lives and other modes of hagiography—English biography can be described as a discursive practice completely dominated by traditional pastoral power: the sacred plot of individual revelation through sacrifice and salvation reproduces over and over again a life-story, the *only* life-story, which Christianity authorizes. Later, in Walton's *Life of Donne,* biographer and biographical subject reaffirm their sympathetic covenant through a series of symbolic maneuvers that retraverses the spiritual topography of pastoral power. As we saw in Chapter 2, by emblematically situating itself and Donne at the altar and then the pulpit, Walton's narrative tries to resolve the conflict between secular employment and sacred calling presented by Donne's life-course. Having appropriated Donne's pastoral functions, the Waltonian biographer seeks to "re-animate" biography as an expression and inscription of traditional pastoral power. As we shall see in Chapter 7, the most influential twentieth-century biographical narrative, Lytton Strachey's *Eminent Victorians,* is as concerned as Waltonian biography with the aesthetic possibilities of the conflict between secular employment and sacred calling. Three of the narrative's four biographical subjects—Nightingale, Arnold, and Gordon—can be considered types of lay clerics, whose efforts to convert careers in medical administration, education, and the military into spiritual vocations emplot melodramatic life-courses that reveal and indict their age. Only Cardinal Manning, the head of the English Catholic Church, is a professional cleric—and, in his pursuit of salvation in this world, he emerges as the most secular of all these eminent Victorians. What was possible, indeed necessary, in Walton—a conversion from secular employment to sacred calling that reaffirms traditional pastoral power—is impossible (if also necessary) in Strachey, where it becomes the discontinuity that instrumentalizes a relentless, ironic reading of the Victorian life-course. This reading indicates the extent to which the modern state's institutional redistribution of individualization had already co-opted biography as a functionary of a new, secular form of pastoral power.

Foucault's dating of this redistribution of pastoral power in and around the eighteenth-century coincides with the modern state's appropriation of biography as an individualizing tactic. The deployment of this emergent discursive practice can be traced in Johnson's *Life of Savage* (1744), one of English biography's most well-known and admired texts, perhaps because, as Paul Fussell has remarked, we can discern in it "Johnson's archetypal Portrait of the Artist."[3] Indeed, throughout Johnson's biographical narrative, Savage tries to use the institutions of authorship and literature as an individualizing tactic through which he can reclaim his cultural identity. As the biography constantly demonstrates, many of Savage's poems, such as *The Author to be Let, The Volunteer Laureate,* and *The Bastard,* are autobiographical works proclaiming, lamenting, and exploiting his marginal status in English society. For instance, the publication of *The Bastard,* Savage's most famous poem, is presented in Johnson's narrative as a powerful instrument of revenge which individualizes its author as it generalizes and depersonalizes his reputed mother, whom it forces to leave Bath and "shelter herself among the Crouds of London."[4] Yet, as we know, Johnson's Savage is more often an unsuccessful, frustrated participant in the mid-eighteenth-century institutions of authorship and literature; his fruitless effort to sustain a literary career, and to define himself in terms of it, is one of the narrative's most consistent thematic structures. That Johnson's biography can transform this more or less marginal figure (a bastard son of nobility and a convicted murderer, as well as an impoverished writer who dies in debtors' prison) into an archetypal portrait of the artist is a tribute of sorts to the secularization of pastoral power and (despite nearly overwhelming odds) to the deployment of its cultural authority to (re)produce individual lives. If discursive practice can institutionalize Savage in this way, then, it would appear, there are hardly any limits to 'biographical subjection' (a phrase which, as we shall see in the next chapter, expresses the force of the generic frame "recognizing the biographical subject"). To appreciate the kind of challenge Savage offers in this respect, and how Johnson's narrative meets that challenge, we turn now to the concept and practice of patronage, another cultural institution through which the sacred was transformed into the secular and with which both Savage and biography were intimately associated.

II

Here is how the scholarship on English literary patronage in the late Middle Ages and early Renaissance describes the situation in which the pre-Gutenberg hagiographer produced biography: "'he wrote the lives of saints who inspired the foundation of, or themselves founded, religious orders . . . for the heads of religious houses to be read by the inmates of those houses.'"[5] Thus the early English patron is not only a royal or aristocratic connoisseur of literature who influences and supports the production of literary texts, but also, as the *OED* and Johnson's *Dictionary* remind us, "a founder of a religious order," or a "special tutelary saint of a person, place, country, craft, or institution" (that is, a patron saint), or "one who holds the right of presentation to an ecclesiastical benefice," in all of which functions the patron is expected to act as "advocate and defender" (the earliest sense of the term in English usage) of the Church.[6] Hence patronage is a cultural practice closely allied to the ecclesiastical institution that governed the distribution of traditional pastoral power. The hagiographer's writing lives of the founding patrons or patron saints of particular religious orders for the heads of religious houses to be read by the inmates of those houses perfectly encapsulates the hermetic character of the conditions under which early English biography was produced.

Although the recent scholarship of Peter Lucas, Elizabeth Eisenstein, and others has informed our concept of the early development of English literary patronage and has pushed back our sense of when it began to change,[7] students of English literary history still tend to identify the traditional system of patronizing literature with the classic studies of Elizabethan authorship undertaken by Phoebe Sheavyn and her followers.[8] Governed by ancient genealogical and class-oriented structures of authority vested in the crown, the church, and the nobility, this patronage arrangement can be described as self-sealing and self-authenticating. Like a religious order or a craft guild, it reproduced itself as a closed, privileged, preserving cell or group that established and enforced its own rules, and that jealously guarded and sponsored the processes of admission and advancement. Further, because the reading public was (compared to later periods) relatively limited and because access to the materials and opportunities associated with both reading and writing were still relatively restricted, authors and readers often shared small, specially informed communities in which formal publication was only one (and often not the most significant) means of distribution. One of the more common patterns of the Renaissance literary career (and there were many variations upon this somewhat idealized representation) involved access to the circulation of literary texts in manuscript; a university or private tutorial education; the opportunity to travel and broaden knowledge and contacts (often as the result of domestic and foreign civil or ecclesiastical service); membership in an exclusive circle of poets, a peerage of talent like the "Sons of Ben," which considered itself the only appropriate judge of literary merit; the selection of a suitably classical topic and poetic convention; the acquisition of a royal, noble, or ecclesiastical patron; and the occasional publication of text surrounded and authorized by dedicatory poems from previously established authors and by lists of similarly authenticated and authenticating literary peers.

As the work of A. S. Collins and (more recently) Paul Korshin suggests,[9] this hierarchical system was changing throughout the eighteenth century. Korshin notes that *"direct* crown support for intellectuals" dwindled away almost entirely under the Georges; that "job-oriented public patronage, paid for out of Treasury funds," offered "few places . . . specifically designated for literary men and scholars"; that "very few" peers "were interested in supporting literature and scholarship on a large scale"; and that "there is practically no evidence of large or continuous literary patronage from members of the rising mercantile class."[10] Yet, as both Collins and Korshin make clear, hierarchical patronage gradually lost its influence over literature not because it ceased to support authorship (indeed, its subsidizing of individual authors seems to have been about the same, numerically, as during the Renaissance) but because the size of the reading public and the number of authors or potential authors increased dramatically. There were, this Malthusian argument runs, simply too many authors to support and too large and diverse a readership to influence. The traditional self-regulating cell no longer 'contained' literature.

Of course, hierarchical patronage did not die out overnight; rather, as Korshin and others suggest, it was dispersed, somewhat haphazardly, over a wider territory. Although the soliciting of subscriptions to individual works (which began in the early seventeenth century but was much more prevalent in the eighteenth) "democratized literary patronage" to some extent, both this method and the nearly universal practice of gathering "incidental bounty" through a dedication directed to someone with whom the author was, in most cases, unacquainted and from whom he or she could expect little or no reward,[11] was hardly sufficient to influence what was becoming a vast,

nearly anonymous reading and writing public. Literature and authorship were now patronized primarily by the booksellers, by what was
called "the trade," a consumer-oriented mercantile monopoly which
acted as agent for both readers and writers. The new "trade" grew in
prominence because, unlike the old "order" or "guild," which had
flourished within small hierarchical communities with common interests, accomplishments, and opportunities, the "trade" could service an expanding, diversifying, democratizing consumer culture.

Hence mid-eighteenth-century authorship was no longer a way of
announcing or re-affirming one's acceptance or position in the traditional socio-political structures of authority. The celebrated observation appended to one of Johnson's *Dictionary*'s definitions of 'patron'
("Commonly a wretch who supports with insolence, and is paid with
flattery") points to this cultural shift. Indeed, we can find signs of
this ambiguous and changing situation distributed throughout Johnson's literary career. For instance, the revised version of *The Vanity of
Human Wishes* depicts the contemporary scholar assailed by "Toil,
Envy, Want, the Patron, and the Jail." [12] The replacement of the word
"Garret" with "Patron" is a powerful symbolic gesture. The original
wording locates the scholar in the two places, the garret and the jail,
where he characteristically toils, envies, and wants. The revised wording disrupts this parallelism: instead of the place, the patron's levee
or "outward Rooms," [13] the revision offers the person who dominates
the place—and whose neglect, the new wording suggests, is responsible for the scholar's ills. The patron also now dominates the line:
customarily isolated from his potential client in a privileged inner
space which garret- and jail-dwellers may not enter, the patron can
be glimpsed in the middle (the inner space) of this line, where he
momentarily reassumes an institutional agency and cultural authority
that, as we have seen, the mid-eighteenth century was increasingly
reluctant to recognize. In stressing the patron's isolation and neglect,
the revised *Vanity of Human Wishes* acknowledges the decline of the
old patronage system's enveloping authority. No longer able to control the production and consumption of literature on behalf of a de-
vitalized form of pastoral power, it is classed now among the forces
that assail writers, its diminished authority directed against those
whom it once governed.

Johnson's famous letter to Chesterfield, which, it has often been
claimed, prompted the garret/patron revision, is another example

from Johnson's own literary career of the ambiguous and changing relationships among authorship, patronage, and cultural authority. Recent scholarship has suggested that the letter ought to be read as a direct response to papers Chesterfield published in *The World,* papers which invited the conclusion that he was still patronizing the *Dictionary* long after the two men had broken and which promoted views on language that Johnson had abandoned.[14] Nevertheless, as we know, Johnson's letter (to which Chesterfield never responded and to which subsequent readers have customarily reacted as if it were a general observation and not a specific response) has often been treated as the modern author's declaration of independence from the old, hierarchical patronage system. Its description of a patron is well-known and frequently quoted: "one who looks with unconcern on a Man struggling for Life in the Water and when he has reached ground encumbers him with Help." Its depiction of an impoverished, unknown Johnson waiting vainly in Chesterfield's "outward Rooms" is engraved in art and memory. And its characterization of the letter's writer, emerging now as Dictionary Johnson, a figure who will himself dominate mid- and late-eighteenth-century cultural discourse, suggests the new attitude with which the mid-century author confronts the traditional structures of authority: "The notice which you have been pleased to take of my Labours, had it been early, had been kind; but it has been delayed till I am indifferent and cannot enjoy it, till I am solitary and cannot impart it, till I am known and do not want it."[15] Indifferent, solitary, and known, adjectives which might describe the patron, are used here to characterize the New Author, whose appropriation of the patron's attitude indicates that he has become (or has the illusion of becoming) his own patron.

That the self-patronizing author is but an illusion is evident from Johnson's own extensive efforts to act as a patron of literature. Holladay and Brack have recently catalogued and enumerated many instances of Johnson's "writing reviews, signing subscription lists, influencing booksellers, contributing to others' works, revising others' works, and [ghost]writing Prefaces and Dedications." They conclude: "Johnson did whatever he could to gain for other authors the attraction of aristocrats, booksellers, subscribers, and the public, all potential sources of income in a period of transition from court to private patronage to purely commercial publication reliant on mass consumption."[16] Thus the autonomous public posture Johnson occasionally assumed ("No man who ever lived by literature, has lived more independently than I have done")[17] was constrained by his patronage of other writers, whose dependence and distress he both relieved and shared.

This situation is implicated in a satirical piece, a letter to the editor subsequently entitled "A Project for the Employment of Authors," which Johnson wrote for the *Universal Visiter* in 1756, the year after the Chesterfield letter. This essay ironically suggests that the recent prodigious increase in the number of authors, who "are spread over all the town and all the country, and fill every stage of habitation from the cellar to the garret," can be alleviated by pressing them into military service, "for which they may seem particularly qualified" by their familiarity with "want" and uncertainty and by their willingness "to obey the word of command from their patrons and their booksellers." The essay's conclusion ("if they should be destroyed in war, we shall lose only those who had wearied the public, and whom, whatever be their fate, nobody will miss") reinforces its major premise ("If I were to form an adage of misery, or fix the lowest point to which humanity could fall, I should be tempted to name the life of an author"). Although this observation can be treated as an overstatement supporting the satire, its sting is not easily salved. The author emerges here not as the indifferently independent self-patronizer of the Chesterfield letter, but, as is more customary in Johnson's work, as "an adage of misery," neglected by his patron, deserted by the public, "worried by critics, tormented by his bookseller, and hunted by his creditors." No longer entailed in the landed estate of hierarchical patronage, the author is now the public's performer, plaything, and pet—"teazed like a bear at the stake, tormented like a toad under a harrow; or hunted like a dog with a stick at his tail."[18]

III

The biographical subject of a text which refers to itself in its opening paragraphs as one of those "mournful Narratives" that "has been written only to enumerate the Miseries of the Learned" (4), Johnson's Savage also becomes an "adage of misery" as he turns to authorship and literature in an effort to re-enter the hierarchical system which, he claims, has inappropriately excluded him. This turning from genealogy to authorship is powerfully and directly presented in Johnson's narrative, where Savage's "Discovery of his real Mother" (the Countess of Macclesfield) prompts "his frequent Practice to walk in the dark Evenings for several Hours before her Door, in Hopes of seeing her as she might come by Accident to the Window, or cross her Apartment with a Candle in her Hand." Banished to the dark but seeking the light of entry, he finds that "he could neither soften her Heart, nor open her Hand," and, in the next sentence, without any previously delineated desire or preparation, determines "He was therefore obliged to seek some other Means of Support, and having no Profession, became, by Necessity, an Author" (12). This relationship between necessity and authorship is sketched throughout Johnson's narrative. For instance, Savage's inconstant "Supply" of funds and increasing friendships "necessarily leading him to Places of Expence, he found it necessary to endeavour once more at dramatick Poetry" (21). Conversely, his selling *The Wanderer* for a mere ten guineas "was not to be imputed either to Necessity by which the Learned and Ingenious are often obliged to submit to very hard Conditions, or to Avarice by which the Booksellers are frequently invited to oppress that Genius by which they are supported" (58). In a sense, such necessity is responsible for the habitual predicament of a common, secular authorship disinherited by genealogy or excommunicated by religion; neither a person who writes for bread nor a client who writes for patronage can be trusted to seek the truth. "The name of an Author would never have been made contemptible, had no Man ever said what he did not think, or misled others, but when he was himself deceived" (46).

Of course, "the Discovery of his real Mother" implies the discovery of Savage's real father (the Earl Rivers), but the father has been long dead and his Will thwarted. Savage cannot reach his father, the *pater* who can act as his *patron* and authenticate his place in the hierarchy. The shared philological root[19] suggests one reason why, in Johnson's narrative, Savage's mother does not acknowledge him: to do so would be to patronize him, to assume the father's role. But her role is to maintain the separation of father and son, and hence to force Savage into authorship and literature, through which she will become the subject and victim of his writing, and through which he will discover the futility of his quest for patronage and learn to resign himself to the divine will, to the supreme Father of all our Being and the original Patron of all our words. Johnson's narrative acknowledges the *pater*/patron relationship in various ways. To Richard Steele, himself an established author who is one of the many patrons and father-figures Savage acquires and then loses, is attributed the statement: *"the Inhumanity of* [Savage's] *Mother had given him a Right to find every good Man his Father"* (13). In a poem by Savage reprinted in Johnson's narrative, Aaron Hill, "an Author of an established Character" (23) who patronizes Savage's early efforts at playwriting, is addressed as "Thou Brother, Father, nearer yet—thou Friend" (22). Here and elsewhere Johnson's narrative suggests that Savage has a natural right to seek paternity and patronage wherever he can find it. As the Duke of Dorset, one of the many noble personages to whom Savage attaches himself, remarks: "it was just to consider [Savage] as an injured Nobleman, and . . . the Nobility ought to think themselves obliged without Solicitation to take every Opportunity of supporting him by their Countenance and Patronage" (20). That Savage seeks this natural right through authorship, that he tries to establish a literary career in terms of the old, eroding system of patronage—and thereby re-enter the nobility, is a significant narrative structure which, as we shall see, Johnson's biography symbolically appropriates and then frustrates.

Johnson's earliest surviving comment on Savage is a Latin epigram published in the *Gentleman's Magazine* in April 1738, about the time of their first meeting and six years before the initial publication of the biography. Although "the epigram cannot be taken to show more than slight and recent acquaintance,"[20] it intimates that, in one way or another, the notion of patronage (and of its uncertain application and authority) was deeply and presuppositionally embedded in Johnson's writing on Savage. The epigram reads: "Humani studium generis cui pectore fervet, / O! colat humanum Te foveatque genus!"[21] Clarence Tracy, who observes that the epigram implies an "antithesis [that] rings through" the *Life of Savage,* translates it as "Devotion to mankind burns in your breast! O! may mankind in turn cherish and protect you!"[22] Tracy's translation suggests the community's responsibility to support Savage, an injunction enriched and implemented by the knowledge that the verb *foveo* in the epigram's second line can also mean to patronize, as well as to make warm, give comfort to, soothe, relieve, fondle, caress, nurse, foster, nurture, minister to, favor, support, encourage, befriend, promote, cherish, and cultivate.[23] Indeed, we might claim that, in its various senses, this verb

informs the biography's depiction of Savage's treatment by the changing patronage system, for Johnson's narrative employs nearly all these
meanings as it elaborates and particularizes the many patron/client
relationships it traces.

For instance, Steele and Robert Wilks the actor are presented as
patrons "by whom [Savage] was pitied, caressed, and relieved" (13).
Elsewhere, a client is somewhat generally described as "one whom [a
patron] has relieved and supported, whose Establishment he has laboured, and whose Interest he has promoted" (16). Connotations of
foveo emerge also in the differences among the various women with
whom Savage is involved. "Instead of supporting, assisting, and defending him," his mother would "delight to see him struggling with
Misery" (6); in contrast, the actions of the Countess of Hertford, who
intercedes with the Queen after Savage's murder trial, provoke the
observation that it is "much more amiable to relieve, then to oppress"
(39). Several senses of the Latin verb characterize the Lord Tyrconnell's
patronage. At first, this is "the Golden Part of Mr. *Savage*'s Life,"
during which he is "courted" and "caressed" (44). Yet, upon their
falling out, it comes to typify the inevitable situation of all client/
patron relationships: "he was only a Dependent on the Bounty of
another, whom he could expect to support him no longer than he
endeavoured to preserve his Favour, by complying with his Inclinations" (66). The group of subscribing friends, who eventually replace
Tyrconnell, fare no better. Jailed for debt in Bristol, Savage discovers
that "his Friends, who had hitherto caressed and applauded, . . . all
refused to preserve him from a Prison, at the Expence of eight
pounds" (124). Finally, in the narrative's summary character sketch,
Savage emerges as one who "appeared to think himself born to be
supported by others, and dispensed from all Necessity of providing
for himself" (137). This is an echo of Savage's preface to the 1726
Miscellaneous Poems, an autobiographical account reprinted in Johnson's narrative: "Thus however ill qualified I am to *live by my Wits,* I
have the best Plea in the World for attempting it; since it is too
apparent, that I was *born to it*" (because he has been "thrown, friend-
less on the World, without Means of supporting *myself;* and without
Authority to apply to those, whose Duty I know it is to support
me") (28).

Born to live by his wits, born to be supported by others—this is
the Savage we have been tracing. Unlike another recipient of "Mr.

Wilks's Generosity" whom the narrative briefly describes—a failed author named Smith who saves the money he receives from a benefit organized by Wilks, uses it to study medicine at Leyden, and eventually becomes "one of the chief Physicians at the *Russian* court" (17)—Savage is unable to capitalize on the several benefits Wilks stages for him or, for that matter, on any patronage arrangement into which he enters. "He was very ready to set himself free from the Load of an Obligation; for he could not bear to conceive himself in a State of Dependence" (138). The biography studiously catalogues the various patrons to whom Savage is such a disobliging client; contempt, dissatisfaction, and neglect characterize the behavior of both parties. Savage cannot abide his patrons' condescension, but he will not allow them to ignore what he sees as their duty to him. The narrative is constantly following Savage's movement from one unsatisfactory patronage scheme to another: "To despair was not, however, the Character of *Savage,* when one Patronage failed, he had recourse to another" (90). Steele is a "Patron [who] had many Follies" (16); Mrs. Oldfield, the actress who comes closest to the ideal combination of substitute mother and undemanding patron, dies; Wilks, the actor, and Hill, the author, cannot provide him access to the nobility; his various aristocratic patrons, like Hertford, Middlesex, and Tyrconnell, presume on the relationship and are in turn abused by their client, who insists on acting as willfully as a 'real' nobleman; political and royal patrons, like Walpole, the King, the Queen, and the Prince of Wales, are either unreliable and niggardly or unapproachable and unavailing; the group of subscribing friends organized by Pope are "*Little Creatures*" (111) who provide him with "a Pension less than that which Mrs. *Oldfield* paid him without exacting any Servilities" (114); the Bristol merchants, "sufficiently studious of Profit," cannot countenance Savage's "Neglect of Oeconomy" (120–21).

Finally, there is Abel Dagg, the Keeper of Bristol Newgate Gaol— "a Pattern of Benevolence . . . whose Heart has not been hardened by such an Employment" (127). Dagg is generous, patient, and undemanding. As the client of this "Pattern" or patron (the two words not only share a Latin root and French derivation but, until the sixteenth century, were both spelled 'patron'—hence the sense, as here and in Johnson's *Dictionary,* of "pattern" as an exemplar to be copied), Savage can write in a letter to a friend: "I am now all collected in myself, and tho' my Person is in Confinement, my Mind can expatiate

on ample and useful Subjects, with all the Freedom imaginable. . . .
if, instead of a *Newgate* Bird, I may be allowed to be a Bird of the
Muses, I assure you, Sir, I sing very freely in my Cage" (125). With
this totemic image of eighteenth-century authorship (Sterne's Yorick,
we remember, emblazons a caged starling on his family arms),[24] Johnson's Savage ends his quest to re-enter the nobility, to regain paternity
and patronage through the traditional system of hierarchical authority. This disintegrating arrangement for producing literature can no
longer confer anything but a revokable symbolic status—what the
narrative calls "uncertain Patronage" (43), a phrase that not only describes Savage's specific situation but also characterizes the general
condition of the new, emerging institution of literature, which authorizes authorship not by enmeshing the writer and his text in a self-
authenticating context of privileged and private production and
consumption but by forcing the writer to assert his independence and
isolation from both the hierarchical authority structures and the reading public. Indeed, it is in the mid-eighteenth century that the reading public begins to establish itself as the consumer which does not
produce, as the authority which endorses authorship (in concert with
the booksellers, its agents) through the brute fact of its massive anonymity. In such a situation, the writer aspiring to be transformed into
an author can deny his essential humanity in two ways—by embracing either the immaterial or the material. That is, he can invoke (as
Johnson does in many of his works) the residual authority and individualizing tactic of the old form of pastoral power, an invocation
expressed by renouncing the material world and resigning himself to
the divine will in order to seek salvation and self-definition in God's
eternal and immaterial realm—as Savage does just before he dies,
when, "all Resignation to the *divine Will*" (123), he sings very freely
in his cage. Or the aspiring author can reside, temporarily and provisionally, in the transient individuality promised to everyone by the
new secular form of pastoral power, can become a mere name, a material nexus of acceptability and marketability in a commodity culture
that canonizes self-advertisement and secularizes salvation.

IV

Biography, itself a form of writing aspiring to literary status, is in a
similar situation. By the mid-eighteenth century it is no longer pa-

tronized exclusively or dominantly by the structures of hierarchical authority through which traditional pastoral power is distributed. For the most part, mid-eighteenth-century English biography must seek patronage and authority from the reading public, the vastness and anonymity of which threaten to consume it, that is, both read it and exhaust it, use it and use it up. For the reading public's appetite is enormous, and yet the stipulative supply of biographical subjects (the received and recognized saints, heroes, and leaders of traditional hierarchical culture) is limited. If biography is to survive it must generate more and different biographical subjects, must learn how to exploit (more extensively than did the predominantly autobiographical, hierarchical cultural practice that Stephen Greenblatt has recently labelled "Renaissance self-fashioning") the individualizing tactic authorized by the new, secular form of pastoral power. As I have suggested, Johnson's Savage is a powerful sign of this transitional situation. A self-proclaimed bastard son of nobility, a convicted and nearly executed murderer, a self-advertised "volunteer laureate" and "author to be let," he is a biographical subject in flux—the subject simultaneously and ambiguously presented and authorized by traditional hierarchical biography, by the new subcultural criminal biography, and by the emerging magazine biography (which Johnson helped to initiate in the *Gentleman's Magazine* and which sought to link high and low culture). A successful failure more notorious than famous, a creation of the exploding subculture of hack-writing (which discovered him at his murder trial, variously supported and disobliged him throughout his subsequent public careers, and in the service of which he battled anonymously and pseudonymously as one of Pope's allies in the War of the Dunces), Savage is a classic transitional figure, a fatherless, unpatronized, disestablished, self-promoting author who became (in Goldsmith's memorable phrase) "a child of the public."[25]

As Neil McKendrick, John Brewer, and J. H. Plumb have recently shown, eighteenth-century England gave birth to "the first of the world's consumer societies." "Bourgeois consumerism" was a crucial pre-condition for the shift from a "client economy" serving the aristocracy to an "open market" in which Mandevillian tradesmen manipulated luxury as a "great chain of enterprise." McKendrick quotes from the *London Tradesman* of 1747, a kind of early trade journal: a tradesman "must be 'a Perfect Proteus, change Shapes as often as the

Moon, and still find something new'; for 'the continual Flux and Reflux of Fashion, obliges him to learn something new almost every day,'" obliges him, McKendrick later asserts, to produce and manipulate agents of supply and demand in his "pursuit of new levels of consumption from an ever-widening market."[26] In this "Perfect Proteus" we glimpse not only a Wedgwood or a Boulton merchandising pottery or buttons but the booksellers (the "Trade") and their factories of hack writers producing, publishing, and distributing reading material to an expanding, seemingly insatiable mass public, whose demand for new, diverse biographical subjects must be supplied. Indeed, McKendrick's description of the modification, during the course of the eighteenth century, in one of the fashion industry's agents of change, the fashion doll, is strikingly similar to the transformation which, I have been suggesting, the biographical subject undergoes during the same period.

The fashion dolls of the early part of the century were wooden, often life-sized mannequins outfitted in the elaborate costuming of the French court. Accurate down to details of hairstyle, underclothing, and the other accessories of fashion, they were sent annually to the English court and then passed on "to the leading London fashion makers." But by the end of the century the English had developed "a flat fashion model cut out of cardboard," which "cost only three shillings . . . and later only a few pence, . . . was printed by the thousand," and was "specifically aimed at different classes and professions." McKendrick comments: "Where the French fashion doll of the first decades of the century served only an *élite,* the English fashion doll of the last decades of that century served a mass consumer market. . . . Its role was now the manipulation and extension of consumer demand. Its dramatic metamorphosis in the course of the century nicely confirms the change from a world where fashion was not only designed to serve the few but was designed to mark them off from the rest of society, to a world where fashion was being deliberately designed to encourage social imitation, social emulation, and emulative spending."[27]

This "dramatic metamorphosis" is similar to the shift in patronizing the biographical subject that we have been tracing. Like the fashion doll, the biographical subject moves out of the client economy of the elite and into the mass consumer market over the course of the eighteenth century. Moreover, like the fashion doll, it marks a new

tactic of individualization: the selection and production of biographical subjects are no longer the sole responsibility and privilege of a
patronage arrangement dominated by the traditional structures of
hierarchical authority. A biographical subject like Johnson's Savage
signifies that biography too has become an agent in the great chain of
enterprise, another institutional channel through which the modern
state can materially produce or reproduce the individual in this world.
Indeed, one of Wedgwood's eighteenth-century lines of merchandise
was "a Biographical Catalogue of distinguished Characters"—medallions and busts of "illustrious Men of various Ages and Countries,"
available "at a moderate price."[28] But, as we have seen, neither antique fame nor distinguished character is a prerequisite for inclusion
in the biographical catalogue of the emerging consumer society. On
the reading public's behalf biography can now authorize practically
anyone (or anything) as a biographical subject: Johnson, Boswell
claims, "is reported to have once said, that 'he could write the Life of
a Broomstick.'"[29] This anecdote heralds a proliferation of mock biography, a parodic form which, after the middle of the eighteenth century, becomes a sign of biography's newly acquired generic authority.
Lives of dogs and cats, of fictional painters, detectives, and spies
(culminating perhaps in Woolf's *Orlando*, who lives for more than
three hundred years as both a man and a woman) reveal how powerful
and how vulnerable is the new form of pastoral power first exerted by
eighteenth-century biography. If *Eminent Victorians* ironically deflates
the received relationship between secular employment and sacred calling, then Woolf's *Orlando* (1928) challenges the discursive project of
English biography itself, by presenting it as a discontinuous narrative
unable or unwilling to deconstruct crucial individualizing tactics like
gender, class, period, or nationality through which both the old and
new forms of pastoral power exerted themselves.

We can briefly trace this failure of nerve in the patron/client relationships delineated by biographer and biographical subject in
Walton's *Donne* and Johnson's *Savage*. The Waltonian biographer characterizes himself as "Pompey's *poor bondman*," that is, as the *"artless"*
servant of a great man who finds himself employed in the *"officious
duty"* of making a *"well-meant sacrifice to* [that man's] *memory."*[30] This
master/servant relationship is, of course, a complex one: the narrative
and enveloping dedicatory materials of Walton's *Donne* imply that
(among other possibilities) it can be interpreted as ruler/subject,

pastor/congregant, model/artist, or author/amanuensis, as well as patron/client. This last interpretation, however, is made explicit in Henry King's *Elegy,* which follows the narrative and which presents Donne as the *"Late . . . great Patron"* of *"Widow'd invention."* Thus, the poem posits, whoever seeks to commemorate Donne, be he elegist or biographer, must seek stylistic and creative *"prerogative"*[31] from his patron of invention, from Donne himself. This or some cognate notion of the biographical subject as the patron of the biographer is characteristic of the royal and ecclesiastical biography of the late-sixteenth and early-seventeenth centuries. Biography emerges there as the client of the dominant socio-cultural authority structures, which patronize it by permitting it to perform its commemorative duty.

Waltonian biography's celebration of the sanctity of its biographical subject's life involves not only a stated acceptance of the subject's prerogative and patronage but also an implicit recognition that, in reanimating his subject, the biographer in effect acts as his patron's patron. Yet this is not an approach Walton's narratives can afford to adopt formally. Rather, the subversive reversal of the patron/client, biographical subject/biographer relationship must emerge as an accidental consequence of a client's associating himself with his intellectual, social, and spiritual superior—the attitude of "the most affectionate and most humble servants" of Waltonian and most seventeenth- and early-eighteenth-century dedications. But, by the mid-eighteenth century, our reading of Johnson's *Savage* suggests, this alternative 'political' relationship between biographer and biographical subject, which always was and is a generic possibility, can become more explicit. Now the biographer can more forthrightly assume the authority to act as his subject's father/patron, a relationship which has been occasionally acknowledged in subsequent commentary—for instance, when the Johnsonian narrator has been treated as a kind of benign father-figure for a disinherited, "artificial bastard," or when the biographer has been chastised for defending the convicted murderer too vigorously (vindicator or legal advocate is one of the senses of the Latin word *patronus* that Johnson's *Dictionary* also ascribes to its English derivative). As we know, these are metaphorical relationships which are characteristic of biographical recognition: biographers are frequently applauded or chastised for vigorous or indifferent defenses of their subjects, as well as for patronizing or parenting subjects who have been disenfranchised or disinherited by discursive politics. Of course, biographical narratives have always been evaluated in this way, but only with more or less 'modern' biographies has this evaluation proceeded from the assumption that the patronage instrumentalizing these relationships is in the gift of the biographer and not the biographical subject.

A biographical subject like Savage would have been nearly impossible in traditional hierarchical culture: his anomalous position in the rigid class structure would have disinherited him as an appropriate patron of biographical invention. But in the emerging consumer culture Savage is an eminently apposite biographical subject, because, lacking both a father and a patron, he requires and justifies biography's newly acquired authority to parent and patronize him and any other child of the public. What must be suppressed now is that, like Steele, Tyrconnell, and the many other patrons who pass through Johnson's narrative, the biographer may be only a transient, substitute father/patron, a temporary agent who tries to assume authority but does not grant it. In a sense, the biographer can be characterized as merely another commodity, a familiar name by which books are bought and sold and through which literary history is incorporated and enfranchised. Mid- and late-eighteenth-century authors can become so closely associated with their texts that, to the reading public at least, they are virtually indistinguishable from them: Johnson is "Dictionary Johnson," Boswell "Corsica Boswell," Sterne "Yorick" or "Tristram Shandy." Linked inexorably to their subjects, biographers, like all authors, are themselves parented and patronized by the new consumer society, which, during this transitional period, aggrandizes and appropriates authorship as yet another agent in the commercialization and secularization of culture.

If Johnson's *Savage* traces one of the individualizing tactics through which mid-eighteenth-century cultural discourse institutionalizes the shift from a sacred to a secular form of pastoral power, then it also indicates how generic conventions are, like fashion, in "continual flux and reflux." As the fatherless, patronless Savage becomes Johnson's *Savage*, so Dictionary Johnson becomes Boswell's *Johnson*, a recontextualization in which Johnson's status as father/patron of biography is recognized and then usurped by a biographer whose self-conscious desire to manipulate generic authority consumes his biographical subject. In the discourse of consumerism, everyone soon comes to realize what Johnson's Savage can never quite accept, "that his Opinion in

Questions of Criticism [is] no longer regarded, when his Coat [is] out of Fashion" (101). If Johnson's *Savage* is a transitional agent of change, an English fashion doll or child of the public demonstrating that the traditional three estates are no longer the sole patrons and beneficiaries of English biography, then Boswell's *Johnson* is the modern state itself—an infinitely reproducing matrix of individualization, a technological marvel of interchangeable parts, a self-patronizing, self-advertising, self-consuming economy of biography which perfectly encapsulates the secular form of pastoral power and which thus situates itself at the conventionally acknowledged center of generic authority. Consequently, the epigram with which this chapter begins—"it was therefore impossible to pay him any Distinction without the entire Subversion of all Oeconomy, a Kind of Establishment which, wherever he went, he always appeared ambitious to overthrow" (98)—can refer not only to Savage's neglect of domestic management but also, in and through Johnson's narrative, to his role as a biographical subject who heralds a new economic, political, social, and literary distribution of the conditions that produce biography and reproduce individuals.

chapter 5

RECOGNIZING THE BIOGRAPHICAL SUBJECT

"Genre lives in the present, but it always *remembers* the
past, its beginnings." (Mikhail Bakhtin)

I

Although "unpublished and virtually unknown until 1962," Roger
North's *General Preface* to his *Lives* of his brothers, written between
1718 and 1722, is now acknowledged to be the most extensive English commentary on biography before Johnson and Boswell, whose
theory and practice of life-writing it anticipates in many ways.[1] North
(c. 1653–1734) lived and wrote during that crucial period at the turn
of the eighteenth century when, as we saw in the last chapter, biography participated in the shift from a sacred to a secular form of
pastoral power and thereby became an individualizing tactic through
which the mass consumer market of the modern state could materially
reproduce the individual. The theoretical approach to biography out-
lined in North's *General Preface* expresses this situation almost exactly.
It rejects traditional forms of hierarchical life-writing—"the most
solemn registers of ages and nations, or the acts and monuments of
famed governors, statesmen, prelates, or generals of armies"—as containing "little if anything comparate or applicable to instruct a private
economy, or tending to make a man either wiser or more cautelous
[cautious] in his own proper concerns" (51). Rather it prefers "private
biography" or "the history of private lives adapted to the perusal of
common men" (51, 70, 76). For, besides conveying "the proper ef-
fects as to good and evil, . . . there is also a copious harvest of discretion and wisdom . . . to be gathered from the patterns of private
men, who have at their great risk proved divers ways of living, and it
may be have found out the best at last, and possibly suffered from
their mistakes. Therefore nothing can be more profitably instructive
to private men than relations of other men's proceedings in like condition" (64–65).

Born into a proud and powerful aristocratic family that he defended and celebrated in his *Lives* of his brothers, North was "a committed member of a small group of High Church, Tory Jacobites" who seems to have fit Steele's prototype of "the ideal country gentleman" ("father to his tenants, and patron to his neighbors"—the language, as we have seen, of the traditional, now disintegrating system of socio-cultural authority).[2] Yet his theoretical approach to lifewriting invokes the language and adopts the assumptions of a different economic and cultural order. The *General Preface* forthrightly approaches biography as an individualizing tactic of a secular form of pastoral power, as a discursive practice devoted to the institutionalization of profitable patterns of private economy. As we have seen, this is a discontinuity with which Johnson's Savage is unable to contend; indeed, Johnson's narrative can be seen as a gloss on the problems that biography confronts in making the transition from a symbolic plot governed by paternal patronage to one negotiated by private economy. Unable to discover, or even discern the need for, a profitable pattern of conducting his own life, Savage is a biographical subject in flux, a bastard child of the public who threatens "the entire Subversion of all Oeconomy."[3] North's notion of private biography suggests how Savage becomes an anomalous (although, in that respect, a representative and instructive) subject for the alternative forms of life-writing induced by the eighteenth-century's secular redistribution of pastoral power. It also shows how the generic frame "recognizing the biographical subject" (the generative scheme whereby individual human lives are reproduced) was forced to accommodate itself to the shift from a patron, in which all cultural and generic authority resides, to a pattern that is evaluated only in terms of its profitability.

As biography becomes a transaction between the private economies of reader and subject, it drifts away from the gaze of sanctioned authority. Although North accepts that "no historical relation hath that force and efficacy as a man's own observations hath," he insists that observation and reading are "*in genere* the same," for "where observation is not to be had, the reading is a proper succedaneum [substitute] to supply the defect, and I must needs say that in many respects it hath the advantage" (56–57). Thus "private biography" becomes a way of turning a potential loss into a potential gain, of filling up the vacancies of a life conducted as if it were outside the purview of hierarchical authority. The defects in an individual's own experience, "and what is [experience] but a tradition or private history of a man's own gathering," can be "gathered and preserved by others" (56). Biography then becomes an agent of the "private economy" of everyday life, a means of supplying and augmenting "business and conversation, by which only the manners of men are formable, and their judgments maturable with regard to good breeding, and conduct of life" (56). "Solitary and deliberate," the experience of reading biographical narrative is "eyes to the blind" (57), a way of perceiving and taking advantage of the previously unglimpsed possibilities of modern life.

The pattern of the biographical subject's life which directs this 'insight' is not founded on the direct patronage of the traditional three estates. Patron and pattern, which were once the same word but did not become 'fully' "differentiated in sense and meaning" until about 1700 (*OED*), no longer enjoy a virtually unchallenged synonymy. North's *General Preface* avouches that the notion of a patron as "an example to be copied," the sense of the word from which 'pattern' develops,[4] cannot continue to dominate biographical recognition. As the profitable pattern of private economy, the biographical subject has lost its traditional patron. A product and producer of an emerging consumer culture, it must now show a profit by demystifying and naturalizing the patterns of everyday life. "If in private biography one would not mislead folks into extravagancies, it is required that the truth be unfolded just as in a legal testimony, whole, sole, and nothing else. And then the prospect will be clear, and a man may plainly discern whether anything is to be gathered there for his use or not. And without this point of sincerity the writing as to all profit is but a will-in-the-wisp" (70). When "all the tokens of veracity" are "artificially {artistically} interwoven with the relation," then "the matter is made, as it were, to speak, rather than the author." Thus "if the riches of observation lie concealed or couched in the style, they follow (as they say) naturally, or as if the reader and not the author supplied them" (70–71).

Here, in the *General Preface*'s language of profit and loss, observation and concealment, artificiality and naturalness, is biography as a discursive practice calibrated to the needs of a secular form of pastoral power. Assuming the pattern of a direct transaction between biographical subject and reader, the profitable biography of private economy is useful, sincere, and natural. It seems to patronize itself, to unfold its truth as if it were, in fact, a profitably instructive conversation between private men in like condition.[5] This is biography as commerce, as an exchange of goods or services invoking (as the word commerce once did) various modes of physical intimacy. If biography can naturalize the world by reproducing the hierarchical arrangement of patron and client in biographical subject and biographer, it can also do so by transforming the biographer into a mere tradesman in a commercial exchange between biographical subject as producer and biographical readership as consumer, or, alternatively, into a self-effacing go-between in an intimate private relationship. Artificially interwoven with the relation, the biographer loses the status of client and becomes (or is revealed to have always been) both a parasite and a supplement—the augmentation that lives off others and yet is necessary to their survival and even their completion.[6] In this sense, as we shall explore more fully in the next chapter, the biographer is like 'profit'—the parasitical supplement produced by economic exchange which replaces or relieves the suffering that, North suggests, afflicts those uninstructed by "the patterns of private men." Of course, the biographer can still appear in biographical narrative, but always as if on sufferance. As we remarked in the previous chapter, the self-patronizing biographer of the mid-eighteenth century is only a transient, substitute father/patron, a temporary agent manipulated by a commodity culture. Private biography, like the traditional public biography, privileges the biographical subject as the pattern, if not the patron, of individual human existence—for, as we shall see, the generic frame "recognizing the biographical subject" is a powerful force in intra-generic politics that does not easily concede tactical advantage. Like the public patrons of the hierarchical forms of life-writing, the private patterns of 'commercial' biography can become the model and the proof upon which the referential authority of biography is founded.[7]

"Recognizing the biographical subject"'s successful negotiation of the crisis it encounters around the turn of the eighteenth century indicates just how important this generic frame has always been to the sense of biographical recognition as an enabling act accompanying the transfer of authority. Despite the shift from a sacred to a secular form of pastoral power, the biographical subject remains "the master-sign and . . . generative model"[8] of individual human existence. A way of being and becoming to which we attach special significance, it continues to denote a cultural process of exclusion and inclusion that we monitor closely. We still recognize the entrance of a biographical subject into written discourse as a momentous occasion, as an event that can, among other things, reaffirm cultural eminence, contextualize social action, alter literary opinion, deputize political influence, or instruct economic conduct. Thus the ambiguous and changing relationship between 'patron' and 'pattern' adumbrated in North's *General Preface* and enacted in Johnson's *Savage* represents not merely a significant passage in the generic history of English biography but an ongoing feature of biographical recognition. Moreover, although North, Johnson, and their contemporaries may have expressed and enacted this generic situation in various ways in their theory and practice of biography, it should be seen not only as an outgrowth of particular social, economic, and cultural circumstances, but also as a specific instance of a crisis that is always already occurring in biographical recognition. For instance, it has been claimed that the Greek "biographic and autobiographic experiments of the fourth century [B.C.]" were "transitional . . . compositions" between "portraits of public figures" and "private lives"; and that Varro's *Imagines* or *Hebdomades,* apparently written between 44 and 39 B.C., "transformed" the "Roman aristocratic tradition" of ancestral biography into a prose form that "now made availble to educated readers" what was formerly "the property of aristocratic families." It has also been claimed that, during the Roman Imperial Age, when Plutarch, Suetonius, and Tacitus produced the biographical narratives to which seventeenth- and eighteenth-century English lifewriting inexorably returns, biography was both "an instrument of Imperial propaganda" and "a vehicle for unorthodox political and philosophic ideas"—it could be "the natural [that is, officially patronized] form of telling the story of a Caesar" or "a capital offense under the tyranny of Domitian."[9] In this broader generic context "recognizing the biographical subject" emerges as a generative scheme for (re)producing individual human lives that is always seeking a 'natural' relationship with sanctioned authority, for the alternative to the similitude of 'patron' and 'pattern' is the capital offense of biographical recognition—the alienation of the decentered subject.

This threat of losing its official sanction and becoming a cultural outlaw motivates, indeed overdetermines, the generic frame "recognizing the biographical subject." As we have noted previously, the crisis it successfully negotiates in English biography around the turn of the eighteenth century is a specific manifestation of a general phenomenon. As Bakhtin remarks, "Genre lives in the present, but it always *remembers* the past, its beginnings."[10] Thus it is that the generic frame "recognizing the biographical subject" can be emplotted as an attempt to restore the similitude of 'patron' and 'pattern,' to 'remember' that which has been dismembered. If successful, this effort will reconstitute the 'natural' economy of the sovereign subject as the model upon which individual human existence is founded, and as the system of exchange and circulation through which observed public presence (the business and conversation of everyday life) and concealed private absence (the solitary and deliberate transaction of biographical discourse) become interchangeable coin of the realm.

II

A brief exploration of two specialized senses of "pattern" helps us establish this approach. "A figure in wood or metal from which a mould is made for casting" (*OED*): this is an old sense of the word, derived from founding, that dates from at least the early sixteenth century, when it was spelled "patron." We can compare it with a sense dating from the nineteenth century, after "pattern" and "patron" "became differentiated in form and sense": "A specimen model of a proposed coin, struck by a mint, but not subsequently adopted for the currency. Distinguished from a *proof*" (*OED*). The earlier meaning suits our conventional sense of the biographical subject as patterned after and patronized by an individual human who existed in concrete time and space, a material figure from which the biographical mold is cast. In this sense, the biographical subject is "founded" upon an original, a patron whose pattern it faithfully reproduces. The later meaning 'casts' doubt on this originary founding. Like "pattern" and "patron," the model and the proof are now to be differentiated. In this sense, the biographical subject is a discursive specimen, a proposal to be considered but not adopted as coin of the realm. A biographical subject which is minted but not proved is a coin without value, an unpatronized pattern distinguished from (and not by) a proof. As we know, biographical recognition generally does not acknowledge that "patron" and "pattern" can be "differentiated in form and sense," that an unfounded, uncirculated biographical subject can become "the master-sign and . . . generative model" of individual human existence. Yet, as we shall see, it is just this possibility that instrumentalizes the generic frame "recognizing the biographical subject," for it *"amounts to saying once again that there is no absolute origin of sense in general."* [11]

But first we must consider the conventional recognition of the biographical subject, which, as we have noted, is founded on the notion of a non-discursive figure that functions as the patron/pattern from which a discursive model is made. That which resists semiotic encoding (because it is in some sense or aspect unknown or unknowable) sponsors and pre-figures what can enter discourse as a biographical subject. This crucial theme of generic recognition supposedly distinguishes the biographical subject from the fictional subject, which we conventionally recognize as an individual human that exists only in and through discourse and is thus thoroughly encodable. Tom Jones pre-exists the narrative first published in 1749 only as type or theme in cultural or literary discourse, and cannot post-exist it except as a character or topic in creative or critical discourse. The *transdiscursive* pattern Tom Jones thus describes as he moves across discourse is never biographical; his "life" is always mock-biographical, "lived" entirely in cultural and literary discourse and read always and only as fiction or criticism. Johnson's Savage, on the other hand, is an *extra-discursive* figure in cultural and literary history. Enjoying the same opportunities as Tom Jones to be portrayed, satirized, analyzed, and typologized in creative and critical discourse, he can also be recognized as an individual human whose existence prior to the narrative first published in 1744 cannot be completely or ultimately reduced to semiosis. [12]

Thus the biographical subject is conventionally patterned after and patronized by an appeal to the materially unknown or unknowable, to a transcendental signified which is formally outside discourse but is knowable only in and through discourse. As paradoxical as this situation may seem when formulated theoretically, it is, in practice, a powerful way of being and becoming in Western culture. As we have seen, extra-discursivity is a privilege accorded to very few English individuals before the Renaissance, and then only to the received saints, heroes, and leaders of a hierarchical authority structure that controlled access to written discourse. By patronizing the biographical subject as the discursive pattern through which individual human existence was to be expressed (and suppressed), hierarchical culture effectively controlled the distribution of extra-discursivity as a function of "pastoral power." When this patronage arrangement disintegrated in and around the eighteenth century, it gave way to a secular, consumer society manipulated by fashion and trade. By democratizing and secularizing the biographical subject (at least in the English-speaking world), the subsequent redistribution of extra-discursivity threatened to reveal that "recognizing the biographical subject" was not a proof of existence but a mere tactic for individuation demonstrating that patron and pattern were not (and never had been) synonymous.

The investment that English commerce made in patronizing 'pattern' elaborates the cultural currency of this redistribution. The new consumer industries marketed their swelling inventories through 'pattern books,' 'pattern cards,' and 'pattern rooms,' thus redefining the conceptual practice of 'pattern' as a commercial strategy associated with material culture. The quickest and most effective means of publicizing and circulating merchandise, 'pattern' was also the greatest threat to the stability and exclusivity of trade. Matthew Boulton, the great button and hardware manufacturer, smuggled his patterns into France "'by the help of wide Breeches and pocketts,'" yet the Soho pattern books, upon which his immense fortune was built, contain nearly 1500 designs from which his customers could choose. Josiah Wedgwood, self-described "vase maker general to the universe," acknowledged that "by selling single patterns [he could] give away without any adiquate [sic] compensation the result of several years study & application, & many hundred pounds expence," but advised his partner that "so far from being afraid of other People geting [sic] our patterns, we should Glory in it," for this "*Generous* plan" to "lay our works open to be imitated" would "place us in a very advantageous light to the Public eye" and "might bring us as much *proffit* [sic] as *loss*." Furniture designers like Chippendale, Heppelwhite, and Sheraton, architects like Robert and James Adam, and other pattern-book producers and distributors also understood how this new marketing strategy worked; how the open distribution of hitherto exclusive trade secrets initiated a transformational and generative process that made profit out of loss; how, as one of Wedgwood's catalogues observed, "the Art of making *durable copies* . . . will thus promote the Art of *making Originals,* . . . for the more Copies there are of any Works, . . . the more celebrated the Original will be."[13]

The extent to which biography in general and the biographical subject in particular can be described as enmeshed in the rampant commercialization of eighteenth-century English culture is illustrated by one of Wedgwood's lines of merchandise—the *"Biographical Catalogue* of distinguished Characters" mentioned in the last chapter. These medallions and busts of "illustrious Men of various Ages and Countries," available "at a moderate price,"[14] indicate just how easily the emerging consumer society could reinscribe the biographical subject in its new 'pattern book' and thus put into question the traditional synonymy of patron and pattern. The project of biographical recognition ever since has been to restore this similitude by suggesting that the new arrangement for patronizing pattern is merely a variation on the old one, that the hegemony over the narrative inscription of individual human lives encoded in traditional hierarchical culture's book of worthies, saints, martyrs, and kings is re-encoded in the new consumer society's biographical catalogue of distinguished characters. As we know, this is an enterprise at which biographical recognition has been generally successful, for it has managed to remain the cultural model for extra-discursivity and to dominate the narrative space in which the theoretical paradox we mentioned earlier is allowed to go largely unexamined. Throughout this period biographical recognition has artlessly and craftily invoked the notion of the ideologically real, or the process by which "the object of the text . . . is 'ever-already' inscribed within ideology." This process of inscription and circumscription delineates "referential space" as "a dialectical interplay of textually present and absent cultural units."[15] Our exploration of pattern and patron re-creates (or *re*creates) this dialectical interplay as it remaps the referential space in which the biographical subject is signified.

Of course, in the lifewriting of traditional hierarchical culture this dialectical interplay was arrested by a more or less explicit appeal to God, the Father (*pater,* hence *patronus,* hence patron/pattern) whose creating Word is the archetypal pattern of discursive patronage. Significantly, this familiar Judaeo-Christian precept entered English biography as the exemplar for the biographical subject rather than the biographer. Before about 1700, that is, prior to the (supposedly) complete differentiation between patron and pattern, the ecclesiastical and royal biography which dominated English lifewriting was fathered by the biographical subject, whose cultural status patronized the narrative design elaborated by the biographer. This is the discursive situation which, as we have seen, "reanimates" Waltonian biography.[16] In this context, it is not misleading to assert that English biography was 'originally written' or underwritten by the biographical subject, through whose patronage the biographer ritualistically reproduced the only pattern deserving imitation. Thus, historically, the generic frame "recognizing the biographical subject" authorized the virtual disappearance of the biographer, except as a scribe or amanuensis through which the biographical subject, always already inscribed in cultural ideology, was to be reinscribed in biographical narrative—or, to pursue our metaphor of "pattern," as a pieceworker who elaborated the form and composed the parts of a decorative design of 'natural' (that is, culturally sanctioned) origin. Moreover, despite the decline of traditional hierarchical culture as the patron of English biography, and its subsequent replacement by an expanding consumer culture that might have been expected to purchase referential space by employing the biographer as a kind of producer or manufacturer of narrative lives, the generic frame "recognizing the biographical subject" still controls the production and distribution of extra-discursivity. Now, as then, the biographical subject is a virtually materialized signified which dominates referential space to such an extent that the biographer occupies it only as a virtually dematerialized signifier retained only as a formal necessity. The ongoing assertion of the 're-membered' union of pattern and patron thus (re-)creates how the generic frame "recognizing the biographical subject" has continued to underwrite English biography.

In the sense that generic recognition is an enabling act accompanying the transfer of authority, "recognizing the biographical subject" demonstrates the particularism characteristic of intra-generic politics. Each generic frame seeks to aggrandize itself at the expense of every other generic frame—to function as an independent power exclusively devoted to a special interest. Hence every genre has an internal (as well as external) politics, denoted by the constantly shifting, indeed, perpetually disruptive power relationships between and among generic frames, which, like the European powers at the end of the Napoleonic Era, wage war and negotiate peace simultaneously. The special interest of "recognizing the biographical subject" is, of course, to aggrandize the biographical subject, especially at the expense of the biographer, whose own extra-discursivity must be resisted as an invader or treated with as a plenipotentiary. Indeed, the extent to which resistance or negotiation succeeds is a factor in extra-generic politics as well, for it also demarcates the closely watched border between biography and autobiography. Biographical narratives characterized by virtually dematerialized biographers seldom challenge internal or external generic politics. On the other hand, those in which the biographer dominates (or seems to dominate) the referential space traditionally patronized by and patterned after the biographical subject are more often accused of disrupting conventional generic politics. As we shall see in a later chapter, this is the charge that is frequently levelled at Boswell's *Life of Johnson,* the narrative which, consequently, has long been recognized as both the greatest and the least representative English biography. Hence the generic frame "recognizing the biographical subject" is a conservative force in biographical recognition, a contextual and intertextual defender of the faith. Consistently opposed to it is another generic frame, "recognizing the biographer," a radically destabilizing element that, should it dominate the dialectical interplay of the ideologically real, would threaten biographical recognition itself.

III

Thus the plot thickens. The threat that patron and pattern may be dismembered—that the biographical subject's dominance of the dialectical interplay of textually present and absent cultural units may be subverted by the biographer's manipulation of (or by) a mass consumer culture which, allied with Romantic ideology, tends to privilege authorial or narratorial presence—is always countered by a form of generic 'reversion,' by a return (as in biology, the science of life) to ancestral type. Even a narrative like Boswell's *Johnson,* where the biographer has supposedly invaded referential space by establishing himself as an opinionated character who goads and manipulates his subject, is prefaced by an assertion explaining that any aggrandizement of the biographer's prerogatives is parented by the biographical subject. "When I delineate him without reserve," remarks the Boswellian biographer, invoking his biographical subject's pattern of patronage, "I do what he himself recommended, both by his precept and his example."[17] This is the kind of ancestral gesture with which biographical recognition is always already underwritten. It need not actually be expressed in any particular biographical narrative, but that it is, frequently and approvingly, indicates how "recognizing the biographical subject" is constantly and more or less self-consciously re-enacting a kind of patrimonial reversion to generic type. Through this transfer of authority a 're-membered' pattern/patron characteristically becomes the only begotten author of individual human existence.

"In various forms," Foucault has written, "this theme has played a constant role since the nineteenth century: to preserve, against all decentrings, the sovereignty of the subject, and the twin figures of anthropology and humanism."[18] As we have seen, the generic frame "recognizing the biographical subject" returns again and again to this theme. In one sense, what Foucault is saying (here and elsewhere in his work) is that 'recognizing the subject' (be it biographical, political, or whatever) is always an activity of subjection, violence committed in the guise of interpretation. As Barthes has observed, "meaning is a force: to name is to subject, and the more generic the nomination, the stronger the subjection."[19] Thus generic framing is always a powerful agent of violent interpretive subjection. What makes "recognizing the biographical subject" an especially forceful frame of biographical recognition is that, like the political subject, the biographical subject conspires in its submission to the ruler, whose sovereignty 'centers' the subject in a discursive formation that is thus already underwritten as an arena of cultural recognition. By submitting to the sovereignty of anthropological humanism, "recognizing the biographical subject" resists Marxist, Nietzchean, Foucauldian, Lacanian, Derridean, and other efforts to decenter the subject, and itself maintains sovereignty over the generic emplotment of the extra-discursive human individual.

Note, for instance, how biographical recognition always anthropomorphizes the biographical subject as an individual human, even (or especially) when that subject is nominally nonhuman or is not conventionally individualized. Books with titles or sub-titles like "biography of a city," "the biography of a book," "a biography of a poem by William Carlos Williams," "a biography of the Constitution of the United States," "studies in the biography of ideas," "a biography of England, 1841–1851," "biography of a small town," "biography of a breed," "Gertrude Stein: a biography of her work," "the biography of a form," "biography of a newspaper," "biography of the gods," "biography of a family," "biography of a marriage," "a biography of Miami Beach," "the biography of a tree," "a biography of the eye," "the biography of a Victorian village," or "a dual biography" give birth to narratives in which the synergy of biographical subject and anthropological humanism instances the dominant (one is tempted to say, the exclusive) pattern for extra-discursivity.[20] What is especially interesting here is what seems to require explanation: how the generic frame "recognizing the biographical subject" can reproduce itself in contexts in which its 'recognition' can only be described as a form of *mis*recognition. Now, in one sense, this is a common enough discursive phenomenon—the metaphorical colonizing of neighboring genres, a mutual interaction that designates, simultaneously, the sovereignty and dependence of all conventional discursive formations. Yet, as we shall see, the very ease and frequency of this transformationalism undermines generic authority by suggesting that all biographical recognition, even that 'centered' by a conventionally appropriate biographical subject, can be construed as misrecognition.

"Every established order tends to produce . . . the naturalness of its own arbitrariness," Pierre Bourdieu explains. "Of all the mechanisms tending to produce this effect, the most important and best concealed is undoubtedly the dialectic . . . out of which arises . . . the *sense of reality,* i.e. the correspondence between . . . social structures and mental structures, which is the basis of the most ineradicable adherence to the established order." As one of those "systems of classification" that reproduce this correspondence, the generic frame "recognizing the biographical subject" thus contributes to the "reproduction of the power relations of which [it is] the product, by securing the misrecognition, and hence the recognition, of the arbitrariness on which [it is] based." Bourdieu's use of the term "recognition" (and the even more instructive "misrecognition") places what we have been calling "biographical recognition" in the context of a whole set of cultural practices that, at their most extreme, permit "the established cosmological and political order [to be] perceived not as arbitrary, i.e. as one possible order among others, but as a self-evident and natural order which goes without saying and therefore goes unquestioned."[21] Indeed, as we have seen, in order to reproduce itself (especially in situations in which such reproduction might reveal the arbitrariness upon which it is based), the generic frame "recognizing the biographical subject" habitually misrecognizes the correspondence between social and mental structures. In this sense, at least, biographical recognition is always biographical (mis)-recognition—a deeply ingrained cultural practice, constituent and symbolic of our sense of reality, producing "a truth whose sole meaning and function are to deny a truth known and recognized by all, a lie which would deceive no one, were not everyone determined to deceive *himself.*"[22] If "recognizing the biographical subject" is to be construed as the generative model of individual human existence, then it is only because it can "generate products that are indeed systematic but are so by virtue of a fuzzy systematicity and an approximate logic which cannot withstand the test of rational systematization and logical criticism."[23]

Thus the 'spread' of the generic frame "recognizing the biographical subject" into discursive formations conventionally 'centered' in historical, biological, critical, and other subjects marks, simultaneously, the frame's fullness and emptiness, precision and ambiguity, authority and powerlessness. It reveals that (mis)recognizing the biographical subject is not only a special case of the metaphorizing of a well-established generic frame but the unavoidable consequence of discursive practice. Every generic frame takes the narrative form of a lie cast in the shape of a truth denying a truth. As we have seen, "recognizing the biographical subject" delineates how a transcendental signified formally outside discourse but knowable only in and through discourse emerges as the master-sign and generative model of extra-discursivity—the 're-membered' pattern/patron as the only begotten author of individual human existence. The application of this truthful lie to subjects that are nominally neither individual nor human shows that this generic frame is a potent generative scheme that, willy nilly, induces anthropological singularity. To enter discourse as a biographical subject may be a powerful way of being and becoming in Western culture, yet, because doing so always *signifies* but cannot necessarily *prove* individual human existence, it is also a potent instrument for existential homicide. That the discursive pattern this generative model traces is almost invariably (mis)recognized as the former and not the latter (as a symbolic birth and not a symbolic death) is a function of the fuzzy logic of cultural practice, of what Bourdieu calls "the collectively maintained and approved self-deception without which symbolic exchange, a fake circulation of fake coin, could not operate."[24]

The notion of the fake circulation of fake coin invokes the alternative approach to the biographical subject suggested by the second definition of "pattern"—"A specimen model of a proposed coin, struck by a mint, but not subsequently adopted for the currency. Distinguished from a *proof.*" This is the situation of what we might call the decentered biographical subject—the perpetually misrecognized biographical subject that cannot be permitted to enter cultural discourse except as a cultural outlaw, as an agent in a system of symbolic exchange which is always converting it into something else. A plural, non-human, trans-discursive biographical subject is a generic impossibility: it delineates a pattern of distribution that is unimaginable and unmanageable. Yet that is so only if we assume that the ontological pattern upon which the biographical subject is conventionally founded provides adequate existential "proof." As soon as we question its status as transcendental signifier we invoke another generative model for "recognizing the biographical subject," one in which individual human existence must be explained rather than taken for granted, one in which the synergy of biographical recognition and anthropological humanism emerges as a deviation from and imposition upon collective cultural experience. In this context there are only decentered biographical subjects, for "the history of the individual is never anything other than a certain specification of the collective history of his group or class, . . . expressing the difference between trajectories and positions inside or outside the class."[25] As an expression of difference the biographical subject has no metaphysical presence in the ordinary sense; rather, it occupies the epistemological gap between presence and absence, singular and plural, self and other. Distinguished from a proof, it is rather a discursive specimen not adopted for currency, a fake circulation of a fake coin.[26] If, as Derrida maintains, *"there is no absolute origin of sense in general,"* then there is no ontological foundation upon which to model the biographical subject. It is always off-center, an unpatronized pattern that can only be (mis)recognized.

Bakhtin claims that this is essentially the situation of the classical Greek type of *"rhetorical* autobiography and biography" from which modern Western lifewriting in large part emerges. "In ancient times the autobiographical and biographical self-consciousness of an individual and his life was first laid bare and shaped in the public square," which, in itself, "constituted the entire state apparatus, with all its official organs." Here "was the highest court, the whole of science, the whole of art"; here "the entire people participated in . . . the laying bare and examination of a citizen's whole life." "[I]n such a 'biographized' individual," Bakhtin argues, "there was not, nor could there be, anything intimate or private, secret or personal, anything relating solely to the individual himself. . . . Everything here, down to the last detail, is entirely public." It is "[o]nly later, in the Hellenistic and Roman era," that "the classical *public wholeness* of an individual" breaks down and is replaced by the private, generic subjects of various life-writing forms like biographical narrative.[27] Arnaldo Momigliano concurs: "biography became a precise notion and got an appropriate word only in the Hellenistic age. The word is *bios* . . . , not a word reserved for the life of an individual man . . . [but] also used for the life of a country."[28] From this perspective, marked by its nostalgia for a lost communal humanism, the biographical subject, as we know it, is always already off-center, a discursive fragment elliptically dispersed into written culture by the disintegration of a thoroughly public world in which the individual was openly and inescapably present and plural. In this view the generative scheme of misrecognizing the biographical subject that characterizes English biography is a re-enactment of the generic history of all Western life-writing: the false circulation of false coin—an absent, singular, discursive specimen introduced into cultural currency as if it were the open individual of classical Greece, "laid bare and shaped in the public square." It is in this sense that an unfounded, uncirculated, decentered biographical subject is the impossible possibility that instrumentalizes the generic frame "recognizing the biographical subject" and becomes the master-sign and generative model of individual human existence.

IV

The capacity of a generic frame to repeat itself is, simultaneously, that which characterizes its authority and that which, because context always differs, perpetually problematizes the notion of essentially repeatable sameness through which generic authority is exerted. As Derrida remarks, "iterability is at once the condition and the limit of mastery."[29] The misrecognized economy of 'patron' and 'pattern' that we have been tracing is a way of emplotting how the generic frame "recognizing the biographical subject" (to use the Derridean phrase) "broaches and breaches" the mastery of its iterability, that is, how it begins discussion of the topic by opening up a gap in it.[30] We can never 'master' a generic frame—either in the sense that we can offer a complete theoretical description of the conditions and limits of its iterability, or in the sense that we can thoroughly appropriate it for our own purposes in biographical narrative. Any effort to broach it will breach it, will place it beyond our control by revealing it to be a culturally motivated vehicle of discursive formation with its own (often hidden) agenda.

Attempts to appropriate this generic frame as if it were not so motivated are as ancient as lifewriting itself, and as unlikely to fix the limits of biographical recognition as Domitian's making it a capital offense to write the life of a disestablished biographical subject. North's concept of an "untainted" biography of private economy that, "out of all roads towards preferment or gain" (79–80), instrumentalizes a direct transaction between biographical subject and biographical readership is just one instance of the keen desire to formulate and control this agenda. North wants to sanitize the profitable patterns of private economy and thus avoid the imputation of falsely circulating false coin. Harold Nicolson's notion of "'pure' biography" ("written with no other purpose than that of conveying to the reader an authentic portait of the individual whose life is being narrated") offers another variation on this theme. "'Impure' biography," in which category Nicolson places Walton's *Lives* and other "masterpieces of English prose," harbors the "'extraneous purposes' by which the purity of biography is infected." Nicolson's 'pure biography' is itself whole and entire, a sanitized organism threatened but never nourished by "the pests and parasites that gnaw the leaves of purity."[31] Both North and Nicolson entertain a utopian vision of biography as uncorrupted and uninfected, a 'natural' locus of private transactions and intrinsic purposes within and yet isolated from cultural practice.

This desire (indeed, this need) to sanitize and isolate biography is itself a way of (mis)recognizing the economy of biographical recognition. The purifications of biographical theorists are a mere variation on the purges of imperial tyrants—instances of institutional or state terrorism that, in trying to legislate the similitude of patron and pattern, expose the arbitrariness of any effort to proclaim the 'naturalness' of generic framing. This is what Derrida calls "the law of genre,"[32] the desire, as North expresses it, "that the truth be unfolded just as in a legal testimony, whole, sole, and nothing else" (70). Of course, as we have seen, theorists and tyrants have no exclusive purchase on (mis)recognition. The biographical subject is persistently and perpetually (mis)recognized; seldom approached as an unfounded and uncirculated coin in the decentered discourse of collective cultural experience, it is habitually treated as the sovereign model of individual human existence in a sanitized system of cultural exchange. As such, it presents itself as a discursive formation that can be easily and harmlessly appropriated. Yet this is, as it were, its protective coloring, its way of seeming to blend 'naturally' into its surroundings. For, although a conservative force in intra-generic politics (and, in that respect, an unlikely agent of change), "recognizing the biographical subject" is a 'radical' element in extra-generic politics in at least two interrelated ways. First, because it is the instrument by which cultural outlaws ('Domitian's enemies,' among whom we might list such recent patterns as the heroines of a new feminist discourse, the leaders of a decolonialized third world, or the hipsters of a revolutionary counter-culture) emerge into social consciousness and thereby assert their difference. Second, because it is the means through which they are co-opted by a discursive formation that stresses the 'original' sameness of all biographical subjects and thereby maintains itself as one of the ways that the dominant authority structure has traditionally reproduced anthropological humanism.

If, as Momigliano claims, "biography developed in the Hellenistic age in conjunction with philological commentaries and surveys," then the "close connection between biography and philology" that he proposes may be traced not only to "the systematic structure of erudite works" of "indisputably antiquarian character"[33] but also to the search for 'roots,' that is, to the 'radical' endeavor to assert, simultaneously, the difference and sameness by which the biographical subject is (mis)recognized. As we know, this "amounts to saying once again [with Derrida] that there is no absolute origin of sense in general," itself an increasingly sanitized 'radical' statement in post-modern discourse. To speak of a decentered biographical subject as "the master-sign and generative model" of individual human existence, as the impossible possibility that instrumentalizes the generic frame "recognizing the biographical subject," is to broach a virtual opportunity that may breach the conventionally acknowledged limits of generic recognition. The economy of symbolic exchange through which we (mis)recognize the biographical subject will then shift, artlessly and craftily, and once again the world will change before we know it. Perhaps it has already done so.

chapter 6

RECOGNIZING THE BIOGRAPHER:
BOSWELL'S *LIFE OF JOHNSON*

"I now relieve the readers of this Work from any farther
personal notice of its authour, who if he should be
thought to have obtruded himself too much upon their
attention, requests them to consider the peculiar plan of
his biographical undertaking."[1]

I

Boswell is the most recognizable biographer in the English-speaking
world; indeed, his name has become synonymous with the word and
with its generic functioning. Thus to recognize the Boswellian biographer is also virtually to emplot the generic frame "recognizing the
biographer." In this long chapter interweaving historical and theoretical approaches we shall explore and exploit this relationship.[2]

On Friday 22 March 1776, during a "jaunt" through Johnson's
native grounds (681), Boswell visited "the great works of Mr. Bolton"
(704). This was Matthew Boulton's Soho Manufactory, the prototypical factory where this "very ingenious proprietor" (704), who was
instrumental in introducing the factory system of industrial production and in developing the merchandising and advertising techniques
of bourgeois consumerism, manufactured sundry hardware items as
well as some of the key components of his partner James Watt's new
steam engine.[3] "I wish that Johnson had been with us," Boswell
writes in the *Life of Johnson,* "for it was a scene which I should have
been glad to contemplate by his light. The vastness and the contrivance of the machinery would have 'matched his mighty mind'. I shall
never forget Mr. Boulton's expression to me: 'I sell here, Sir, what all
the world desires to have—POWER.' He had about seven hundred
people at work. I contemplated him as an *iron chieftain,* and he seemed
to be a father to his tribe" (704). This passage, in which the Boswellian biographer records his admiration of an early example of large,
concentrated manufacturing and compares Johnson's mind to the

vast, ingenious contrivance of its machinery, is both constituent and symbolic of how the *Life* itself is a great works, a vast contrivance that tries to match Johnson's mighty mind and that merchandises what Boulton sells—power. Here, as throughout the *Life,* Boswell reminds his readership that he is the ingenious proprietor of the great works of biographical power and that, like Boulton, he is an apostle of self-advertisement, a master of the art of pleasing who cannot restrain himself from proudly conducting tours of his manufacturing process. As we shall see, this habitual display of his biographical power transforms Boswell into the prototypical modern biographer, the iron chieftain who shows himself to the best advantage and seems to be a father to the tribe of biographers who followed him.

The strange hybrid term with which Boswell describes Boulton (and which, as I have suggested, also characterizes the Boswellian biographer) is itself instructive. 'Chieftain,' of course, is a nostalgic word with which Boswell invokes the recently disestablished patriarchal authority structure of the Scottish Highlands, the passing of which both he and Johnson lamented in their narrative accounts of their famous Highland tour. Thus the term 'iron chieftain' attempts to deny the discontinuity between different socio-economic situations, to bridge the gap between the agrarian patriarchy of the ancient clans and the industrialized nation-state of the emergent consumer society. The Boswellian biographer can be placed in much the same context. The "new species of biography" (1372n4) that he is claiming to produce, and with which his first readers credited him, displaces the long line of classical lifewriting that, in his introductory materials, he traces back through Johnson and Mason to Plutarch. Boswell wants to be the iron chieftain of biography, both the father/patron of its traditional undertaking (which provides a monument that preserves the memory of its biographical subject) and the ingenious proprietor of its modern manufacturing (which accumulates credit, and thereby enhances its value, by displaying the great works of biographical power). Moreover, the appropriation of the term 'iron chieftain' allows us to think of Boswell metaphorically as a capitalist, although one who is (in Marxist terms) uncharacteristically also a laborer. Boswell's biographical labor—which, as we shall see, is represented throughout the *Life,* his journals, and correspondence—functions, as it were, as the (metaphorical) material base of a (metaphorical) economic superstructure. We can never really see Boswell's labor but only his representation of it, a reification that is already part of a capitalist scheme of accruing credit. Thus the term 'iron chieftain' metaphorically denies yet another discontinuity, that between labor and capital, for it allows the Boswellian biographer to be represented both as the sign of labor and as the venture capitalist who exploits this labor. In this way the *Life of Johnson* becomes the work that 'corrects' English biography by perfecting its composition and disciplining its readership to participate in an alternative 'economy' of biographical recognition.

The situation of the Boswellian biographer can be traced in one of the first gaps he bridges in the *Life,* the transition between the initial two paragraphs of the "Advertisement to the First Edition," which also was included among the prefatory materials to subsequent editions. The first paragraph invokes the traditional notion of those *"distinguished persons in all quarters,"* who, *"resembling . . . the grateful tribes of ancient nations, . . . throw a stone upon the grave of a departed Hero"* by supplying his biographer with information, and thus (in the language that we have learned to associate with Waltonian biography, in which Boswell was well versed) *"share in the pious office of erecting an honourable monument to his memory."* The second paragraph, among the most frequently cited passages in Boswell's writing, begins with a sentence that is already engaged in the process of correcting a readership unacquainted with the vast contrivance of modern biographical machinery: *"The labour and anxious attention with which I have collected and arranged the materials of which these volumes are composed, will hardly be conceived by those who read them with careless facility."* His readership, which has not yet learned how to recognize (and thus value) this new species of biography, must be introduced to it through a reflexive display of his labor and anxious attention, a nearly inconceivable compositional process that *"I myself, at some distance of time, contemplate with wonder."* Marked by *"a scrupulous authenticity"* that *"I have spared no pains to ascertain,"* it *"has occasioned a degree of trouble far beyond that of any other species of composition. Were I to detail the books which I have consulted, and the inquiries which I have found it necessary to make by various channels, I should probably be thought ridiculously ostentatious. Let me only observe, as a specimen of my trouble, that I have sometimes been obliged to run half over London, in order to fix a date correctly; which, when I had accomplished, I well knew would obtain me no praise, though a failure would have been to my discredit"* (4).

The notion of credit, with which this passage ends, is a crucial one in the *Life* and is closely connected to labor, value, close attention, correction, and other notions through which 'Boswell' became recognized as the iron chieftain of modern biography. Credit is one of the period's salient concepts; its unprecedented extension throughout public and private commercial networks helped to bring about a "financial revolution" that, by the end of the eighteenth century, had made London the banking center of the world, enabled almost constant warfare with England's European neighbors, provided the support for risky colonial development, promoted an emergent bourgeois consumerism, and fueled a nascent industrialization.[4] J. G. A. Pocock has shown that, as political controversialists of the late seventeenth and early eighteenth centuries sought "a bourgeois ideology, a civic morality for market man" (432), credit became "the appropriate form" for "the epistemology of the investing society" (440). When "men must constantly translate their evaluations of the public good into actions of investment and speculation," they come to "realize that their well-being depends upon mutual support," and thus "credit is converted into confidence, into a mutual trust and a belief in one another" (440). Although credit was also associated with instability and corruption, it became "the ultimate determinant of national prosperity" (451), "a stabilizing, virtuous, and intelligent agency" (454) that was eventually "translated into virtue, in the entirely moral and societal sense of that word" (456). Credit was now "a huge new force in human affairs" (454): "the precondition" for "the health of all society and the practice of all the moral activities which society entails" (456). Thus the "business" of the "individual" in an investment society dominated by Credit was "to get on with his social life, practice its virtues, and make his contribution to the credit and confidence which men repose in one another." Yet, because credit is volatile and fantastic, dependent upon opinion and passion, the individual's "world will be primarily conventional and subjective, and only experience (and the state of the market) will tell him how far his opinions concerning reality are founded upon truth." Thus, Pocock concludes, "we have perhaps reached the point of defining that 'privatization' which modern historians are fond of detecting in the philosophies of commercial society" (460).

The task of Boswellian biography, indeed, of all lifewriting after the "financial revolution" unleashed this "huge, new force in human

affairs," is to accumulate so much credit that biographical truth becomes (virtually) impervious to the volatile instability of a credit
economy. If biography is to participate in the conventional and subjective privatization of human experience, then "the labour and
anxious attention" that enable a biographer "to ascertain with a scrupulous authenticity" become a form of credit convertible into mutual
trust and belief—a virtuous, stabilizing, and intelligent agency upon
which biographical recognition itself can be founded. Thus it is no
surprise to discover that the *Life of Johnson* is firmly committed to the
concept of credit. For instance, it is dedicated to Sir Joshua Reynolds,
Johnson's close friend, whom it describes as "one who is master of the
subject of it, and whose approbation, therefore, must ensure it credit
and success" (1–2). Moreover, its biographer takes great pains to
distinguish the conventional subjectivity of his truth from that of
his rivals, especially Mrs. Piozzi: "This is one of the numerous misrepresentations of this lively lady, which it is worth while to correct; for if credit should be given to such a childish, irrational, and
ridiculous statement of the foundation of Dr. Johnson's faith in Christianity, how little credit would be due to it" (51n1). Here Boswell
plays not only on two intertwined senses of 'credit' but also on two
related notions of 'correct' (to emend an error and to discipline a
child), a complex conceptual relationship that, as we shall see later,
comes to govern the 'economy' of biographer and biographical readership.

Indeed, 'credit' emerges in many contexts in the *Life*. A brief (partial) survey here before looking closely at two crucial occurrences will
provide an overview. Boswell evaluates "the credit of Savage's narrative, as conveyed to us" (124); asserts that, in *Candide,* Voltaire
"meant . . . to discredit the belief of a superintending Providence"
(241–42); notes that, before meeting Johnson, he had "given credit
to reports of his bigotry" (287); observes that "A printer having acquired a fortune sufficient to keep his coach, was a good topick for
the credit of literature" (519); begins his account of the famous
Wilkes episode by describing it as "a very curious incident . . . which
I am persuaded wiH, with the liberal-minded, be much to [Johnson's]
credit" (764), and concludes it by recounting how "Mr. Burke gave
me much credit for this successful *negociation*" (776); claims that
"Johnson was by no means of opinion, that every man of a learned
profession should consider it as incumbent upon him, or as necessary

to his credit, to appear as an authour" (861); asks his readers "to grant me their indulgence for here inserting" Sir William Forbes' opinion of "my original Journal" (upon which the *Life* is partly based) because "it is so much to my credit as the biographer of Johnson" (881); notes that Johnson "was unwilling to allow [Bishop Hurd] full credit for his political conversion" (1212) or "Mr. David Hume any credit for his political principles" (1214–15); justifies including an anecdote contributed by one of his many correspondents because it "is not a little to the credit of Johnson's candour" (1213); lets Professor J. Young of Glasgow "have the credit" of "the most perfect imitation" of Johnson's criticism (1373); and inquires, "Why then shall credit be refused to the *sincerity* of those who acknowledge their persuasion of moral and religious duty, yet sometimes fail of living as it requires?" (1376). Boswell also frequently quotes Johnson's use of the term: "'We must confess the faults of our favourite [Shakespeare], to gain credit to our praise of his excellencies'" (352); (to Boswell, concerning a law case or "cause" in which Boswell acted as an attorney), "'I am glad if you got credit by your cause'" (502); (to Boswell, concerning the celebrated MacPherson controversy) "'No man has a claim to credit upon his own word, when better evidence, if he had it, may be easily produced'" (578); "'Many things which are false are transmitted from book to book, and gain credit in the world'" (755); "'Let a man whose credit is bad, come to a Quaker, and say, "Well, Sir, lend me a hundred pounds"; he'll find him as unwilling as any other man'" (1228); "'I will, indeed, allow him courage, and on this account we so far give him credit'" (1295).

In this context what Boswell calls "a droll little circumstance" assumes particular significance: "as if he [Johnson] meant to reprimand my minute exactness as a creditor, he thus addressed me;—'Boswell, *lend* me sixpence—*not to be repaid*'" (1213). As I have been suggesting, Boswell's minute exactness as a creditor characterizes not only his lending and borrowing money but also his gathering and arranging biographical information: he is as "*scrupulous*" and "*anxious*" (4) about the latter as he is about the former. Acknowledging "debts" of assistance, emending the mistakes of others, cross-checking his many sources, he is constantly adding to "my Johnsonian store" (881), trying "*to render my Book more perfect . . . and to enrich the Work with many valuable additions*" (6). This minute exactness, much criticized in his own day and subsequently as indulgent and prideful self-advertisement,[5] must also be seen as the inevitable consequence of a mode of biographical composition deeply committed to a credit economy. Here, and indeed throughout the *Life*, Boswell is correcting (teaching and disciplining) his readership to recognize and thus value how the modern biographer accumulates credit, how (through a minutely exact display of his symbolic capital) he establishes mutual trust and belief in the authenticity of his work. "Once one realizes that symbolic capital is always *credit*," Pierre Bourdieu asserts, "it can be seen that the exhibition of symbolic capital . . . is one of the mechanisms which (no doubt universally) make capital go to capital."[6] In this respect, Boswell is a kind of venture capitalist, who, in 'exhibiting' (a museum word Boswell often uses) his "Johnsonian store," is also exhibiting and *increasing* his credit as Johnsonian biographer.

The Advertisement to the second Edition describes one of the ways that this process works and reveals its consequences. Unable *"to restrain the effusion of delight"* he feels *"on having obtained* [literary] *fame,"* Boswell reports how *"I have been regaled with spontaneous praise of my work by many and various persons eminent for their rank, learning, talents and accomplishments; much of which praise I have under their hands to be reposited in my archives at* Auchinleck. *An honourable and reverend friend . . . said to me, 'you have made them all talk Johnson,'—Yes, I may add, I have* Johnsonised *the land; and I trust they will not only* talk *but* think, *Johnson"* (8). Boswell is explaining here another way that a biographer accumulates credit: by producing a work which is spontaneously praised by many and various eminent persons. Such praise is valuable because it signifies the literary fame all authors desire and, when put in writing and deposited in archives, provides a kind of documentary proof upon which the biographer can draw, as if it were a fund or line of credit. Having once obtained fame, the biographer can treasure it up, adding it to the stock of his personal, family, or national honor. If Boswell has in fact Johnsonized the land, then, as the person who has the greatest stock of and in Johnson, he has the greatest credit. The entire nation is in his debt: he is the one to whom the national debt is owed and also the one who has put the most in the national sinking fund.[7] In this sense the Boswellian biographer becomes the custodian or manager of a nation's stock of extra-discursive human individuality, or, alternatively, of this stock's transactionality, of its participation in an economy of lending and borrowing.

II

Our recognition of the Boswellian biographer as a venture capitalist participating in a credit economy (and thus constantly reinvesting in his capacity to reinforce belief in individual human existence) is ᴄased, as I have already indicated, on our recognizing that the (represented) biographical labor he exploits is displayed everywhere in his work. Boswell's *Life of Johnson* begins and ends, is indeed characterized throughout, with references to and invocations of 'labor.' Of the one hundred or so direct references to the term that I have found in the *Life,* over a quarter of them depict Johnson as engaged in what he, Boswell, and their friends and correspondents consistently label 'literary labor.' For instance, early in his career Johnson is depicted as "a mere literary labourer" (86) who "was constantly engaged in literary labours" (240). His work on the *Dictionary* is a "prodigious labour" (135), a "laborious task" (212), a "wonderful atchievement of genius and labour" (272n1), which Johnson in his prayers ("'O GOD, who hast hitherto supported me, enable me to proceed in this labour, and in the whole task of my present state'" [180]) and his countrymen in spoken and written testimonials habitually represent as "'executed with the greatest labour and judgement'" (199). Indeed, official solicitations on Johnson's behalf almost always stress laboring. Strahan, the printer, whom Boswell describes as "long in intimacy with Johnson, in the course of his literary labours," tries to get Johnson into the House of Commons by writing a letter in which he characterizes Johnson as someone who "'can undergo any degree of labour'" (451). Johnson's honorary master's and doctoral degrees from Oxford are awarded to one "'even now labouring at a work of the greatest usefulness'" (200n1, where it is translated from the Latin) and to "'this distinguished man [who] has won such repute by his subsequent labours'" (604n1, where it is translated from the Latin). Johnson, who thought of himself as indolent, frequently comments on laboring. "'Mankind have a great aversion to intellectual labour'" (281); "labouring men who work hard, and live sparingly, are seldom or never troubled with low spirits" (316); "'no man loves labour for itself'" (420); "'It is laudable in a man to wish to live by his labours; but he should write so as he may *live* by them, not so as he may be knocked on the head'" (516); "'Endeavouring to make children prematurely wise is useless labour'" (662); "'O GOD, who hast ordained that whatever is to be desired should be sought by labour, and who, by thy blessing, bringest honest labour to good effect, look with mercy upon my studies and endeavours'" (784); "'One night's drunkenness may defeat the labours of forty days well employed'" (1270).

Of course, the 'labor' of the *Life* is not confined to Johnson or to his writing. Boswell notes Malone's "*very laborious and admirable edition of* Shakspeare" (5), "these painful labourers [the Dictionary amanuenses]" (135), Johnson's efforts "to assist other labourers in literature" (244), "the labours of other able and ingenious criticks who have followed" Johnson in editing Shakespeare (351), Beattie's "'labours in the service of virtue and religion'" (455), the "wonderful research and labour" of Campbell's *Political Survey of Great Britain* (695n1), and "a Prelate, whose labours were certainly of considerable advantage both to literature and religion" (1286n1). Boswell is also constantly reminding us of the physical, spiritual, and emotional handicaps under which Johnson labored: "all his labours, and all his enjoyments, were but temporary interruptions of [his hypochondria's] baleful influence" (47); "notwithstanding a great deal of ill health that he seemed to labour under" (1001); "so far as his indolence allowed him to labour" (1046); "Notwithstanding the complication of disorders under which Johnson now laboured" (1260); (Dr. Gillespie writes Boswell) "'the bad state of health your very learned and illustrious friend, Dr. Johnson, labours under at present'" (1267); (Johnson writes a friend) "'I not only perform the perpetual act of respiration with less labour'" (1340); (Boswell quotes Nichols) "'the paralytick affection, under which our great Philologist laboured through life'" (1385n1).

A virtual compendium of labor, the *Life* also reflects and depicts the labor of its own composition. In his journals, correspondence, and other papers related to the making of the *Life*,[8] Boswell will note: "Laboured at *Life* all day" (29 March 1787), "Did a great deal of *Life*, having laboured all day" (30 November 1787), "today I resume my pen and shall labour vigorously" (to Temple, 25 February 1788), "after a shameful interval of neglect, ... I laboured with alacrity at the *Life*" (25 February 1788), "At home and laboured at *Life*" (28 March 1788), "Resumed the labour of *Life*" (28 April 1788), "At home all day—not out of my slippers. Laboured at *Life*" (29 April 1788), "Laboured at *Life* forenoon" (30 April 1788), "During all this time I have laboured at the *Life*" (to Malone, 17 November 1788),

"You cannot imagine what labour, what perplexity what vexation I have endured in arranging a prodigious multiplicity of materials, in supplying omissions, in searching for papers buried in different masses—and all this besides the exertion of composing and polishing" (to Temple, 28–30 November 1789). These passages, particularly the last, indicate that 'labor' is the general term Boswell uses for the various activities involved in biographical composition. It entails and characterizes such tasks as "gathering," "sorting," "arranging," "supplying," "searching," "composing," "writing," and "polishing," and later, after the book is in press, "correcting" (see, for example, 3 February 1791).

Thus it is not surprising to discover that the Boswellian biographer begins the published *Life* by dedicating "his labours" to Reynolds (1), then goes on (in the prefatory "Advertisement to the First Edition") to describe *"the labour and anxious attention with which I have collected and arranged the materials of which these volumes are composed"* (4), and (in the "Advertisement to the Second Edition") to celebrate *"the success of a Work which had employed so much of my time and labour"* (6). Nor that in the "Advertisement to the Third Edition" Malone laments Boswell's death (and the authorial revisions it interrupted) as having come *"unfortunately in the midst of his labours"* (9). A little later, in the introductory remarks, Boswell distinguishes his approach from the "dark uncharitable cast" of "Sir John Hawkins's ponderous labours" (20–21), and attempts to justify his work "to those who are weak enough to think this a degrading task, and the time and labour which have been devoted to it misemployed" (26). Farther along, in his main narrative, he excuses his failure "to trace [Johnson's] acquaintance with each particular person" as "a task, of which the labour would not be repaid by the advantage" (172–73), and compares the "good store of *Johnsoniana* . . . treasured in [Langton's] mind" to "Herculaneum, or some old Roman field, which, when dug, fully rewards the labour employed" (1066).

Boswell's contributors and correspondents, whom he had invited "to unite their labours of love with mine" (to Bowles, 14 June 1785) and thus pay their respects to "the object of my present labour" (to Hastings, 27 February 1790), did so literally and figuratively. During the *Life*'s composition they hoped "That All Imaginable Success may attend your meritorious labours" (Maxwell, 12 May 1787) and wished him "all happiness and all health to finish the labourious Task you

have imposed upon yourself" (Hector, 19 June 1787). Upon its publication they wrote to "congratulate you on the close of your usefull
and laborious researches" (Hector, 16 May 1791), to honor "the man,
whose assiduous and arduous labours have collected the various
smaller scyphons of the great literary Tree" (Rashleigh, 30 May
1791), to applaud the "candor, conscpiccuous [sic] in yoor [sic] labors" (Elphinston, 30 July 1791), to acknowledge "a degree of labour
and attention which very few persons will be found willing to submit
to" (Elford, 16 March 1792), to represent "that Publick, whose Approbation has so amply rewarded your Labours" (anonymous, 10 December 1792), to inquire "if my labors shall in any degree contribute
to the improvement of a new Edition" (J. Campbell, 19 April 1793),
to "express the strongest approbation of your labours" (Davies, 11
September 1793), and to hope that "you will not soon lay down your
pen, but favour the public with more of your labours" (Holt, 23
September 1791). As we might expect, Boswell responded accordingly. He thanked Burke for informing him "what the Sovereign and
Yourself said of my Labours" (16 July 1791), assured another correspondent that "my recording the conversations of so extraordinary a
man as Johnson . . . was a *peculiar* undertaking attended with much
anxiety and labour" (to Scott, 9 August 1791), explained to three
others that "spontaneous praise" is "the best reward of my labours"
(to Churton and Elford, 5 April 1792; to Le Fleming, 3 March 1795),
and told yet another that "the hope of giving instruction and entertainment is a great motive to my literary labours" (to Fawcett, 12
October 1792).

Although these examples clearly show that Boswell used the term
in all its various senses, 'labor' as a concept in classical economics is
especially germane to our inquiry. Most eighteenth-century discussions of economic theory cite Locke's *Essay of Civil Government,* which
derives the notion of property from that of labor. "God commanded,
and {man's} Wants forced him to *labour.* That was his *Property* which
could not be taken from him where-ever he had fixed it. . . . Man
(by being Master of himself, and *Proprietor of his own Person,* and the
Actions or *Labour* of it) had still in himself *the great Foundation of
Property."* Moreover, because *"labour makes the far greatest part of the
value* of things, . . . 'tis *Labour* indeed that *puts the difference of value*
on every thing." This, Locke acknowledges, is a pre-lapsarian vision
of a true barter economy, before *"Money* was any where known," when

"all the World was *America*."[9] Locke approaches here what Kurt Heinzelman calls "the psychomachia of labor—its conflict of soul—
[which] occurs precisely at the moment when labor has to price itself,
to account for itself as productive work, and to represent itself in its
money form, as an exchange value." Money thus mediates the relationship between property and labor and "displaces nature as an object
of economic value."[10]

Classical "theories of labor displacement are derived from Adam
Smith,"[11] a fellow member of The Club under whom Boswell studied
at Glasgow and of whom he spoke "more highly than of any other
teacher he had ever had."[12] Heinzelman offers a succinct summary of
"Smith's three definitions" of "labor as value, measure, and price" in
Book I of *The Wealth of Nations*, which "came out of the lectures in
Moral Philosophy that Boswell heard in 1759–1760" and which later
(in a note in the *Tour*) Boswell asserted he "value[d] the greatest part
of"[13]: (1) "The value of any commodity . . . to the person who possesses it, and who means . . . to exchange it for other commodities,
is equal to the quantity of labour which it enables him to purchase or
command"; (2) "Labour, therefore, is the real measure of the ex-
changeable value of all commodities"; (3) "Labour was the first price,
the original purchase-money that was paid for all things." As Heinzelman points out, "Smith's labor theory of value is founded upon the
original homogeneity of production and exchange, of labor bestowed
and labor commanded," when "labor was price, value, and measure
all at once" in "an earlier, preindustrialized, essentially agrarian (and,
historically, wholly imaginary) economy of barter." Consequently, "in
the post-barter world of modern economy (which is the subject of *The
Wealth of Nations*), money becomes the actual measure of value," and
"labor becomes just another factor in production, merely a sign of
value, and not even the primary one."[14]

III

As it explores how the constantly shifting relationships between labor, property, and value affect the credit economy of the generic frame
"recognizing the biographer," Boswellian biography experiences, over
and over again, the psychomachia of labor. As we shall see, 'Boswell,'
not only as the iron chieftain of modern biography but also as Scottish
laird, crusading attorney, and published author, had a sophisticated

appreciation of the many ways in which later eighteenth-century culture encountered these relationships. But first we should establish the *Life*'s concern with 'value,' a term that appears even more often than 'labor' and, in this and other respects, supersedes and displaces it. 'Value' occurs more than one hundred and fifty times in the *Life*, where it measures or estimates the worth or merit of money, religion, people, books, rank, fame, praise, statuary, ale, land, kindness, imagination, acting, medals, education, invitations, the art of making candles, and many other miscellaneous topics. More pertinently, it frequently calculates the 'value' of Johnson and his conversation, of Boswell and his character, of the *Life* and biography, upon the last of which, Boswell observes, Johnson "set the highest value" (181).

Boswell was acutely aware of Johnson's value as a friend and, of course, as a biographical subject. "My readers will, I trust, excuse me for being thus minutely circumstantial, when it is considered that the acquaintance of Dr. Johnson was to me a most valuable acquisition, and laid the foundation of whatever instruction and entertainment they may receive from my collections concerning the great subject of the work which they are now perusing" (282). Coming just after Boswell's eagerly anticipated first meeting with Johnson (which was itself preceded by a conversation with Tom Davies, who eventually introduced them, a conversation that "increased my impatience more and more to see the extraordinary man whose works I highly valued" [276]), this is a crucial passage in which the biographer instructs his readership about the value of acquiring the biographical subject. It is an acquisition (indeed, as we shall see, a literary property) in which, Boswell never lets us forget, he is constantly reinvesting and thus increasing both his credit as a biographer and the value of his biography. For instance, he inserts in the middle of the *Life* a letter he wrote Johnson in 1775, after Boswell's *Account of Corsica* and Johnson's *Journey to the Western Islands* had firmly associated him with Johnson in the public mind: "'I am now so connected with you, that any thing that I can say or do to your honour has not the value of an additional compliment. It is only giving you a guinea out of that treasure of admiration which already belongs to you, and which is no hidden treasure; for I suppose my admiration of you is co-existent with the knowledge of my character'" (587). Co-existence with his biographical subject is, of course, what the biographer values most, a treasure in which he shares and that he does not wish to remain hidden. The notion Boswell seeks to foster, here and elsewhere in the *Life*, is that Johnson is his property, both because Boswell realized and invested in Johnson's value as an acquaintance and cultural acquisition, and because 'Johnson,' as biographical subject, is the represented (and exploited) product of Boswell's biographical labor, the commodity for which his work is exchanged. Of course, as we have seen, in a modern credit economy labor is "merely a sign of value, and not even the primary one." The 'value' of Johnson is not only and not predominantly the exchange-value of Boswell's biographical labor, but the exchange-value of 'Johnson' in the literary and cultural marketplace. This is the property in which Boswell, as capitalist, has invested and from which, as biographer, he hopes to profit. The force of this supplementarity, as I have suggested in a previous chapter, opens a rupture in biographical recognition that privileges the generic frame "recognizing the biographer" and induces an alternative 'economy' of biographical recognition.

But we are getting a little ahead of ourselves. The 'value' of Boswell's *Life* depends first of all on the 'value' of its subject, of which the biographer is constantly reminding his readership. Johnson's mother "'knew her son's value'" (28); "the elder Mr. Langton and his lady . . .[were] fully capable of understanding his value" (338); Mr. Thrale "understood and valued Johnson" (350); "the booksellers . . . knew the value of his name" (Malone's note, 803n1); Lord Chancellor Thurlow "highly valued Johnson" (1317). What Boswell and nearly everyone who met Johnson valued most highly, of course, was Johnson's conversation. Boswell's prefatory comment—"What I consider as the peculiar value of the following work, is, the quantity that it contains of Johnson's conversation" (23)—is constantly reinforced by, for example, his noting how, "in the course of their works," Johnson's friends "received many valuable hints from his conversation" (166), or his observing how seldom the great, "who *knew* the value of the conversation of Johnson," sought "the rich intellectual entertainment which Johnson could furnish" (1154). Indeed, "considering how highly the small portion which we have of the table-talk and other anecdotes of our celebrated writers is valued," Boswell feels "I am justified in preserving rather too many of Johnson's sayings, than too few" (26). As we have seen, Johnson's value redounds upon Boswell, who is anxious to reinvest and display it in the *Life*. He reprints or excerpts letters in which Johnson writes him, "'I have always loved and valued you'" (403), "'I value you as a worthy man'" (640), and "'I set a very high value upon your friendship'" (824). He also quotes a conversation in which Johnson, provoked by Boswell, remarks, "'I do value you more for being a Scotchman. You are a Scotchman without the faults of a Scotchman. You would not have been so valuable as you are, had you not been a Scotchman'" (991). Johnson's observation (and Boswell's retailing of it) is astute. As an outsider who (as a result of the Union of 1707) is also an insider in English culture, as a patriarchal Scottish laird who has learned how to manipulate England's consumer society, as a sometime visitor and affable travelling companion who has introduced Johnson to different and (in some cases) remote social circles and customs, Boswell is, like Hume, Smith, and Ferguson, that new phenomenon—a cosmopolitan Scotsman, who has overcome parochial interests and is reinvigorating what George III and the Bute ministry hoped would become a 'British' culture. This is, as it were, Boswell's cultural value, which is also his generic value: the iron chieftain of modern biography must be simultaneously inside and outside, "a Scotchman without the faults of a Scotchman."

Thus Boswell's value as a biographer is founded in part (as in Waltonian biography) on his subject's worth(iness), and in part on his own realization of how to invest that valuable treasure. The Journal records how Boswell had "a constant plan to write the *Life* of Mr. Johnson" from at least 1772 (31 March 1772), and the *Life* frequently cites this plan and its execution. "He recommended to me to keep a journal of my life, full and unreserved. He said it would be a very good exercise, and would yield me great satisfaction when the particulars were faded from my remembrance. . . . I had kept a journal for some time. . . . From this habit I have been enabled to give the world so many anecdotes, which would otherwise have been lost to posterity" (307). Boswell often reminds his readership of this journal and its special value. "I find in my journal the following minute of our conversation, which, though it will give but a very faint notion of what passed, is in some degree a valuable record" (284); "His lordship [Bishop Douglas], however, knows too well the value of written documents to insist on setting his recollection against my notes taken at the time" (399n1); "I must, again and again, intreat of my readers not to suppose that my imperfect record of conversation contains the whole of what was said by Johnson, or other eminent persons who lived with him. What I have preserved, however, has the value of the most perfect authenticity" (617). As we have already observed, Boswell was acutely aware of the value of his journal and the other materials that he had acquired and produced. By displaying these great works of biographical power, he hoped to instruct his readers how to estimate that value and thus appreciate his achievement.

This is a feature of his work Boswell acknowledged during its composition. "My next consideration is Dr. Johnson's *Life,*" he wrote his wife on 3 July 1786; "as I have collected a great variety of materials, it will probably be a Work of considerable value." He wrote Hugh Blair on 27 April 1786: "I am preparing for my Great Work the *Life of Dr. Johnson,* which will be, I trust, a very valuable acquisition to the Philo[lo]gical World. . . . I will venture to promise that my Life of my revered Friend will be the richest piece of Biography that has ever appeared. The Bullion will be immense, whatever defects there may be in the workmanship" (145–46). We can see emerging here, in the "Work of considerable value," the "valuable acquisition," the "richest piece of Biography," and the "Bullion" of "immense workmanship," the 'economy' (in language and generic conception) that we have been tracing. The pattern holds throughout the compositional process and even after publication. "I flatter myself," he wrote Anna Seward on 11 April 1788, that "My Life of that illustrious Man . . . will exhibit him more completely than any person ancient or modern has yet been preserved, and whatever merit I may be allowed, the World will at least owe to my assiduity the possession of a rich intellectual treasure." Note how the "treasure of admiration" belonging to Johnson and "co-existent with the knowledge of my character" in Boswell's letter of 1775 (587) has now (through assiduous preservation and exhibition) become co-existent with the "rich intellectual treasure" of "my Life," an exchange of value made explicit in a letter of 28–30 November 1789 to Boswell's old friend Temple. This is the letter (quoted earlier) in which Boswell describes the arduous biographical "labour" of "arranging," "supplying," "searching," "composing," and "polishing." The passage continues: "Many a time have I thought of giving it up. However though I shall be uneasily sensible of its many deficiencies it will certainly be to the World a very valuable and peculiar Volume of Biography, full of literary and characteristical Anecdotes . . . told with authenticity and in a lively manner." Thus the value of Boswell's 'work' (as both an 'act of labor' and a 'literary composition')[15] transforms the co-existent treasure of Johnson's life into a valuable volume of biography. This is the capital that Boswell is constantly reinvesting in the great works of biographical power, the capital that finances the manufacturing process ("I see that *the whole* will be of London manufacture," Boswell wrote Malone on 18 September 1788) through which this iron chieftain induces an alternative economy of biographical recognition.

The *Life*'s reflexive display of this process teaches a lesson in how the modern biographer accumulates credit. We have already seen how some of Boswell's first readers recognized and applauded his 'labor'; the *Life* also taught them to 'value' it. Whether or not they were friends, contributors, or recipients of presentation copies, Boswell's contemporary readership responded in the language with which the *Life* had instructed them to recognize and 'evaluate' the biographer. Over and over again they thank him for "your valuable Gift of the *Life of Doctor Johnson*" (Hastings, 14 May 1791), "your valuable volumes" (Warton, 15 May 1791), "so valuable a Present" (Douglas, 16 May 1791), "the valuable Present" (Lumm, 16 May 1791), "a very valuable Present" (Lofft, 17 May 1791), "a most valuable Work . . .[that offers] a new Species of Biography" (Knox, 1 June 1791), "your late valuable Production" (Adey, 21 July 1791), "your Valuable *Life of Johnson*" (Maxwell, 15 November 1792), "your kind and most valuable present, . . . so valuable a memorial of my ever respected Friend" (Hoole, 6 August 1793), "Your very valuable present of the Second Edition of the *Life of Dr. Johnson*" (Churton, 20 September 1793). At two guineas for the two-volume quarto set, the published work was expensive (as we shall see, Boswell much fretted its price and sale), and to a certain extent his correspondents (particularly those who received presentation copies) are rating its market value. But, as they well knew, the market in which the *Life* traded participated in an economy neither local nor merely financial. "I can hardly express the pleasure I feel in considering the fame and the profit it must procure you," Temple wrote on 4 July 1791. "Johnson had enemies, who of course will try to depreciate your work," Dr. Burney wrote on 16 July 1791, but "*Biography* now claims you as her chairman." Other correspondents, employing variations on the economic metaphor we have been tracing, struck similar notes. "Besides the intrinsic value of the work, every serious person must think it seasonable in this Paroxism of the times [apparently, the French Revolution], when certain notions are but too much propagated" (Holt, 23 September

1791); "it constitutes a fund of the highest intellectual entertainment. . . . Your plan require'd not only great Ability, and Capacity of selection, but a degree of labour and attention which very few persons will be found willing to submit to" (Elford, 16 March 1792); "It contains, in my humble Opinion, the first Specimen of biographical Composition. . . . the Present from Yourself would stamp a Value upon it, much superior to what it could derive from any Quarter besides" (De Coetlogon, 15 September 1792); "It contains a rich fund of instruction and entertainment, for which the public is greatly indebted to you" (Fawcett, 22 September 1792); "I shall consider its own singularly intrinsic value much increased, by being honor'd with it *immediately from the author*" (Abercrombie, 10 October 1792); it provides "so ample a fund for the entertainment of your Readers" (J. Campbell, 19 April 1793); the volumes' "value, intrinsically great, I must ever consider as enhanced in a high degree, when I view them as a testimony of regard from Mr. Boswell" (J. Campbell, 21 September 1793); "I was much pleased with receiving your handsome present of the *Life of Johnson* not so much on account of the Value of the Book as that I esteemed it a mark of your regard and friendship" (Claud Boswell, 21 September 1793).

Sensitively attuned to the financial, cultural, generic, legal, and other aspects of the literary marketplace, Boswell had tried for over three decades to manipulate them to his advantage. He understood well the value of the literary property he had invested and acquired in Johnson's life. Nevertheless, the situation he encountered in the few months before the first edition was published illustrates how, when the interests of labor, value, and property intersect, even the investment credit of the iron chieftain of modern biography could be threatened. By January 1791 Boswell's purchases of land to enhance his patriarchal estate, a habit of investment that yielded little and yet (because of familial pride) he could not resist, had left him financially strapped (with what today we might call a 'cash-flow' problem). Offered one thousand guineas for his "property" (that is, his copyright) in the *Life,* a very large sum for the time, he had to choose between taking the offer or raising a similar sum (as he put it) "upon the credit of the work" (to Malone, 29 January 1791) and thus "as Sir Joshua [Reynolds] says *game* with my Book" (to Malone, 25 February 1791). His "distressing perplexity how to decide as to the property of my Book" (to Malone, 25 February 1791) was complicated by his publisher's decision (arrived at reluctantly) to print the book in two quarto volumes at two guineas, an expensive proposition in a literary marketplace already saturated with Johnsonian biography. "A certain person who delights in mischief has been *depreciating* it, so that I fear the sale of it may be very dubious. *Two Quartos* and *Two Guineas* sound in an alarming manner" (to Malone, 25 February 1791). Yet "I am very very unwilling to part with the property of it" (to Malone, 10 February 1791), "for, indeed I should be vexed to sell my *Magnum Opus* for a great deal less than its intrinsick value" (to Malone, 25 February 1791).[16] Although he remained "in great anxiety about the sale of my Book" because "I find so many people shake their head's {sic] at the *two quartos* and *two guineas*" (to Malone, 12 March 1791), Boswell "resolved . . . to keep the property of my *Magnum Opus*" after his publisher and printer "each advance[d] £200 on the credit of my Book" (to Malone, 8 March 1791) and thus, as he later remarked, "assisted me with their credit" (24 November 1792).

Confronted with a financial crisis apparently forcing him to choose between the two properties he holds dearest, his patriarchal estate and his life of Johnson, Boswell is indeed "in a distressing perplexity." Characteristically, he can part with neither. Rather, he "games" with the "credit" of the book, a risk calculated on the "credit" he has already accrued (as the author of the *Account* and the *Tour*) and will earn (as the author of the *Life*) with 'the Trade' and his readership, as well as on the vagaries of a literary marketplace that can "depreciate" an unread book because it appears to be too long, too expensive, and too late. Because he has already invested so much in "Johnsonising the land," Boswell has accumulated the credit to (literally and figuratively) Johnsonize his land. One property becomes interchangeable and dependent upon the other; Boswell is willing to gamble everything on credit, on that volatile yet stabilizing agency that was, for the Scottish laird attempting to Johnsonize all his property and "the land" as well, truly "the ultimate determinant of national prosperity." As the publication date of the *Life* (which is also the anniversary of his meeting Johnson) nears, Boswell has managed to become "coexistent" with his biographical subject in almost every way possible.

IV

The participation of Boswell's literary and hereditary property in a mutual economy of generic and cultural exchange emerges in the *Life* in a passage in which the biographer discusses Johnson's habit of writing essays for other people to publish in their own names. "I am not quite satisfied with the casuistry by which the productions of one person are thus passed upon the world for the productions of another. I allow that not only knowledge, but powers and qualities of mind may be communicated; but the actual effect of individual exertion never can be transferred, with truth, to any other than its own original cause. . . . an authour may give the profits and fame of his composition to another man, but cannot make that other the real author. A Highland gentleman, a younger branch of a family, once consulted me if he could not validly purchase the Chieftainship of his family, from the Chief who was willing to sell it. I told him it was impossible for him to acquire, by purchase, a right to be a different person from what he really was; for that the right of Chieftainship attached to the blood of primogeniture, and, therefore, was incapable of being transferred. . . . whatever agreement a Chief might make with any of the clan, the Herald's Office could not admit of the metamorphosis" (179–80). Thus authorship, and the notion of literary property it induces, is like a highland chieftainship, an original filiation that cannot be transferred. This, of course, is the traditional notion of patriarchal propriety with which Boswell, the 'iron chieftain,' 'naturalizes' Boulton and his modern factory, and which, I have been claiming, enables 'Boswell' to bridge the gap between different economies of generic recognition and become the very name of the modern biographer.

Yet, as Boswell remarks elsewhere in the *Life* (commenting on literary frauds), "The *Filiation* of a literary performance is difficult of proof; seldom is there any witness present at its birth" (255). There is no Herald's Office of literary filiation, although literary tradition, the literary academy, and copyright laws more or less attempt to fulfill its function. In any event, treating authorship as a hereditary right endangers Boswell's own project, unless he can show he is the rightful heir to the literary property he is claiming or unless he can problematize this traditional notion of authorial primogeniture. The first of these tactics is a familiar one in Boswellian studies, to which I shall devote only a few passing observations. Citing such passages as the one in which Boswell "expressed a regret that I could not be so easy with my father, though he was not much older than Johnson" (302), and the eventual meeting between Johnson and Lord Auchinleck towards which the *Tour* seems to be pointing, many scholars have noticed that Boswell, constantly at odds with his own father, presents himself as the substitute son of the childless Johnson.[17] Yet Boswell was not one of the three executors of Johnson's will, nor, for that matter, even mentioned in it, an omission which, when he first learned of it, made him "a little uneasy,"[18] but which he tried to justify, in both his journal and the *Life,* by claiming that Johnson had already shown him "proofs of his regard" and "that it was not necessary to crowd his Will" (1383n). Nevertheless, reinforced by the publication of personal memoirs by Johnson's other friends, the impression lingers (now as it did then) that the 'herald's office' of literary filiation is not necessarily prepared to sanction this mode of transferring literary property. Boswell will have to find another way to claim his inheritance.

The same passsage that extenuates Boswell's lack of testamentary affiliation laments that, on his deathbed, Johnson precipitately burned "large masses" of his personal papers rather than entrusting "some faithful and discreet person with the care and selection of them" (1381–83). The implication, of course, is that Boswell is this person, for this is one of the roles he plays throughout the *Life* (although the integrity and extent of both his faithfulness and his discretion have been constantly challenged). As the greatest investor in the paper mass through which Johnson's 'greatness' (his 'mass' in later eighteenth-century culture) will have to be reproduced, Boswell suggests that only a person like him can be the rightful heir to this valuable literary property. But, and here is a point the *Life* makes over and over, there is no one like him: "Had his other friends been as diligent and ardent as I was, he might have been almost entirely preserved. As it is, I will venture to say that he will be seen in this work more completely than any man who has ever yet lived" (22). This is a claim that not even Boswell's enemies were prepared to deny, and it is upon this claim, and the symbolic capital with which it credits him, that, we could say, Boswell (who had renounced his own birthright in the Auchinleck estate for an annual allowance and then later reluctantly signed an agreement entailing the estate on his father's heirs)[19] purchases or earns the chieftainship of Johnson's life. But didn't he claim such a "metamorphosis" was impossible, and how did he do it?

Boswell comes into possession of this supposedly untransferrable property through a symbolic manipulation of the law of copyright, a recently established legal right necessitated by the London booksellers' domination of the rapidly expanding publishing industry. "The only case in which Boswell participated" that has "retain[ed] legal significance" was Hinton v. Donaldson (as it was known in Scotland, where it began; in England, where it was eventually decided, it was Donaldson v. Beckett), which, as Frank Brady remarks, "remains the basis of British and American copyright law."[20] In 1773 Boswell was one of Donaldson's three defense attorneys before the Scottish Court of Session; in 1774 he was responsible for the publication of a pamphlet detailing the judges' decision, which he rushed into print in an effort to influence the House of Lords' verdict. The many legal issues on both sides in what was known at the time as the Literary Property Cause are complex and need not be rehearsed here.[21] What does interest us is that one of the arguments concerned a distinction between the "author" and the "proprietor" of a literary composition, and whether the "incorporeal doctrine" of such a composition could be transferred and thus become (as one of the Scottish justices noted) "affected by creditors."[22]

Sir David Rae, Lord Eskgrove, who represented Hinton, offered an argument that construed literary production as trade and the author as a kind of venture capitalist who transfers his property in perpetuity.[23] Adopting Blackstone's definition of literary property, which was itself based on Locke's definition of property as the process and product of labor, Rae claimed "an original incorporeal right in the composition, entitling the author to the sole right of printing and publishing his own sentiments," a right that "will appear to be neither ideal nor imaginary, but . . . solid and substantial" (9). "In the more refined state of society," he went on, *property,* in its just sense, now comprehends the interest of a party in any thing which is capable of ownership, whether it is corporeal or incorporeal. In this sense of the word, it cannot be denied, that a man has a property not only in his lands or his goods, but also in his life, his fame, his labour, and the like" (9–10). Because "a man has a just and lawful property, or right, in the fruits of his own labour or ingenuity, . . . to distinguish . . . between those labours which are merely manual . . . and those which flow from the intellectual labours of the mind . . . is to represent the nature of right, or property, in a view unworthy of the enlightened times in which we live" (10–11). Thus "an author should have, what is called a *copy-right,* or a property in his own ideas and sentiments expressed in writing, which can entitle him to the sole use

and disposal thereof" both before and after publication (13). Noting
that "not only the writing of books, but the printing and publishing them, is become a trade or business" (14), Rae argues that the
author (and, by implication, his assignees, for it is the booksellers
who purchase his copyright and thus have the greatest interest in
preserving its continuity) "can never forfeit" his "property in his
work" (15).

The argument made by Donaldson's defense team, written by Ilay
Campbell and supported in all its major points by the justices' statements in Boswell's pamphlet, arises from a traditional hierarchical
conception of literary production.[24] Denying the "incorporeal right,
detached from any physical existence, . . . express[ed] by the word
copy, or *copyright*" (5), Campbell reasoned that the author of a published literary composition was not its proprietor, for "the work of
the mind, or what is called the *doctrine,* [and] is said to be the foundation of the author's claim of property" (18–19), "is merely a *metaphorical property,* and an abusive signification of the word" (6). Thus
copyright, understood as "*doctrine,*" is not "a tangible substance, capable of possession, . . . which carries along with it the sole privilege
and power of disposal even after publication" (15), but the right, also
granted to "the inventor of a machine" (22), "to determine, whether
the world shall see his production or not," and the right, "if he once
makes it *public,* [for] every acquirer . . . to make what use of it he
pleases" (23). The author is entitled only to the profit of the first
edition he publishes and to "the further advantage accruing from the
reputation of it, which may often be considerable," for "even those who
apply themselves to history, to poetry, or to *belles lettres,* have generally
met with patronage and support from rich and powerful men, according to the merit of their works. This was of old, and this ought still
to be, the true idea of an author's profit; and it is an idea far superior
to the modern invention of copy-money: An invention which has
tended much to degrade the author's character, and to make him
subservient to booksellers and printers" (15).

These two (supposedly) different notions of literary property produce or are produced by two (seemingly) different approaches to authorship. The side which Boswell took in this debate is more or less
consistent with the *Life*'s depiction of authorship as an untransferrable
highland chieftainship, but the way in which the *Life* has made 'John-

son' Boswell's literary property in cultural history suggests that Boswell somehow managed to possess and retain Johnson's incorporeal property (his copyright) in his own life. He can do so because the *Life* falls into the gap between the two sides in the Literary Property Cause: it reveals that every use of the word 'property' is also an abuse, that literary property can be transferred only because it does not exist. What I mean here is that literary property is not a special case of property in general, a right extended from the tangible to the incorporeal—but the condition of all property, a metaphorical signification always already absent from the laborer and his labor. Rae's collapsing of the distinction between manual and intellectual labor makes this clear enough, as, in its way, does Campbell's denying the difference between a book and a machine. Property is always a metaphorical 'composition,' always an "incorporeal right, detached from any physical existence," which owes its privilege to its culturally assigned power of *appearing* "to be neither ideal nor imaginary, but . . . solid and substantial." In this respect property is always *in*substantial, and thus is invariably "express[ed] by the word *copy.*"

If property is always already metaphorical, then the arguments on both sides in the Literary Property Cause are problematized. There is no untransferrable property (no "original cause," as Boswell puts it) for Campbell and the Herald's Office to sanctify and protect, no tangible substance from which Rae can extend the privilege of enlightenment and profit to intellectual labor. Property, like copyright, becomes an implicit and explicit social agreement to (mis)recognize certain epistemological problems. Of course, as we have seen in a previous chapter, this is also an appropriate way of characterizing what I have been calling generic recognition; every generic frame is, in this respect, (mis)recognized. In order to recognize the biographer, for which, since the *Life of Johnson,* the eponym has been 'Boswell,' we must (mis)recognize him as the displaced, property holding sign of symbolic capital in a credit economy. Boswell's *Life* teaches us how to follow the plot of this generic frame. It exhibits how an incorporeal property in which the biographer does not believe is gradually accreted to the Boswellian archive, how the acquisition of a valuable acquaintance is made even more valuable by "*labour and anxious attention,*" how the credit accrued by this investment induces a coexistence which is a virtual 'copy-right,' and how the reinvestment of

this right in biographical narrative not only reproduces and com-
modifies the biographical subject but also reproduces and profits the
biographer.

V

"Ich lebe auf meinen eigenen Kredit hin," "I live on my own credit"—this
is the clause from the preface to Nietzsche's *Ecce Homo* with which
Derrida characterizes the autobiographer. In the sense that the *Life of
Johnson* can be said to have emerged from Boswell's prolific autobiographical writing (a common assertion), and to the extent that Boswell is recognized as perhaps the most self-reflexive of English
biographers, Derrida's characterization applies to him as well. Like
the Derridean autobiographer, the Boswellian biographer does not
claim his identity "by right of some contract drawn up with his contemporaries." Rather, "it has passed to him through the unheard-of
contract he has drawn up with himself. He has taken out a loan with
himself and *has implicated us in this transaction.*" Thus "it is also our
business, this unlimited credit that cannot be measured against the
credit his contemporaries extended or refused him," because he "never
knows in the present . . . whether anyone will ever honor the inordinate credit that he extends to *himself* in his name, but also necessarily in the name of another." "The life that he lives and tells to himself
. . . cannot be *his* life in the first place except as the effect of a secret
contract, a credit account which has been both opened and encrypted," and "as long as the contract has not been honored—and it
cannot be honored except by another, for example, by you," then "this
life will be verified only at the moment the bearer of the name, the
one whom we, in our prejudice, call living, will have died." Consequently, "if life returns, it will return to the name but not to the
living, in the name of the living *as* a name of the dead." This is
because "at the very least, to be dead means that no profit or deficit,
no good or evil, whether calculated or not, can *ever return again* to the
bearer of the name. Only the name can inherit, and this is why the
name, to be distinguished from the bearer, is always and a priori a
dead man's name, a name of death. What returns to the name never
returns to the living." Thus, like the Derridean autobiographer, the
Boswellian biographer "advances behind a plurality of masks or names
that, like any mask and even any theory of the simulacrum, can pro-

pose and produce themselves only by returning a constant yield of protection, a surplus value in which one may still recognize the ruse of life. However, the ruse starts incurring losses as soon as the surplus value does not return again to the living, but to and in the name of names, the community of masks."[25]

Thus the "inordinate credit" that, as we have seen, Boswell is constantly accruing in his private and public life-writing projects is a "surplus value" that cannot ultimately "be measured against the credit his contemporaries extended or refused him." Profit or loss returns only to the name, to the eponym by which, I have been claiming, we recognize the modern biographer. Although "he has taken out a loan with himself and *has implicated us in this transaction*," the "secret contract," the "credit account which has been both opened and encrypted" ("behind a plurality of masks or names" in which, he hopes, we "may still recognize the ruse of life"), can be honored only "by another, for example, by you [or me]." Thus, despite Boswell's efforts to Johnsonize the land and thereby control the credit economy of extra-discursive human individuality, what I have called the 'Boswellian archive' is, in fact, a credit account that, in the name of "a dead man's name," can be inherited and claimed only by us (in a work such as this). Boswell's 'virtual copyright' on Johnson's name, which is also more or less co-existent with his own (that is, Boswell's) name, becomes our property, or at least (as I have indicated above) can be (mis)recognized by us as the displaced, property holding sign of symbolic capital in a credit economy. The biographer's profit, or the biographer *as* profit, returns to his name, or to "the name of names," only if we complete the transaction, if we open and encrypt the credit account that he has (so laboriously) established.

We have been doing so throughout this chapter. For instance, we have noted how the Boswellian biographer accumulates credit by ascertaining with scrupulous authenticity, by revealing how his work has been manufactured, by acquiring and co-existing with the biographical subject, by valuing and being valued by the biographical subject, by eliciting spontaneous praise, by acknowledging his debts to the assistance of others, by perfecting and enriching a diverse store of knowledge, by correcting the misrepresentations of others, by exhibiting his diligent and ardent preservation. To this list we might add such associated activities as 'deciding disputes' (a quasi-juridical function in which Boswell, the reluctant attorney, frequently engages),[26] or 'supplying blanks' (that is, filling up the silent vacancies of the subject's life with *"Collectanea"* [434], as Boswell often does), or 'rendering up the whole task of the biographical subject's life' (a paraphrase of an entry Boswell quotes from Johnson's diary [180], which suggests, as we have seen, that the biographer's task or labor is to "render up, at the last day, an account" of the "whole task of [his subject's] present state"). These are just some of the ways that we recognize the Boswellian biographer's "minute exactness as a creditor" (1213), and, in so doing, render up the credit account that he has taken out (but that only we can complete) in his name. Certainly, this catalogue of credit transactions can be extended, but perhaps it will be more instructive if we study its thematics by analyzing three enterprises that pervade the *Life of Johnson*—close attention, preservation, and correction.

Elaborating upon *Capital*'s effort "to describe the labor process in 'a form that stamps it as exclusively human,'" Heinzelman explains how "Marx identifies the origin of labor's psychomachia in its internal conflict, its need for 'close attention,' and its imaginative exercise of willed subordination. . . . Labor is a dialectical progression of imagination and will, and this process renders unto labor its moral value. 'Besides the exertion of the bodily organs, the process demands that, during the whole operation, the workman's will be steadily in consonance with his purpose. This means close attention.' Thus, both material product and mental cognition are realized together in the physical act of labor, for the original purpose of the work process is to bind together mind and body into a language which is cognate with action."[27] "*The labour and anxious attention with which* [Boswell claims in the Advertisement to the First Edition] *I have collected and arranged the materials of which these volumes are composed*" (4) participate in this "dialectical progression of imagination and will," for "*the stretch of mind and prompt assiduity*" (4) that this work requires "bind together mind and body into a language which is cognate with action," and produce in turn a "work" that Boswell can describe as one in which his subject "will be seen . . . more completely than any man who has ever yet lived" (22). This 'work' (in both senses) "*has occasioned a degree of trouble far beyond that of any other species of composition*" (4); it induces (or is induced by) 'close attention,' a habit of mind and body that, to paraphrase Boswell explaining a practice Johnson often planned but rarely executed, materializes as "a methodical course of study" through

which the biographer has "fixed his attention steadily upon something without, and prevented his mind preying upon itself" (53). As
we know, Boswell is characterizing his own as well as Johnson's work
habits and mental preoccupations, for he feared that he shared with
Johnson "a mind gloomy and impetuous" that "cannot be fixed for
any length of time in minute attention" (70). Remarking in the *Life*
on "'the morbid melancholy' in Johnson's constitution," he asserts
that "attentive observation and close inquiry have convinced me, that
there is too much of reality in the gloomy picture" (242–43). Thus
'close attention' ("attentive observation and close inquiry") convinces
him that, like Johnson, he ought to be "engaged in a steady continued course of occupation," a project that is for him, as the *Dictionary*
is for his subject, "sufficient to employ all his time for some years"
(136) and able to bring him the *"literary fame"* (8) (the 'close attention'
of his contemporaries and posterity) that he so desires. He finds it, of
course, in lifewriting, a compulsive habit to which he (sporadically
but voluminously) attends throughout his adult life.

The *Life* offers many explicit examples of the crucial importance of
'close attention' to a biographer who is building up a credit account.
Indeed, the amount and intensity bestowed differentiate a kind of
calculus by which friendship, respect, admiration, accuracy, wholeness, achievement, greatness, piety, and other personal or social qualities are to be computed. "It may easily be imagined that this, my
first interview with Dr. Johnson, with all its circumstances, made a
strong impression on my mind, and would be registered with peculiar
attention" (277n1). "I opened my mind to him [Johnson] ingen-
uously, and gave him a little sketch of my life, to which he was
pleased to listen with great attention" (286). "When at table, he was
totally absorbed in the business of the moment; his looks seemed
rivetted to his plate; nor would he, unless when in very high company, say one word, or even pay the least attention to what was said
by others, till he had satisfied his appetite" (331). "Posterity will be
astonished when they are told, upon the authority of Johnson himself,
that many of these discourses [the *Rambler* essays], which we should
suppose had been laboured with all the slow attention of literary
leisure, were written in haste as the moment pressed, without even
being read over by him before they were printed" (145). "[T]he ap-
pellation of *Methodists* was first given to a society of students in the
University of Oxford, who about the year 1730 were distinguished

by an earnest and *methodical* attention to devout exercises" (324n1).
"Johnson listened with the closest attention" to General Oglethorpe's
"'account of the siege of Belgrade'" (485). Boswell writes Johnson,
"'all the attention that I can give shall be cheerfully bestowed, upon
what I think a pious work, the preservation and elucidation of Walton, by whose writings I have been most pleasingly edified'" (566).
Lord North writes Oxford requesting a doctorate for Johnson: "'The
many learned labours which have since that time employed the attention and displayed the abilities of that great man, so much to the
advancement of literature and the benefit of the community, render
him worthy of more distinguished honours in the Republick of letters'" (603). "The last paragraph of this note is of great importance;
and I request that my readers may consider it with particular attention. It will be afterwards referred to in this work" (1105).

The last of these examples shows that the calculus of 'close attention' also computes reader response. Boswell is constantly involved in
directing such response, in teaching and disciplining his readers how
to 'attend' to this new species of biography. We shall investigate this
process in greater detail later, when we treat the theme of 'correction.'
For now it is sufficient to note that, from the very beginning of his
narrative, Boswell has been providing his readership with instances
of 'close attention' upon which response can be modelled. As one of
Boswell's contemporary readers wrote him, "Your plan requir'd not
only great Ability, and Capacity of selection, but a degree of labour
and attention which very few persons will be found willing to submit
to" (Elford, 16 March 1792). Indeed, if Boswell's workmanlike "will"
had not been "steadily in consonance with his purpose," the *Life*
would not be able to command and receive the attention with which
it is credited. "From this habit I have been enabled to give the world
so many anecdotes, which would otherwise have been lost to posterity" (307). Moreover, "this habit" justifies (or is justified by) the
"minute detail" (1223), the "particulars" of "all the little circumstances of his [subject's] life" (474), to which Boswell's (and his readership's) attention is constantly directed, and for which Boswell
invokes Johnson's authority. "I mentioned that I was afraid I put into
my journal too many little incidents. JOHNSON. 'There is nothing,
Sir, too little for so little a creature as man'" (307). This is an anecdotal version of Johnson's *Rambler* 60 (quoted at length in Boswell's
introductory remarks): "'The business of the biographer is often to

pass slightly over those performances and incidents which produce vulgar greatness, to lead the thoughts into domestick privacies, and display the minute details of daily life. . . . There are many invisible circumstances, which . . . are more important than publick occurrences'" (24). Boswell uses these "sentiments of the very man whose life I am about to exhibit" (24) to counter "the objections which may be made to the minuteness on some occasions of my detail of Johnson's conversation," and to announce that "I remain firm and confident in my opinion, that minute particulars are frequently characteristick, and always amusing, when they relate to a distinguished man" (25). This is an opinion Boswell repeats often in the *Life:* "That the most minute singularities which belonged to him . . . may not be omitted" (343); "it is a small characteristick trait in the Flemish picture which I give of my friend, and in which, therefore I mark the most minute particulars" (869); "I record this minute detail, which some may think trifling" (1223); "The minute diversities in every thing are wonderful" (846); and, perhaps most relevantly to our immediate concerns, "Johnson gave a very earnest recommendation of what he himself practised with the utmost conscientiousness: I mean a strict attention to truth, even in the most minute particulars" (898–99).

A pun on 'attention,' directed toward the "great work" of a disappointed biographer, suggests how familiar this theme was in Johnsonian circles and probably throughout later eighteenth-century culture. Boswell writes in the *Life:* "Biography led us to speak of Dr. John Campbell, who had written a considerable part of the *Biographia Britannica* ["the outstanding work, the collection of collections," of eighteenth-century antiquarian prosopography[28]]. Johnson, though he valued him highly, was of opinion that there was not so much in his great work, *A Political Survey of Great Britain,* as the world had been taught to expect; and had said to me, that he believed Campbell's disappointment, on account of the bad success of that work, had killed him. He this evening observed of it, 'That work was his death.' Mr. Warton, not adverting to his meaning, answered, 'I believe so; from the great attention he bestowed on it.' JOHNSON. 'Nay, Sir, he died of *want* of attention, if he died at all by that book'" (695). Lurking in this humorous word-play is a deadly serious matter that threatens every biographer, every writer: "great attention" to a "great work" may be met with a "want of attention," a great lack or loss that cannot be supplied or recovered. He may die by that book, that work may be his death. He may become, as Campbell has, a *mere* name—and yet, as Derrida argues, "the name, to be distinguished from the bearer, is always and a priori a dead man's name, a name of death." This is why 'Campbell,' the disappointed lifewriter whose work was his death, is perhaps as appropriate an eponym for the biographer as 'Boswell': indeed, it is more obvious in his case that the credit he extended to himself in his name did not return to the living. 'Campbell' is the very name of death, yet it is to this name (and this name only) that profit and loss can return. Thus his is also "the name of names" under the sign of which we, to whom alone the biographer's credit account is still open, can "recognize the ruse of life." To recognize the biographer is to understand that 'Boswell' and 'Campbell' are constantly displacing one another, for attention must be *paid,* and, in paying attention, we are unavoidably "incurring losses." If 'Boswell,' whose attention produced attention, is the name of the biographer as profit, then 'Campbell,' who "died of *want* of attention," is the name of the biographer as loss. We can only recognize one because we can recognize the other—that is, if we are paying attention.

VI

A passage from the *Life* recapitulates many of the themes we have been tracing and introduces yet another. "We resumed the conversation of yesterday. He put me in mind of some of it which had escaped my memory, and enabled me to record it more perfectly than I otherwise could have done. He was much pleased with my paying so great attention to his recommendation in 1763, the period when our acquaintance began, that I should keep a journal; and I could perceive he was secretly pleased to find so much of the fruit of his mind preserved; and as he had been used to imagine and say that he always laboured when he said a good thing—it delighted him, on a review, to find that his conversation teemed with point and imagery" (923). To Johnson the labor of his conversation appears unlabored only in "review," as it receives the "great attention" of Boswell's biographical labor, which itself insists on being labor that shows the signs of labor, a non-spontaneous exertion of great difficulty that leaves its traces everywhere in its display. This, as we have seen, is how the biographer establishes credit, an activity induced and represented in this passage by the trope of preservation—the Boswellian record preserves the fruit of Johnson's mind. "To preserve" is "to keep safe from harm or injury," "to keep in existence, keep from decay, make lasting (a material thing, a name, a memory)," "to retain (a possession, acquisition, property, quality, etc.), "to keep (organic bodies) from decomposition" (*OED*). Its applicability to the credit economy of biographical recognition is obvious: having acquired the biographical subject as his property, the biographer seeks to retain him, to keep his name and memory in (discursive) existence by warding off harm and decay. Thus preservation, the prevention of decomposition, enables and characterizes (re)composition, the (re)combinative process of arrangement and construction through which literary production is conventionally recognized. This is the compositional process Boswell is describing when he suggests that only he possesses the "persevering diligence" necessary to "form" the "many particulars of the progress of [Johnson's] mind and fortunes . . . into a regular composition" (19).

As we know, composition in the name of preservation is a traditional description of the biographer's task. Although Boswell uses various other metaphors or allusions to describe this task—for example, "the Flemish picture which I give of my friend" (869); "I infuse every drop of genuine sweetness into my biographical cup" (1023); "every little spark adds something to the general blaze" (868); *"this extensive biographical work . . . may in one respect be assimilated to the* ODYSSEY" (7)—'preservation' is the figure he uses most often.[29] "To record his sayings after some distance of time, was like preserving or pickling long-kept and faded fruits, or other vegetables. . . . I shall present my readers with a series of what I gathered this evening from the Johnsonian garden" (862). Variations on this image reappear elsewhere. "I could perceive he was secretly pleased to find so much of the fruit of his mind preserved" (923). "During my stay in London this spring, I find I was unaccountably negligent in preserving Johnson's sayings. . . . It is not that there was a bad crop this year; but that I was not sufficiently careful in gathering it in" (1012–13). This last image, inscribed under 1 April 1779, reemerges under 4 October 1779, where Boswell rejoices that he "was to have a second crop, in one year, of London and Johnson" (1030).

As the examples above suggest, Boswell often employs the metaphor of preservation to characterize and authenticate his reproduction of Johnson's conversation. "I cannot too frequently request of my readers, while they peruse my account of Johnson's conversation, to endeavour to keep in mind his deliberate and strong utterance. . . . I wish it could be preserved as musick is written" (599–600). "I must, again and again, intreat of my readers not to suppose that my imperfect record of conversation contains the whole of what was said by Johnson, or other eminent persons who lived with him. What I have preserved, however, has the value of the most perfect authenticity" (617). "I did not see Dr. Johnson for a considerable time, and during the remaining part of my stay in London, kept very imperfect notes of his conversation, which had I according to my usual custom written out at large soon after the time, much might have been preserved, which is now irretrievably lost" (632). "Let me then comfort myself with the large treasure of Johnson's conversation which I have preserved for my own enjoyment and that of the world" (997). The trope of preservation, which promotes the impression that the decomposition of Johnson's speech acts has been arrested in and through the (re)composition of Boswell's biographical project, is a significant instrument of Boswell's elaborate masking (which is also a revealing) of the constant rupture, the ongoing displacement of presence and absence, that (for Derrida) characterizes all language use.[30] Although the preserving energy of this compositional engine is displayed throughout the *Life,* perhaps nowhere does the ingenious proprietor of the great works of biographical power advertise it so proudly and confidently as in his introductory claim, "Had his other friends been as diligent and ardent as I was, he might have been almost entirely preserved" (22), a somewhat tempered version of his assertion, in a letter of 11 April 1788 to Anna Seward, that the *Life* "will exhibit" its subject "more completely than any person ancient or modern has yet been preserved." As we have seen, it is upon the credit established by such claims that Boswell purchases a virtual copyright on Johnson's life. Yet this claim is supplemented (and at least momentarily displaced) some ten paragraphs later by the last sentence of the passage Boswell quotes from *Rambler* 60 (on "the business of the biographer"): "'We know how few can pourtray a living acquaintance, except by his most prominent and observable particularities, and the grosser features of his mind; and it may be easily imagined how much of this little knowledge may be lost in imparting it, and how soon a succession of copies will lose all resemblance of the original'" (25). With this traditional metaphor borrowed from printing, the manufacturing and duplicating process through which Locke, Hume, and so many other neo-classical writers theorize about human understanding, Johnson (and through him, Boswell) delineates the limits of biographical power: as Derrida puts it, "the ruse starts incurring losses as soon as the surplus value does not return to the living."

The profit and loss of composition by preservation can be measured by the trope of recollection, another obsessive Boswellian habit of mind and body which, under the rubric 'memory,' has been frequently remarked in Boswellian studies.[31] The extent and precision of Boswell's remarkable memory, the subject of most of this scholarship, does not much concern us here; rather we seek to understand how, as 'recollection,' he transforms the labor-power of memory into the capital of biography. In the *Life* Boswell describes a habitual activity, how he "sat up all the night . . . , recollecting and writing in my journal what I thought worthy of preservation; an exertion, which, during the first part of my acquaintance with Johnson, I frequently made" (326). Despite (or perhaps because of) Boswell's acknowledged talent for mimicry, the process requires practice and what Walton might have termed 'sympathetic employment': at first "I found it extremely difficult to recollect and record his conversation with its genuine vigour and vivacity," but "in progress of time, when my mind was, as it were, *strongly impregnated with the Johnsonian ether,* I could, with much more facility and exactness, carry in my memory and commit to paper the exuberant variety of his wisdom and wit" (297). Naturally, he highly values this achievement: "As I had not the least recollection of it [a purported conversation between Johnson and another person, at which Boswell was present], and did not find the smallest trace of it in my *Record* taken at the time, I could not in consistency with my firm regard to authenticity, insert it in my work" (952–53n1). Not surprisingly, this valued and valuable habit of mind and body invariably produces profit. "'My Journal [he writes Johnson in a letter inserted in the *Life*] is stored with wisdom and wit; and my memory is filled with the recollection of lively and affectionate feelings, which now, I think, yield me more satisfaction than at the time when they were first excited'" (882). Note how recollection is supplemental; it always yields more, always increases the value of original feeling. This, of course, is a basic capitalist phenomenon: because "the laborer 'everywhere gives credit to the capitalist' by accepting the delay between work and wage," and because "in capitalist production, the money owner exploits the credit which the laborer bestows upon him," "'the consumption of labour-power is *at one and the same time* the production of commodities and of surplus-value.'"[32] Boswell in recollection is the biographer as capitalist, here exploiting the credit of his own labor by delaying (and thus increasing) the gratification and profit of composition. As he once wrote Percy (boasting "that mine is the best plan of Biography that can be conceived"), "I am of opinion that my delay will be for the advantage of the Work" (9 February 1788). Recollection, "the act of recalling to the memory," is also "a gathering together again," that is, a recomposition that "restores composure or confidence" (*OED*)—and thus yields more satisfaction. Drawing on the inordinate credit account he has extended to himself, the Boswellian biographer is constantly and confidently recollecting and recomposing. In this way he tries to control the 'consumption of his labor-power,' to produce a commodity and a profit simultaneously.

One form (or, more precisely, reification) which the surplus-value of recollection takes in the *Life* is the 'monument,' a tribute of sorts to Walton, upon "'the preservation and elucidation'" of whose "'pious work'" (as we have previously noted) Boswell was prepared to bestow "'all the attention that I can give'" (566). Although he never undertook this project (an edition of Walton's *Lives* preceded by a life), the *Life of Johnson*'s constant use of Waltonian language (for example, forms of 'employment' appear more than fifty times, of 'undertaking' nearly thirty, both in the various senses Walton inscribes) preserves and elucidates Walton's pious work and is thus a monument to his as well as Johnson's memory. As we have seen in a previous chapter, the intertwined senses of biography as a memorializing monument to the biographical subject pervade Waltonian biography. Boswell borrows this traditional image (Walton takes it from classical biography, particularly Plutarch) and uses it, at the very beginning and the very end of his book, as the virtually concrete form of his labor. The first paragraph of the Advertisement to the First Edition ends with Boswell's acknowledging the assistance of those who "*share in the pious office of erecting an honourable monument to* [the "departed Hero"'s] *memory*" (4). The last footnote shows how "Bayle's account of Menage may also be quoted as exceedingly applicable to the great subject of this work: '. . . we cannot sufficiently commend the care which his illustrious friends took to erect a monument so capable of giving him immortal glory'" (1401–2n). Moreover, in 1785, as he turned from the *Tour* to the *Life,* Boswell habitually represented his project to his correspondents as "the Great Literary Monument which I am ambitious to erect to the memory of our illustrious departed Friend" (to Bowles, 14 June 1785), and as "my Great Biographical Monument," which "I tell everybody . . . will be an Egyptian Pyramid in which there will be a compleat mummy of Johnson that Literary Monarch" (to Seward, 30 April 1785). Variations on this last image, in which monumentalizing is directly associated with preservation as the prevention of bodily decomposition, reappear in other letters from this period: "it is my design, in writing the Life of that Great and Good Man, to put as it were into a Mausoleum all of his precious remains that I can gather" (to Walker, 1 July 1785), and (Campbell, 19 April 1793), "they will find their great Friend and Master as it were embalmed in your Narrative."[33]

If Boswell could efface himself (he can't and won't), he would transform memory into monument, and thus actualize the compositional process by which close attention preserves recollection. But Boswell is the iron chieftain of modern biography, an apostle of self-advertisement to whom attention must also be paid. Hence this apology, which ends with a Waltonian echo and begins with a promise broken only a few pages later (1372n4): "I now relieve the readers of this Work from any farther personal notice of its authour, who if he should be thought to have obtruded himself too much upon their attention, requests them to consider the peculiar plan of his biographical undertaking" (1363). As this belated and belabored extenuation suggests, the *Life* is a monument not only to the memory of Johnson and Walton but also, as the composition of his biographical labor, to the memory of Boswell.

VII

This chapter began with two assertions adumbrating its claim that to recognize the Boswellian biographer is virtually to emplot the generic frame 'recognizing the biographer.' The first of these assertions, to which we have directed most of our attention, depicts Boswell as the iron chieftain of biography, both the father/patron of its traditional undertaking (which provides a monument that preserves the memory of its biographical subject) and the ingenious proprietor of its modern manufacturing (which accumulates credit, and thereby enhances its value, by displaying the great works of biographical power). The second, to which we now turn, presents the *Life of Johnson* as the work that corrects English biography by perfecting its composition and by disciplining its readership to participate in an alternative economy of biographical recognition. In many ways, as we shall see, we have already encountered the discursive practice of 'correction,' for it operates a crucial generic strategy we find everywhere in Boswellian biography and English lifewriting.

We will approach correction as a discursive practice and epistemological concept marked by 'perfecting' and 'disciplining.' 'Perfecting' induces the Boswellian biographer to such activities as fixing and revising, as well as preparing copy for the press. 'Disciplining' leads to instruction and punishment. As Jerome Christensen has argued, correction (as in the first sense above) is a privileged term for describing "the commerce of letters" in which Enlightenment authors participate.[34] "[T]he correction of texts is a way of dealing with corruption . . . [, a way] made available by the technology of the very culture that . . . was responsible for the corruption of classical values. Figurative extension of the correction made possible by the printing press allowed one to imagine that cultural advance, although ostensibly disruptive, contained within it its own principle of self-restraint." Thus "[c]orrection most closely coincides with the privileged metaphor of composition: it is the dynamis of composition, a substitution for writing, an adjustment of production into refinement." Patterned on the ancient "'copy theory of knowledge,'" which was retrospectively appropriated by the modern technology of the printing press, correction "supervenes" the (largely unexamined, or at least unchallenged) "substitution of the contingent fidelity of copyists and printers for the automatic reliability of the press." This is the "suppression" which, as we have seen, permits Enlightenment men of letters like Hume (Christensen's example) and Boswell to deny "any alterity in the past," to "practice their art of preservation" as they elide the discontinuities between alternative cultural and generic situations.

Governed by the more or less explicit metaphor of printing, correction is the conceptual practice of perfecting, "the substitution of what is right for what is erroneous" (*OED*), not only in printer's copy but also in "character or conduct" (*OED*). Hence it is the 'perfect' instrument for regulating the discourse of biography, that "ancient

practice," which, according to Dryden (in an influential, late seventeenth-century discussion that popularized the recently introduced
word 'biographia' or 'biography'),[35] allows "the writer [to be] more
capable of making a perfect work," because it contracts "examples of
virtue . . . into individuals" and thus circumscribes a "narrow compass" of human conduct that "strike[s] upon our minds a stronger and
more lively *impression*."[36] As Christensen notes, "The printing press
makes possible the metaphor of the impression and the associated
'copy theory of knowledge.'" Boswell's susceptibility to this metaphor
emerges in the *Life* in a passage in which Johnson cautions him, "'Do
not, Sir, accustom yourself to trust to *impressions*. . . . By trusting to
impressions, a man may gradually come to yield to them, and at
length be subject to them, so as not to be a free agent, or what is the
same thing in effect, to *suppose* that he is not a free agent.'" Now
Johnson is referring here to "'Favourable impressions at particular
moments, as to the state of our souls,'" which "'may be deceitful and
dangerous'" because "'no man can be sure of his acceptance with
God'" (1159). But the striking force of the printing press, the impression its impression has already made on theological, psychological, and philosophical discourse, is clearly implied. Of course, unlike
Hume's, the free agency of Johnson's skepticism, his distrust of yielding to the deceit and danger of impressions, is ultimately Christian.
Nevertheless, he shares with the atheistic Hume a faith in the final
corrigibility of impressions, though for Johnson this eventuality
results only from divine intercession. Despite his hypochondria, Boswell was never so skeptical of impressions, in fact, (in the eighteenth-
century sense of the term) 'enthusiastically' roamed Europe seeking
them, and celebrated them everywhere in his lifewriting. Johnson is
right to caution him: Boswell *does* trust too much to impressions. He
needs to be constantly reminded that only (what Christensen calls)
"corrective labor" can extenuate the tyranny of impressions, and thus
give the man of letters in general and the biographer in particular the
appearance (at least) of a divinely ordered free agency impelling the
production and reproduction of human life.

How the "corrective labor" of Enlightenment discourse habitually
pays homage to this possibility, and in so doing capitalizes what we
have been calling the credit economy of generic recognition, is illustrated by a passage Christensen paraphrases from William Walsh's
History of the Art of Printing (Edinburgh, 1713). "Walsh, who main-

tains that the 'Correctness of a Book is that which makes it valuable, and delightful to the Reader, yea, registrates Honour to the Memory of the Printer,' attributes the reasons for the decay of printing in Scotland to the general failure of printers to keep a corrector. Walsh chides his brethren for the false economy of failing to employ a laborer who 'adds both to our Credit and Interest,' especially when 'there are Abundance of young Men fit for this Work among us, who want Bread.'" Always seeking to add to his credit and interest, Boswell too comes to understand that the correctness of a book is what makes it valuable and delightful to his readers. Like Walsh, he eventually realizes that the labor of correction is supplemental: it enhances the value of literary work, memorializes and accrues credit for the capitalist who exploits this labor, copyrights affiliation, preserves the close attention of composition, and suppresses (as it expresses)—that is, (mis)recognizes—discontinuities between present and past, self and other, biographer and biographical subject. As susceptible as he is to impressions, Boswell discovers that corrective labor can seemingly guarantee profit and (at least the appearance of) perfection.

Boswell's desire to perfect by correction is enunciated throughout the *Life*. "Had Dr. Johnson written his own life, . . . the world would probably have had the most perfect example of biography that was ever exhibited" (19). Nevertheless, Boswell can claim of his own work: "I cannot perceive a more perfect mode of writing any man's life. . . . Had his other friends been as diligent and ardent as I was, he might have been almost entirely preserved" (22). Of course, he is acutely aware of the different scales of perfection. "I must, again and again, intreat of my readers not to suppose that my imperfect record of conversations contains the whole of what was said by Johnson, or other eminent persons who lived with him. What I have preserved, however, has the value of the most perfect authenticity" (617). Moreover, the Advertisement to the Second Edition acknowledges that perfecting was an ongoing activity not only in the Johnsonian circle but in the larger sphere of readers, who (as Boswell's voluminous correspondence shows) appreciated and contributed to the perfection of his biographical mode. "[T]*he very favourable reception with which it has been honoured . . . has excited my best exertions to render my Book more perfect; and in this endeavour I have had the assistance not only of some of my particular friends, but of many other learned and ingenious men, by which I have been enabled to rectify some mistakes, and to enrich the Work with many valuable additions*" (6). As all these passages suggest, perfecting is a means of correction that (re)collects the contingent enterprises of biographical composition into an axiological project; like Boswell's pleasure in "recollect[ing] all the passages that I heard Johnson repeat: it stamps a value on them" (738).

We can characterize these enterprises in several ways. One is 'fixing,' by which Boswell means 'ascertaining with scrupulous authenticity,' and which, as we have seen, he illustrates in the Advertisement to the First Edition by relating how "*I have sometimes been obliged to run half over London, in order to fix a date correctly; which, when I had accomplished, I well knew would obtain me no praise, though a failure would have been to my discredit*" (4). The credit that he does receive (or at least to which he aspires) is something like the credit that Johnson (reluctantly) accrued for his work on the *Dictionary:* "'Now whereas this distinguished man [his doctoral diploma from Oxford reads in part] has won such repute by his subsequent labours, notably in refining and fixing our language, . . . he is justly reckoned a chief and leader in the republic of letters'" (604n, where it is translated from the Latin). Boswell would willingly be registered in the herald's office of literary affiliation as the chief(tain) who has fixed the language (of biography). "I am absolutely certain that *my* mode of Biography," he wrote Temple (24–25 February 1788), "is the most perfect that can be conceived, and will be *more* of a *Life* than any Work that has ever yet appeared." Correction by fixing is the effect, if not the cause, of close attention, that "methodical course of study" which "fixed his attention steadily upon something without, and prevented his mind from preying upon itself" (53). In this way the "minute particulars" of everyday life, the very stuff of Boswellian biography, are fixed by fixing, that is, authenticated and stabilized by assiduous scrutiny. A methodical course prevents the mind's impressions (the 'original' copies through which dates and other facts are ascertained) from preying on each other, as if the biographer were the gamekeeper of cultural documentation, who, by inhibiting the free range of a natural habitat, fixes (encloses and domesticates) facthood within the 'preserve' of generic discourse. This is one of the generic consequences of Dryden's observation, derived from Aristotle, that, in biography, "the writer is more capable of making a perfect work, if he confine himself to this narrow compass."[37]

Another of the characteristic enterprises of correction as composi-

tional perfection is 'revision,' by which Boswell usually means something like refinement, that is, purification by reduction or elegance
by polishing. "The whole series of the Composition is to be revised
and polished," he wrote Malone on 17 November 1788. Two months
later he informed Temple: "Whenever I have completed the rough
draught, by which I mean the Work without nice correction, Malone
and I are to prepare one half perfectly, and then it goes to press" (10
January 1789). Throughout 1789 and 1790 Boswell and Malone corrected for perfection; the term that he habitually used (more than
forty times, on the evidence of surviving journal entries and correspondence) to describe this activity was 'revision.' As the process
dragged on and Boswell chafed at the regimen, he would note simply
"Revising *Life*" (6 November 1789) or "Malone's evening, revising"
(27 September 1790). Laboring under the strain of his biographical
labor, of the various activities of arranging, supplying, searching,
composing, and polishing (see letter to Temple, 28–30 November
1789), Boswell solicited the elegant perfection, the 'natural correctness,' with which Johnson was usually credited (as in this passage
from a letter by William Bowles, quoted in the *Life*): "'his conversation might have been all printed without any correction. At the same
time, it was easy and natural; the accuracy of it had no appearance of
labour, constraint, or stiffness; he seemed more correct than others,
by the force of habit, and the customary exercises of his powerful
mind'" (1246–47). Although Johnson himself thought "he always
laboured when he said a good thing" (923), his conversation has "no
appearance of labour," a counter-intuitive impression belying the ordinary sense (at least in certain late-eighteenth-century discursive
communities) that what is most correct will appear most labored.
Johnson's conversation is remarkable because it appears most correct
and least labored, a seemingly impossible combination that redefines
'natural' language-use and provides a standard of perfect eloquence to
which others can aspire.

   Can the same claim be made for Boswell's *Life of Johnson,* the work
which corrects English biography in and through Johnson's language?
Yes and no. No, because, as we have seen, the biographer must display the signs of his biographical labor if he is to correct the economy
of biographical recognition for his readership. Yes, because this aspect
of his work is not always recognized, indeed often (mis)recognized:
many readers have been willing to deceive themselves that, merely a

compulsive recorder who attached himself to Johnson, Boswell was neither a conscious nor conscientious biographer or biographical innovator. The discovery and ongoing publication of the Boswell papers over the past sixty years, which has induced investigation, acknowledgement, and appreciation of Boswell's compositional techniques, certainly have undeceived us (at least in this regard), but, in the process, something has been lost as well as gained. Boswell's (and through him, Johnson's) purchase on 'natural correction' has been depreciated: the more we know about Boswell's revision of his work the less likely we are to credit him (or Johnson) with the 'natural' gift of unlabored correctness. Depreciated and demystified, Boswell's work seems less accidental and more familiar. Revised yet again, it participates now in another more creditable but less perfect economy of biographical recognition.

Malone also assisted Boswell in preparing copy for the press, the practice that, we have already remarked, provides the governing metaphor of perfecting by correction. They were involved in this process from early 1790 until 6 April 1791, when Boswell could finally write Temple, "'My *Life of Johnson* is at last drawing to a close. I am correcting the last sheet.'" Working closely with the press's "correctors" (among whom he mentions a Mr. Selfe and a Mr. Tomlins), Boswell "was always doing a little towards the correction and improvement of my Manuscript or *Copy* as it is called of Johnson's *Life*" (25 August 1790). The printer's use of the word 'copy' to refer to the manuscript, which Boswell noted both here and earlier (11 January 1790), returns us to the notions of copyright and the 'copy theory of knowledge.' With the emergence (which is also, as we have seen, a suppression) of this word and its promise of mechanical replication, the *Life* enters another arena of correction, one in which its (virtual) property, the copyright that Boswell has acquired on Johnson's life, will be refracted beyond his eyes' power of correction. His fretting over the sale of his copyright before publication is merely a symptom of what will happen to it afterwards. Despite the claims of the second and third editions ("corrected, and considerably enlarged," "revised and augmented"),[38] the illusion of control over the corrigible perfectibility of all the mechanically replicated copies of his manuscript is diffusing. His biography, his "*Copy* as it is called," has entered the public domain, where pirated editions ("There has lately been published An Irish Edition of your Valuable *Life of Johnson*, not very ac-

curately printed, for we want here good Correctors of the Press,"
Maxwell wrote him on 15 November 1792) and other acts of literary
piracy (plagiarism, imitation, annotation, criticism, et al.) disperse
the *Life* into a discursive domain too vast and too diverse to sustain
the phantasm of even an imperfect correction.

VIII

Correction is also the discursive practice and epistemological concept
of disciplining. This is biography as a house of correction, an institutional theater for punishment and instruction. As Michel Foucault
has contended, "the architectural figure" of total surveillance that
characterizes the modern prison and other cultural institutions is the
Panopticon, the model penitentiary which Jeremy Bentham was de-
vising and promoting at the same time that Boswell was composing
and correcting the *Life* (*Panopticon: or, the Inspection-House* was also
published in 1791). A "transparent, circular cage" surrounding a
"high tower," the Panopticon is not only a (projected) physical structure but also a cultural formation that institutionalizes "surveillance
and observation, security and knowledge, individualization and totalization, isolation and transparency."[39] The extent to which biography is implicated in this description of panopticism is striking. For
one thing, biographical recognition is a cultural formation that institutionalizes its subjects in exactly the same ways: for instance, on the
basis of our exploration of 'recognizing the biographer,' we could
claim that 'close attention' induces surveillance and observation,
'preservation' ensures security and knowledge, 'copyright' reproduces
individualization and totalization, and 'perfection' replicates isolation
and transparency. Indeed, most of these themes emerge in Boswell's
familiar description of his biographical method, a description that
now seems more than a little 'panoptic': "I cannot conceive a more
perfect mode of writing any man's life, than not only relating all the
most important events of it in their order, but interweaving what he
privately wrote, and said, and thought; by which mankind are enabled as it were to see him live, and to 'live o'er each scene' with him,
as he actually advanced through the several stages of his life" (22).
Here, as in Foucauldian panopticism, the house of correction is
metaphorized as a theater which relates, orders, and (most impor-
tantly) observes ('lives over each scene'), so that what was "privately

wrote, and said, and thought" is reconstituted as public knowledge and thus subjected to public correction.[40]

In this context it is not surprising that biographical recognition played a major role in the prison reform inspired by panopticism. Because "biographical investigation is an essential part of the preliminary investigation for the classification of penalties" and then "a condition for the classification of moralities in the penitentiary system . . . , [t]he introduction of the 'biographical' is important in the history of penalty," for "it establishes the 'criminal' as existing before the crime and even outside it." Thus panopticism's desire "to reconstitute all the sordid detail of a life in the form of knowledge, to fill in the gaps of that knowledge and to act upon it by a practice of compulsion" constitutes "a biographical knowledge" that functions as "a technique for correcting individual lives."[41] But the confluence of Benthamite panopticism and Boswellian biography did not in and of itself cause this new flood of "biographical knowledge"; if anything, it widened an already flowing course of discursive relationships. Foucault's speculative observation, that "the practice of biography became widespread at about the same time [the early nineteenth century] as the constitution of the individual delinquent in the punitive mechanisms,"[42] is (for England, at least) somewhat belated. The great expansion in the production and distribution of biographical narratives began a century earlier, prompted in part by the reading public's fascination with criminal biographies, which were often based upon information supplied by prison chaplains and other more or less official functionaries, and which included among their progeny not only Defoe's *Moll Flanders* and Fielding's *Jonathan Wild* but also Johnson's *Savage* (which drew upon lives published twenty years earlier during Savage's murder trial).[43] In this respect, biographical recognition, as a cultural and generic "technique for correcting individual lives," predates its introduction into panoptic prison reform and is, in a sense, always already collusive with disciplinary correction.

Another house of correction, which in its manipulation of discipline and instruction to impel socialization resembles the prison in many ways, is the school—and it is in defense of a schoolmaster accused of "'immoderate and cruel correction'" that the *Life* makes its most detailed statement on the relationship between punishment and education. Having asked Johnson's assistance in defending a client before the House of Lords, Boswell prints in full the dictation he took at the time. The thrust of Johnson's response is a meditation on "'correction,'" which, "'in itself, is not cruel,'" except "'by being immoderate. . . . But when is correction immoderate? When it is more frequent or more severe than is required . . . for reformation and instruction.'" Thus "'Correction must be proportioned to occasions. The flexible will be reformed by gentle discipline, and the refractory must be subdued by harsher methods.'" Moreover, "'It has been said [Johnson continues, extenuating one of the charges], that he used unprecedented and improper instruments of correction. Of this accusation the meaning is not very easy to be found. No instrument of correction is more proper than another, but as it is better adapted to produce present pain without lasting mischief'" (487–88). Except for its unhesitating endorsement of correction, this statement says nothing, and hence everything. Johnson does little but define terms, and then correct the definition, and then correct it again. Correction, he maintains, must be moderate. What is immoderate correction? More or less than is required for reformation and instruction—which is just another way of saying "what is needed for 'correction.'" Correction must be proportioned to occasions and its instruments adapted to circumstances, yet no occasion and no instrument is more proper than another unless the punishment educates—which is just another way of saying "unless the result is 'correction.'" Such sentences can be parsed or served only in a prisonhouse of language, in a panoptic theater of predetermined cultural values in which nothing can be discerned because everything must be observed. Unable to even imagine a world without correction, Johnson cannot articulate anything outside its purview.[44] In Bourdieu's memorable phrase, such a deeply engrained practice of everyday life *goes without saying because it comes without saying.*[45] All attempts to see through it will invariably reaffirm its impenetrability. Correction is . . . well, 'correction.'

How then does the Boswellian biographer inhabit the inescapable house of correction, play the part of the moderate schoolmaster who metes out the discipline of punishment and instruction? For one thing, he pays homage to the classical Horatian justification of literary production: "the hope of giving instruction and entertainment is a great motive to my literary labours" (to Fawcett, 20 October 1792). For another, he chastises those who have committed errors and who thus require emendation and improvement. Indeed, he presents such correction as one of the prime motives of his work. "To correct these erroneous Accounts will be one of his principal Objects," his May 1787 advertisement in the London papers declared.[46] About the same time he was explaining to the King why the *Life* was delayed: "'It will be some time yet. I have a good deal to do to correct Sir John Hawkins'" (11 May 1787). As we have seen, Boswell inevitably profited from delay. As he wrote Blair, one "motive of having Sir John Hawkins to precede me [is] that I might profit by his gross faults" (2 August 1787). If emending and improving Hawkins is one of Boswell's principal objects, then correcting Hester Thrale Piozzi is a personal and professional obligation by which he incidentally accrues credit. "As a sincere friend of the great man whose *Life* I am writing, I think it necessary to guard my readers against the mistaken notion of Dr. Johnson's character, which this lady's *Anecdotes* of him suggest" (1327). "It is with concern that I find myself obliged to animadvert on the inaccuracies of Mrs. Piozzi's *Anecdotes*. . . . [M]y duty, as a faithful biographer, has obliged me reluctantly to perform this unpleasing task" (1333). "I have had occasion several times, in the course of this work, to point out the incorrectness of Mrs. Thrale" (1329). "This is one of the numerous misrepresentations of this lively lady, which it is worth while to correct; for if credit should be given to such a childish, irrational, and ridiculous statement of the foundation of Dr. Johnson's faith in Christianity, how little credit would be due to it" (51n1). As we have noted previously, this last example plays on various senses of both 'correction' and 'credit.' We might add now that nowhere perhaps is Boswell more schoolmasterly and more paternalistic in his correcting. He treats this "lively lady" (who was also a wealthy and learned lady, yet who, after her husband's death, was thought to have squandered her social and cultural credit by marrying an impoverished foreign musician) as if she were an unruly schoolchild; only the discipline of his emendment and improvement can restore the credit due. That credit was never far from his mind in this matter is indicated by the journal entry for 22 February 1791: "Courtenay came about ten . . . and obligingly assisted me in *lightening* my animadversions on Mrs. Piozzi in my *Life of Johnson*—for my own credit." Even (or especially) as he corrects his own correction, Boswell accrues credit.

Finally, instruction by moderate correction is the practice through which the Boswellian biographer disciplines his readership to participate in the alternative economy of biographical recognition displayed everywhere in the *Life*. If he is not explicitly addressing his readers to value his laborious task or pay close attention to his modes of preservation or recollect his compositional tactics, he is implicitly "request[ing] them to consider the peculiar plan of his biographical undertaking" (1363). To enumerate many more examples of this habitual reflexive display would be redundant; we have been doing so throughout this chapter. Boswell is an obsessive corrector: school is always in session. Perhaps just one more instance, and not an especially memorable or poignant one. Let its very ordinariness stand for the whole and close out our account. Boswell explains why at one point he groups Johnson's conversation "without specifying each scene": "Where the place or the persons do not contribute to the zest of the conversation, it is unnecessary to encumber my page with mentioning them. To know of what vintage our wine is, enables us to judge of its value, and to drink it with more relish: but to have the produce of each vine of one vineyard, in the same year, kept separate, would serve no purpose. To know that our wine, (to use an advertising phrase,) is 'of the stock of an Ambassadour lately deceased,' heightens its flavour: but it signifies nothing to know the bin where each bottle was once deposited" (753). Besides recollecting the compositional tropes of the value of his Johnsonian property and the fruits of preservation, this passage shows us a Boswell thoroughly immersed in the apparatus of the emerging consumer society. He employs an advertising phrase and an analogy of (literal and figurative) consumption to point the lesson 'how to value the labor of his reproduction of Johnson's conversation.' Coincidentally, in an essay generally considered crucial to the evolution of his "definition of the historical biographer's task," Lytton Strachey (whose *Eminent Victorians* we explore in the next chapter) employs a similar metaphor to characterize "'the first duty of a great historian [or biographer],'" which "'is to be an artist.'" "'The function of art in history [or biography],'" writes Strachey, is analogous "'to the process of fermentation which converts a raw mass of grapejuice into a subtle and splendid wine.'"[47] We need not attach too much significance to this coincidence; it is enough merely to note, once again, how Boswell's correction consumes English biography. The subtle and splendid wine that Strachey decants is of Boswellian vintage.

In the Roman Empire the designation 'corrector' was sometimes given to a governor of a province, a powerful public official who oversaw the discipline and instruction of all the lives under his chief-tainship.[48] In the example just cited, as throughout the *Life,* the Boswellian biographer aspires to this sovereign station, to be the public corrector who governs the province of biographical recognition. Appropriately, Adam Smith places sovereigns in "the same class" as "men of letters of all kinds": their labor is "unproductive of any value, and does not fix or realize itself in any permanent subject, or vendible commodity, which endures after that labour is past, and for which an equal quantity of labour could afterwards be procured." Furthermore, "before the invention of the art of printing, the only employment by which a man of letters [who was generally maintained and "educated at the publick expence"] could make any thing by his talents [and thus partially return this investment], was that of a publick or private teacher," a pursuit that Smith, a traditionalist in these matters, insists "is still surely a more honourable, a more useful, and in general even a more profitable employment than that other of writing for a book-seller, to which the art of printing has given occasion."[49] Aspiring to the sovereignty of public corrector, the Boswellian biographer belies his class and emerges from the *Life* as the kind of venture capitalist *The Wealth of Nations* elsewhere induced. By linking the profitable employment of public teaching with the vendible commodity of the art of printing, his biographical labor realizes itself in a permanent subject of enduring value that continues to correct English biography. This is how 'Boswell' has become the very name of the biographer.

chapter 7

RECOGNIZING THE LIFE-COURSE:
STRACHEY'S *EMINENT VICTORIANS*

"Sexuality is not the most intractable element in power
relations, but rather one of those endowed with the greatest instrumentality: useful for the greatest number of maneuvers and capable of serving as a point of support, as a
linchpin, for the most varied strategies."
—Michel Foucault

I

In a famous passage, Tristram Shandy, who calls himself a "biographer" (the word was used for both the writer of a life and a writer of
personal history until the term 'autobiographer' entered the language
at the end of the eighteenth century), describes the narrative "lines I
moved in through my . . .[previous] volumes," which he illustrates
with an assortment of crooked striations marked by an "indented
curve" and other oddly shaped squiggles. In the future, he promises,
"I make no doubt but I shall be able to go on . . . in a tolerable
straight line," which he then depicts in "a line drawn as straight as I
could draw it, by a writing-master's ruler." Delighted by this prospect, he then rhapsodizes on his new narrative strategy (which, of
course, he does not pursue), characterizing it variously as: "This *right
line,*—the path-way for Christians to walk in! say divines—The emblem of moral rectitude! says *Cicero*—The *best line!* say cabbage-
planters—is the shortest line, says *Archimedes,* which can be drawn
from one given point to another."[1] In his seriously whimsical way
Tristram is adumbrating a theory of the life-course, a cultural and
generic formation from which the 'line' of his narrative, marked constantly by the "frisk of a digression," habitually departs. Inherited
from classical authors (for instance, "'*Recta via,*' or 'the right path of
life,' is a phrase often used by Cicero")[2] as well as from Biblical and
hagiographical tradition, the 'straight line of moral rectitude' which
Tristram projects (and rejects in favor of a frisky curve of digressive

play) delineates one of English lifewriting's most characteristic strategies for emplotting the life-course.

Certainly, the image of "the lines of life" (the phrase with which both Shakespeare and Jonson characterized the life-course)[3] as 'straight' paths, roads, gates, or ways is a familiar one in Western culture. Among the thousands of examples we could cite let these few suffice. *Matthew* (III, 3): "The voice of one crying in the wilderness, / Prepare ye the way of the Lord, make his paths straight." The opening of Dante's *Divine Comedy:* "In the middle of the journey of our life I came to myself within a dark wood where the straight way was lost." Part of the title of an anonymous work published in London in 1658: "The strait-gate and narrow way to life, which hath been alwayes, and still is the good old way." From George Borrow's *Lavengro* (1851): "O ye gifted ones, follow your calling, for, however various your talents may be, ye can have but one calling capable of leading ye to eminence and renown; follow resolutely the one straight path before you." Finally, these bathetic but instructive lines from the Victorian poet William Maccall: "Straight is the line of Duty, / Curved is the line of Beauty, / Follow the straight line, thou shalt see / The curved line ever follow thee."[4] Intersecting in the nineteenth century with the emergent cultural notion of the 'career,' these straight lines are subsumed in a 'doctrine of pursuits' that comes to regulate the generic recognition of the 'life-course.' As we shall see, it is to a 'subtler strategy' that ironically and aesthetically 'curves' or skews these straight lines that Lytton Strachey's *Eminent Victorians* is committed.

The word 'career,' meaning "a person's course through life (or a distinct portion of life), especially when publicly conspicuous, or abounding in remarkable incidents," enters the language around 1800, as does the cognate sense, "a course of professional life or employment, which affords opportunity for progress or advancement in the world" (*OED*). These connotations gain currency throughout a century in which careerism and professionalism emerge as significant social and cultural transformations that more or less redefine the discourse of interpersonal relationships. "In the United States and England, as in most other European societies," writes M. S. Larson, "the professional modernization that started in the nineteenth century was oriented toward a society in which community and aristocratic tradition were no longer sufficient to guarantee *credit* and *credibility*,"[5] relatively modern conceptual practices which, as we saw in the last chapter, are crucial to biographical recognition. Coinciding "with the rise of industrial capitalism, with its early crises and consolidation and, toward the end of the nineteenth century and the beginning of the twentieth, with the evolution of capitalism toward its corporate form" (6), a new "'monopoly of credibility'" was achieved by "the professional sectors of the middle class, seeking to improve their position in the emergent stratification systems of capitalist society" (16–17). Claiming a *"cognitive exclusiveness"* (15) maintained through standardized training, accreditation, and marketing, the "organized professions" thus come to "possess the structural means to incorporate and regulate individual ambition into *a career,* that is, an organized trajectory of individual advancement" (74). "A pattern of organization of the self" as well as "a powerful factor of conformity with the existing social order" (229), the conceptual practice of the professional career, in alliance with biographical recognition, traces the cultural path of the life-course, which emerges now as their reciprocal emplotment. "While biography is looking backward on one's life, an after-the-fact search for order and meaning, career is looking forward, with a sense of order to come" (229). Thus, for the mid-Victorian, as Burton Bledstein has shown, the career was "the new course," "striking for its totality and self-sufficiency," connecting "the entire coherence of an intellectually defined and goal-oriented life," and guaranteeing the credit of "character," which "was the internal and psychological symbol of continuity that corresponded to the sociological course a person ran in a career."[6] A letter from Thomas Arnold, one of Strachey's subjects, to a former Rugby student expresses this attitude exactly: "It is a real pleasure to me to find that you are taking steadily to a profession, without which I scarcely see how a man can live honestly."[7] This then was "the middle-class professional world of the Victorians"—the encompassing phrase with which, in an autobiographical essay about his childhood, Strachey characterized his parents' home.[8]

The extent to which the professional career organized and validated the nineteenth-century life-course is explored throughout *Eminent Victorians,* where 'professional careerism' becomes a socio-economic structure dramatized and satirized by the narrative's rhetorical amplification.[9] Thus, for instance, "the history of Manning's career" (13) is a refraction of "the light which his career throws upon the spirit of his age" (11), revealing how his renunciations of "a political career"

(15) and then of a "splendid career" (63) in the Anglican Church conduce the "long and strange career" which "come[s] at last to fruition in a Princedom of the [Roman Catholic] Church" (111). Along the way, the narrative explains how, traditionally, the taking of Anglican orders "was in fact simply to pursue one of those professions which Nature and Society had decided were proper to gentlemen and gentlemen alone" (18), and how the Oxford Movement was changing this arrangement by "imput[ing] an extraordinary, a transcendent merit to the profession which Manning himself pursued" (31). It also analyzes Manning's alliance with Monsignor Talbot, the Pope's private secretary, which "was destined to have the profoundest effect upon Manning's career" (73–74), and which, in its cruel treatment of Newman (who had earlier abandoned "his Anglican career" [41]), "showed, more clearly perhaps than any other incident in his career, the stuff that Manning was made of" (88). This stress on the cultural and narrative authority of professional careerism continues throughout *Eminent Victorians'* other biographical sketches. To summarize briefly: "the experience which [Florence Nightingale] gained as a nurse at Kaiserwerth formed the foundation of all her future action and finally fixed her in her career" (133), that "particular profession for which Florence was clearly marked out by her instincts and her capacities" (131) and which became (she wrote) what "'I have always longed for'"—"'a profession, a trade, a necessary occupation, something to fill and employ all my faculties'" (134); Arnold's spectacular "career at Rugby" (195) is characterized by the dignity, sternness, and perplexity he habitually displays while acting "in his professional capacity" (212); Gordon's inability "to lay aside the activities of his profession" (236) leads him on "a very different course" (236), an eccentric path crossing (among others) the "extraordinary career" of the Sudanese Mahdi (247) and the "enormous career" of Gladstone (279), and leading, at "the very end of [Gordon's] career" (233), to the disaster at Khartoum.

As this catalogue suggests, we can follow the curving line of biographical recognition through various intersecting senses of the terms 'career,' 'course,' and 'pursuit' (*OED*). Derived from a late Latin word meaning "carriage road" and a French word meaning "race-course," 'career' evolves in English from (the now obsolete) senses "road," "race-course," and "a short gallop at full speed," to a "rapid and continuous course of action," and hence to a virtual definition of the

ordinary cultural sense of the life-course—"a person's course or progress through life" or "a course of professional life or employment."[10]
This progress can be traced also in various senses of the word "course,"
derived from a Latin word meaning "running" or "race," and entailing
among its main senses "the action of running or moving onward" and
"the path, line, or direction of running." Thus we can speak of a race-
course or a water-course, the course of a ship or a mountain chain,
and, by extension, a course of time, events, or actions, most especially, "the continuous connected purport or tenor of a narrative;
drift," "a line of (personal) action," "life viewed as a race that is run;
career." Metaphorically, the words "career" and "course" run headlong
into one another, describing how life, the race-course, the 'race that
is run,' intersects with narrative, the water-course, the 'drift,' "the
direction or line pursued by an ocean current." These lines (supposedly) meet through the action of 'pursuit' (from Latin for "to follow"),
which arrives at "something that one engages in or follows, as a
profession, business, recreation, etc.," through various "courses" of
"following," "chasing," "overtaking," "attacking," "suing," "prosecut-
ing," "seeking," "tracing," "attending," and "complying."

The intersection of all these terms and their various connotations
is a nineteenth-century literary commonplace. From Wordsworth's
Prelude to Matthew Arnold's "The Buried Life" the 'course of life' is
the wandering stream along which "thy race be run," or "the un-
regarded river of our life" which will "Pursue with indiscernible flow
its way."[11] Other modes of literary discourse, such as the novel or the
essay, are similarly marked: for instance, the symbolic water-course of
Our Mutual Friend and so many other Victorian novels, or the headlong career and meandering road of the emblematic journey in De
Quincey's "The English Mail-Coach." There is even a geometric figure, first described in the mid-nineteenth century, depicting this intersection—the *curve of pursuit,* "the curve traced by a point moving
with constant velocity, whose motion is directed at each instant towards another point which also moves with constant velocity (usually
in a straight line)" (*OED*). What all this points to is a familiar premise
of conventional generic wisdom: if the life-course is a straight line (of
duty), then narrative overtakes it by tracing a curve of pursuit (a line
of beauty) that, although adrift and in constant motion, is ultimately
compliant, as it seeks, chases, attacks, and prosecutes in order "to
proceed in accordance with," that is, to reproduce and celebrate in

biographical discourse the straight lines of moral rectitude and professional careerism already inscribed in cultural discourse.[12] Thus 'pursuit' becomes the *doctrine,* the theory or science, of the life-course:
that which overtakes the generic frame and forces it to comply with
the cultural practice of the career.

Appropriately enough, the first book-length study of biography
published in England, James Field Stanfield's *An Essay on the Study
and Composition of Biography* (1813), asserts: "In our contemplation of
biography . . . the *doctrine of* PURSUITS will be the main subject to
claim our attention. . . . Pursuits, directed to certain ends, adjusted
by precise regulations and specified means of advancement, furnish
the inquisitive mind with a class of grateful as well as profitable
studies. Professional biography, scientifically executed, gives both the
materials and form of these studies; and leads the general student or
the kindred artist through all the combinations of skill, perseverance,
established practice, and inventive enterprise, to the professor's point
of excellence, by the actual course the attainment of the object was
accomplished."[13] By "professional biography," Stanfield refers to a
particular "species of biography" designed "to describe, not only the
professional reputation of the character [of the biographical subject],
but also, the means by which that reputation was attained" (18–19).
Consequently, "the term Profession is meant to be extended to every
class of men who pursue a regular vocation, or who are, in some
exclusive way, influenced by a certain designation of purpose" (312).
Eventually, professional biography becomes part of Stanfield's general
attempt to posit an "inductive table" of "comprehensive principles"
through which he could "generalize the spirit of biography" (322–
23)—an early, quixotic effort to describe biographical recognition
depreciated by a contemporary reviewer for its "almost unremitting
and overwhelming parade of scientific phraseology," which "is as pro-
lix and indefinite, and cloudy, for the most part, as it is artificial and
academical."[14] This is not an unfair criticism, and Stanfield's work,
published in a limited edition, has remained obscure.[15] Yet, in one
respect at least, it forestalled future developments in biographical
practice, for, in response to the hero worship of the emergent professional middle-class, professional biography elucidating a 'doctrine of
pursuits' came to dominate mid-Victorian lifewriting. Thus Walter
E. Houghton summarizes the import of James Anthony Froude's classic essay, "Representative Men" (1850): "The great need of the age,

therefore, is a whole series of biographies of lawyers, merchants, land-lords, workmen, each of which is the type of his profession at its best." [16]

Froude's essay is worth pausing over, because, in expressing this need, it also suggests how professional careerism, the motive force of this new 'doctrine of pursuits' that promises to regulate and stabilize the life-course, can (re)produce 'representative men' and 'representative lives.' [17] The present moment in which he writes is an instant of "utter spiritual disintegration" (470) between an older (essentially Catholic) cultural synthesis perfectly articulated in the 'Lives of the Saints,' and what he hopes will be a new Anglo-Protestant age exemplified by the morally heroic lives depicted in professional biography, which will be "laid out in the name of God, as once the saints' lives were" (480). But just now, "in all this [transitional] confusion" (473), "we have no biographies," that is, "no written lives of our fellow creatures. . . . in which the ideal tendencies of this age can be discerned in their true form" (470–71). Here Froude is trying to 're-member' the similitude of patron and pattern which, as we saw in a previous chapter, was being dismembered just as the bourgeois consumerism of industrial capitalism (upon which professional careerism depends) was beginning to emerge. Thus he writes: "the age of saints has passed; . . . we must walk in their spirit, but not along their road; and in this sense we say, that we have no pattern great men, no biographies, no history, which are of real service to us" (472).

Froude's great fear is that, in "our journey through life," we will end as we began, "like strangers set to find their way across a difficult and entangled country." Without a course articulated by a doctrine of pursuits, without a straight line of moral rectitude that we can follow as if it were a career, without "the *track*" that the "pioneers of godliness, have beaten in . . . , a real path trodden in by real men" [18]—we will remain strangers in a strange land. This prospect of perpetual defamiliarization, of an eternal alienation in an entangled country, prompts Froude's espousal of a professional biography that synthesizes spiritual and secular conduct as it re-members the lives of the saints in the new journey through life, the career. As we shall see, the Victorian refraction of this beatific vision into dutiful, sanctimonious panegyrics, "those two fat volumes with which it is our custom to commemorate the dead," induces the "subtler strategy" of Strachey's "haphazard visions" (6–7), a different kind of 'undertaking' that

reimposes 'strangeness' on the eminent Victorian life-course by ironically skewing the straight line of professional biography.

One of the most interesting features of this life-course is, as we
have already noted, that it was being respiritualized and resecularized
simultaneously. Industrial capitalism sponsored not only professional
careerism but such socio-economic practices as the buying and selling
of life assurance, which gained widespread acceptance only in the
early Victorian period. According to the contemporary pamphlets of
its promoters, "the whole object" of life assurance was to standardize
the life-course, or at least its 'expectancy,' "to render that certain
which nature has made uncertain."[19] Life assurance was merchan-
dised, moreover, on the crucial, regulatory premise that, "in a commercial country like Great Britain, it is a well-known fact that the
great majority derive their income from professional pursuits."[20] This
was a great comfort to life-assurance societies, for the reliability of
burial registers and bills of mortality as well as the sophistication of
the theory of probability, upon which they based their rates and div-
idends, were recent and still fallible instruments. The standardization
and regularity of the life-course under the influence of professional
careerism made their 'tables of mortality' much more dependable.[21]
Another influence on the life-course that imparted to it a predictive
structure of biological determinism was Darwinism, probably the
most powerful late-Victorian cultural movement, which treated all
subjects as if they were developing organisms tracing a 'natural' life-
course more or less analogous to that which *Origin of Species* and *The
Descent of Man* ascribed to the human animal in general. Such an
'evolutionary perspective,' wrote John Addington Symonds in 1890,
"lent the charm of biography or narrative to what had previously
seemed so dull and lifeless—the history of art or letters."[22]

The 'charm of biography' was a spell cast over all of Victorian life,
inscribing a doctrine of pursuits by which the assured and evolving
career of industrial capitalism could intersect with the "track of godliness" traced by the body of Christ.[23] We can witness this apotheosis
in the rolling thunder of Carlyle's essays, in the more pedestrian prose
of Samuel Smiles' conduct books, and in the "romantic, didactic, and
philosophic" styles of Edwin P. Hood's treatise on *The Uses of Biography.* In an essay published in 1832 Carlyle recognizes the life-course
as a "miraculously lamplit Pathway" illuminated by the life of Jesus:
"as the highest Gospel was a Biography, so is the Life of every good

man still an indubitable Gospel."[24] In *Self-Help* (1859), *Character* (1872), and *Duty* (1880), Smiles, who also wrote a series of exemplary lives of engineers, propounds the same message and finds the same "right way of life": "at the head of all biographies stands the Great Biography—the Book of Books. And what is the Bible . . . but a series of biographies . . . culminating in the greatest biography of all—the Life embodied in the New Testament?"[25] Biography also enchants Hood. His book, printed in 1852, recognizes the life-course not only as "the inductions" of "well-preserved mental fossils" illustrating "the science of life," but also as "the chronicle of goodness" in which "the lives of the eminently holy, and brave, and truly Christian and heroic men, are like a pathway descried above us in our way up the difficult hill"—a hill marking yet another obscure eminence in Froude's "entangled country," towards which we are led by the strai(gh)tened life-courses of biographical recognition, those miraculously articulate "voices" emanating from the silence of written discourse, "saying to us, 'This is the way, walk ye in it.'"[26]

Another way of understanding the remarkably potent force of Victorian biography is to see it as participant in the spreading of another kind of gospel, what Michel Foucault calls 'bio-power.' From the middle of the eighteenth century, Foucault maintains, "one of [the] primary concerns" of the emerging middle-class "was to provide itself with a body and a sexuality—to ensure the strength, endurance, and secular proliferation of that body through the organization of a deployment of sexuality," for "one of the primordial forms of class consciousness is the affirmation of the body." In the nineteenth century, as the body politic became increasingly middle-class, "political power . . . assigned itself the task of administering life"; one of the dominant modes of this administration "focused on the species body, the body imbued with the mechanics of life and serving as the basis of the biological processes." Eventually, "the administration of bodies and the calculated management of life" emerged "in the field of political practices and economic observation" through "the problems of birthrate, longevity, public health, housing, and migration"— through, that is, "an explosion of numerous and diverse techniques for achieving the subjugation of bodies and the control of populations, marking the beginning of an era of 'bio-power.'" Foucault continues: "This bio-power was without question an indispensable element in the development of capitalism," which "would not have been possible without the controlled insertion of bodies into the machinery of production." Consequently, "methods of power and knowledge assumed responsibility for the life processes and undertook to control and modify them. Western Man was gradually learning what it meant to be a living species in a living world, to have a body, conditions of existence, probabilities of life, an individual and collective welfare." Thus we can use the term "*bio-power*" to designate what brought life and its mechanisms into the realm of explicit calculations and made knowledge-power an agent of transformation of human life."[27]

Concerned "to show how deployments of power are directly connected to the body,"[28] Foucault suggests how 'bio-power' is the motive force of the 'doctrine of pursuits' and why the new 'gospel of biography' situates the track of godliness in the rising eminence of the professional career. Administering the body and controlling its insertion into the machinery of production, the recognition of the life-course becomes a crucial cultural practice, an agent for transforming human life. Appropriated by the nation-state of industrial capitalism as an articulation of its knowledge-power, nineteenth-century biography explicitly calculates the probabilities of life, ensures the strength, endurance, and proliferation of the middle-class body, and plots the trajectory of this body in cultural discourse. The life-course thus becomes, so to speak, another form of life assurance, a strategy for "proliferating, innovating, annexing, creating, and penetrating bodies in an increasingly detailed way" (107), which, like "the deployment of sexuality" (107), was 'incited to discourse' in the nineteenth century as "a means of access both to the life of the body and the life of the species" (146). If "a normalizing society is," as Foucault maintains, "the historical outcome of a technology of power centered on life" (144), then the path traced by the body in and through the conventional Victorian life-course is the virtual imprint of bio-power—an eminent career subscribing to a doctrine of pursuits that administers the body by controlling and sacramentalizing its insertion into cultural production.

What would happen if the deployment of this strategy for recognizing the trajectory of the body were to come under a subversive administration exercising a bio-power that seeks to 'de-actualize' the 'cultural reality' endorsed in the Victorian doctrine of pursuits? This is the possibility that *Eminent Victorians* articulates, as it strategically (mis)recognizes the path traced by the body in the conventional Victorian life-course. In exposing the 'strange truth' of this traditional 'ministry of eminence,' Strachey's narrative defamiliarizes generic recognition—placing it, once more, in an entangled country, where "obscure recesses, hitherto undivined" (6) divert the course of the miraculously lamplit pathway of the professional career. In reformulating 'bio-power,' *Eminent Victorians* interposes in English biography an alternative sexuality for an alternative body politic—a 'subtle' transgression that (dis)embodies the 'pose' of eminence regulating the generic recognition of the life-course.

II

The famous story has been told many times. In January 1916, the Great War on the Western front already a bloody stalemate devastating an entire European generation, Parliament passed England's first conscription act. Pacifists like Lytton Strachey and many of his Bloomsbury friends began to prepare their cases for exemption on the grounds of conscientious objection. Summarily dismissed by his local Advisory Committee, Strachey knew that his forthcoming appearance before the Hampstead Tribunal, whose proceedings he had already visited a number of times, was to be in the role of sacrificial victim, a scapegoating more or less demanded by a frightened and vengeful public contemplating interminable conflict. "Clearly they had decided beforehand to grant *no* exemptions, and all the proceedings were really a farce," he wrote to a friend. "It made one's flesh creep to see victim after victim led off to ruin or slaughter." Thus, Michael Holroyd reports, he "prepared for his examination before the Hampstead Tribunal with all the thoroughness of a general laying plans for some military offensive," even "drawing up imaginary cross-examinations" and rehearsing repartee. He knew he would lose, but he wanted to make his point.

Accompanied by family and friends, he orchestrated a strange and memorable encounter. Although not yet famous as the author of *Eminent Victorians*, which he was working on but was not to publish until two years later, Strachey was known, indeed, had been known since his undergraduate years at Cambridge, as a talented writer whose appearance, conduct, and opinions expressed aesthetic, political, and sexual preferences generally considered shocking and deviant. Now that he was in his mid-thirties, "his eccentricity was . . . far more deliberate and assertive." Tall and thin, his body tilting and bending at unusual angles, his long red beard muffling a distinctive, witty, acerbic, high-pitched voice, often dressed in the flowing capes and unexpected colors of the artist friends for whom he posed in unsettling and distorting portraits by which he was primarily known and through which a modern, 'decadent' movement in painting and sculpture was being expressed, Strachey was at this point only a marginal literary figure, the author of some respected reviews and a spirited book of criticism on French literature. His reputation (such as it was) rested less on his writing than it did on his status as a cultural icon, as a strange body through which eccentric modern ideas—decadent aestheticism, pacifism, homoeroticism—were being projected. Accompanied by family and friends, this body now entered the council chamber of the Hampstead Town Hall.

Carrying "a tartan travelling rug" and flanked by his supporters, who "lined themselves up opposite the eight members of the Tribunal," Strachey, suffering from piles, took up a light blue air cushion ceremoniously carried by his character witness, and, "to the astonishment of the chairman, . . . applied [it] to the aperture in his beard and solemnly inflated. Then he deposited this cushion upon the wooden bench, lowered himself gingerly down upon it facing the mayor, and arranged the rug carefully about his knees." This performance, in its mock solemnity, heightened awareness of bodily discomfort, and ceremonial insistence upon trivial, eccentric detail, was itself a comment upon the administration of official justice and the ethos of war, and provoked the tribunal's military representative to "[fire] a volley of awkward questions from the bench." It was this examination that produced the oft-quoted exchange with which Strachey, despite (or, indeed, because of) his eventual emergence as an important and influential biographical writer, was to be ever after identified. "'Then tell me, Mr. Strachey, what would you do if you saw a German soldier attempting to rape your sister?' Lytton turned and forlornly regarded each of his sisters in turn. Then he confronted the Board once more and answered with gravity: 'I should try and interpose my own body.'"[29]

This situation and this remark, reminiscent of the atmosphere and style of Oscar Wilde's trials some twenty years before (a connection to which we shall return), describe a crucial, exemplary moment, not only in Strachey's public career but also in our discussion of the discourse of English biography—for it is through a reading of *Eminent Victorians* which habitually returns to this cross-examination between a militant administrator posing awkward questions and a homosexual pacifist interposing his body into even more embarrassing answers that we shall (re-)emplot the generic frame 'recognizing the life-course.' In doing so we shall map out the 'subtler strategy' by which the historian-biographer of the famous "Preface" to *Eminent Victorians* plans to "attack his subject in unexpected places," to "fall upon the flank, or the rear," to "shoot a sudden, revealing searchlight into obscure recesses, hitherto undivined" (6). As has often been noted, Strachey's prefatory adoption of military language was a powerful sign of contemporary protest: appearing in the waning months of the Great War, the book was greeted (and attacked) by a war-weary public as an exposure of the values and beliefs that had led to this disillusioning holocaust. As we shall see, *Eminent Victorians* strategically (mis)recognizes the interposition of the body in the conventional Victorian life-course; by revealing the 'strange truth' of the traditional 'ministry of eminence,' it proposes to cure "the deep disease of the body politic" (137), to register a conscientious objection against (as Strachey told his local Advisory Committee) "the whole system by which it is sought to settle international disputes by force," a "profoundly evil" system that, in peace and war, disembodies the spirit of a people.[30]

The theme of 'embodiment' is a traditional one in the discourse of English biography. As we have seen in a previous chapter, Walton uses it to characterize a sympathy of souls embodied in Donne's writing and then re-embodied in his own narrative. In his appropriation of this (and other) thematic structures distributed and popularized by Walton's *Lives,* Strachey returns to the traditional language of English biography, as he calls into question the Victorian recognition of the life-course, and as he re-deploys the bio-power energizing the nineteenth-century's doctrine of pursuits. *Eminent Victorians'* thematizing of 'embodiment' is clearest perhaps in "Gordon," where the term recurs several times; but, in various ways, the theme pervades the other narratives as well and receives its most forceful application in "Nightingale" (which we shall examine in detail later). In "Gordon," for example, the Mahdi appears to his frenzied adherents as "the embodiment of a superhuman power" (252); Sir Evelyn Baring seems

to Gordon to be "the embodiment of England—or rather the embodiment of the English official classes" (285); "in Lord Hartington [his
countrymen] saw, embodied and glorified, the very qualities which
were nearest to their hearts" (294). In each case here 'embodiment' is
the seemingly concrete expression, in the person of an individual
human, of an abstract principle—a familiar cultural practice with
which biography has always been associated, and which, as we shall
see in our close examination of "Nightingale," transforms the body
into a cultural artifact, a lever or fulcrum across which human sentience is projected and reciprocated, and through which values and
beliefs are both reified and de-actualized.

To 'embody' is also 'to invest or clothe a spirit with a body' (*OED*),
a principle of faith with which Walton, influenced by hagiography
and ecclesiastical biography, also emplotted his *Lives*. Gordon, a religious dipsomaniac who, "in his intoxicated heart" (274), "consider[ed] himself a special instrument in God's hand" (238), "evolved"
this traditional conviction into a "mystical and fatalistic" and "highly
unconventional" creed, in which "human beings were the transitory
embodiments of souls who had existed through an infinite past and
would continue to exist through an infinite future" (235). Such religious eccentricity is characteristic of all the eminent Victorians whose
life-courses are traced in Strachey's narrative: driven by ambition,
egotism, and self-righteousness, each is dissatisfied with received religious precepts, each seeks to reinvest his or her spirit in a plenipotentiary body traversing conventional limits. Thus Cardinal Manning
emerges as "some embodied memory of the Middle Ages" (112). His
ultra-orthodox faith founded upon (as Gladstone writes him) "the
great principle of communion in the body of Christ" (34), the essential Christian practice that ritualistically reaffirms spiritual embodiment, Manning discovers in the Church of England a spiritual body
which (he writes) "seems to me to be diseased" (53). A "superstitious
egotist" (63), he reinvests his spiritual embodiment in the "healthy"
(53) faith of "the Roman Pontiff," himself an embodiment, "the head,
heart, mind, and tongue of the Catholic Church" (96). This obsessive
quest for a single (secular and religious) embodiment that unifies
physical and spiritual health is a powerful theme in *Eminent Victorians*:
Arnold's "great work" was to be an unfinished book that "point[ed]
out the remedies of the evils which afflicted society" by promoting
"the absolute identity of the Church and the State" (206–07); Night-

ingale, as we shall see, sought to minister to "the deep disease of the body politic" not only by composing the eight-hundred-page report that systematized the Army medical corps but also by writing a massive three-volume metaphysical treatise logically deducing the laws of Omnipotent Righteousness.

Eventually, as we (re-)emplot the generic frame 'recognizing the life-course,' we shall explore the trajectory of these embodiments in biographical space-time, the paths they trace in cultural discourse. For now it is sufficient to note that, in all these examples, 'embodiment' entails 'incorporation into a system of complex unity' (*OED*), the union of disparate elements in one (nominally organic) body. Thus, throughout *Eminent Victorians,* "outward appearance" is usually "the index of . . . inward character" (193–94), a relationship that induces the notorious poses into which Strachey's subjects invariably arrange themselves and which, in the first edition, were represented by carefully selected illustrations. The description of Arnold's characteristic pose is the longest and most detailed; let it stand for the rest. "[E]verything about him denoted energy, earnestness, and the best intentions. His legs, perhaps, were shorter than they should have been; but the sturdy athletic frame, especially when it was swathed (as it usually was) in the flowing robes of a Doctor of Divinity, was full of imposing vigour; and his head, set decisively upon the collar, stock, and bands of ecclesiastical tradition, clearly belonged to a person of eminence. The thick, dark clusters of his hair, his bushy eyebrows and curling whiskers, his straight nose and bulky chin, his firm and upward-curving lip—all these revealed a temperament of ardour and determination. His eyes were bright and large; they were also obviously honest. And yet—why was it?—was it in the lines of the mouth or the frown on the forehead?—it was hard to say, but it was unmistakable—there was a slightly puzzled look upon the face of Dr. Arnold" (194). All these details conspire to identify (and stigmatize) Arnold as "a person of eminence," to unify divers features of his appearance, conduct, and intellect in a pose of systematic embodiment with which Arnold, like the other titular subjects of *Eminent Victorians,* is to be recognized. This is, in Stanfield's language, "the professor's point of excellence," the position marked by "the professional reputation of [his] character" in the "doctrine of pursuits."

Strachey's habitual use of 'the pose that embodies' participates not only in the traditional association between biography and portrait painting (a relationship which has been often remarked and need concern us only in passing) but also (and more pertinently to our inquiry) in 'posing' as 'attitudinizing' and 'questioning.' A 'pose' is not only 'a deliberately assumed attitude or posture of the body in which a figure is placed for effect or artistic purposes,' it is also a way of 'puzzling or perplexing, of placing in difficulty with a question, of interrogating.' Each of these 'posings' traces the affinity between Strachey's appearance before the Military Tribunal and the character portraits in *Eminent Victorians*. In leaving Arnold with "a slightly puzzled look on [his] face," the narrative suggests that its questioning of this and its other subjects induces an interrogation of the poses, the virtual embodiments, by which they have been traditionally recognized. Moreover, in examining the 'whole system' that produced these well known and much imitated poses, the narrative itself assumes a recognizable and disruptive pose that shades over into a position, 'the manner in which a body is disposed, figuratively represented as a mental attitude, and thus the point of view which one occupies in reference to a subject' (*OED*). Much has been made of Strachey's ironic point of view; we shall approach it as a pose of disruptive, interrogatory embodiment, as a way for Strachey to "interpose my own body" in the Victorian life-course.

'To interpose' is not only the specific action of 'stepping in between persons at variance or in a person's behalf,' the archaic sense of the term Strachey invoked in his figurative defense of his sister at the Hampstead Tribunal, but also the general action of interfering, interrupting, and intervening, as in a narrative (*OED*). The *OED*'s citation of Gibbon's use of the term is particularly instructive: "The Historian, who, without interposing his own sentiments, has delivered a simple narrative of authentic fact." Indeed, this is the historical approach that Strachey, a profound admirer and imitator of Gibbon, champions in the preface to *Eminent Victorians*: "That is what I have aimed at in this book—to lay bare the facts of some cases, as I understand them, dispassionately, impartially, and without ulterior intentions. To quote the words of a Master—'Je n'impose rien; je ne propose rien; j'expose'" (8). What is interesting here is that both Gibbon and Strachey are conventionally recognized as adopting an ironic, detached position which is passionately dispassionate, yet which, in the guise of impartial exposure, imposes and proposes everything. Strachey's carefully staked out position is then one of interposition, a subtler strategy of rear and flank attacks that, in constantly interrogating Victorian poses, inserts his body (or this attitude that is a projection of his body) into the narrative.[31]

In calling his strategy 'subtle' (and in "[attacking] his subject in unexpected places," such as "the flank, or the rear") Strachey has already associated it with decadent aestheticism in general and with homoeroticism in particular, both of which, since the last two decades of the nineteenth century, had mounted direct attacks on Victorian conventionality and were identified with Oscar Wilde.[32] There is perhaps no more famous pose, and no more famous portrait of a pose, in English literature than that in Wilde's *The Picture of Dorian Gray* (1890–91), the book which, during Wilde's trials on the charge of 'posing as a sodomite,' was used to demonstrate "a pervading atmosphere of homosexuality" in Wilde's life and work.[33] The picture, which ages and undergoes bodily distortion and decomposition while its subject remains unchanged, is not only "the visible emblem of [Dorian's guilty] conscience"[34] but also a representation of the (mis)recognized life-course, an inversion of conventional cultural expectations more or less associated with 'sexual inversion,' the 'scientific' term with which Havelock Ellis and John Addington Symonds labelled homosexuality in the last decade of the nineteenth century.[35] The novel habitually allies this inverted pose with 'subtlety,' with a 'strange, rarified, elusive, artful, insidious penetration' (*OED*) that works, imperceptibly and secretly, to disrupt and distort conventional expectations, "to elaborate some new scheme of life," to interpose "a new Hedonism that was to recreate life."[36]

Dorian is led along this course by Lord Henry Wotton, who declares, "'Being natural is simply a pose, and the most irritating pose I know'" (4), and whose 'poisonous' influence on Dorian is expressed as a 'subtle' penetration. Thus, contemplating "the exercise of influence" over Dorian, Lord Henry relishes the opportunity "to convey one's temperament into another as though it were a subtle fluid or a strange perfume" (35), for he realizes "there were poisons so subtle that to know their properties one had to sicken of them" (57). Watching over Dorian with a "subtle smile" (19) and mesmerizing him with the "subtle magic" (19) of his words, Lord Henry hastens Dorian's corruption by sending him a "yellow book" in which "the sins of the world" pass as if "in dumb show before him" (125); the book's "curious jewelled style" is marked by "metaphors as monstrous as orchids, and as subtle in colour" (125), and by "the subtle monotony" of dreamlike, musical sentences (126). "Abandon[ing] himself to [the] subtle influences" of "certain modes of thought that he knew to be really alien to his nature" (132), giving himself over to "pleasures subtle and secret, wild joys and wilder sins" (105), Dorian traces an alternative life-course, and becomes, like Lord Henry and the hero of the yellow book from whose influence Dorian cannot free himself, "a kind of prefiguring type" elaborating (for Wilde and for many English 'sexual inverts') "the story of his own life, written before he had lived it" (127). "'You don't know the danger I am in, and there is nothing to keep me straight'" (99), Dorian cries, as the "subtle affinity be-tween the chemical atoms, that shaped themselves into form and colour on the canvas, and the soul that was within him" (95) disem-bodies and re-embodies his pose.

A 'subtle affinity'—between a writer's work and his life, between one's public pose and one's moral nature, between the body in and of a person's writing and the trajectory of that person's body in and through the course of his life—was also the crucial issue in Wilde's three trials. Wilde was publicly forced to admit, under intense cross-examination, that he had indeed 'posed as a sodomite,' that, as his counsel conceded in open court, "Lord Queensbury [his opponent] in using the word 'posing' was using a word for which there was suffi-cient justification."[37] The motif of 'posing,' in fact, was dominant throughout the trials, and was forever after associated with Wilde, who had, after all, first come to public attention in the early 1880s by posing for newspaper and magazine illustrations and photographs, and who had long been attacked as a 'poseur' who affected the deca-dent aestheticism of the Art-for-Art's Sake movement. Wilde himself willingly played with this motif in his witty (but ultimately mis-guided) trial repartee—"I have no wish to pose as being young"; "I do not pose as being ordinary"—and, before the last trial, his enemies used the word to signal his impending disintegration: "They say he has lost all nerve, all pose, all everything."[38]

Thus the subtle strategy of the rear attack was, literally and figu-ratively, associated with the 'pose of the sodomite,' with an ancient sexual practice converted by the late-nineteenth-century scientific and cultural establishment into a physical embodiment and social style unnaturally disseminated and propagated by decadent aestheticism. A comment from an early review of *Dorian Gray* expresses this attitude as it registers the disapproval with which many of his contemporaries viewed Wilde's interposition of his own body into the conventional recognition of the life-course: "it is not made sufficiently clear that the writer does not prefer a course of unnatural iniquity to a life of cleanliness, health, and sanity."[39] It is this language, and the cultural synthesis (the 'doctrine of pursuits') it articulates, that *Eminent Victorians* explores as it demonstrates the subtle affinity between 'a life of cleanliness, health, and sanity' and 'a course of unnatural iniquity,' as it disembodies and re-embodies the eminent poses through which the Victorians who interrogated Oscar Wilde ministered to the spiritual and physical well-being of the body politic,[40] as it displays what many of Strachey's readers have always thought he shared with *Eminent Victorians'* artist figure, the sincere and childlike Cardinal Newman—"a perverted supersubtlety of intellect" yoked to "a temper of mind that was fundamentally dishonest" (37). Nowhere is this strategy more forcefully deployed than in Strachey's narrative of the life-course of Florence Nightingale.

III

When Strachey's Florence Nightingale arrives at Scutari, across the Bosphorus from the Crimean battlefields, she immediately realizes that, before tending to the injured bodies of the soldiers, she must cure "the deep disease of the body politic" (137). Diagnosed as "the enormous calamity of administrative collapse" (137), this is a seemingly agentless affliction, "that worst of all evils—one which has been caused by nothing in particular and for which no one in particular is to blame" (136). That the body politic should submit itself to the curative administration of this person in this time and place is a coincidence that induces the full tactical deployment of *Eminent Victorians'* 'subtler strategy.' Dr. Arnold "wait[s] in vain" for "a miraculous interposition of God's Providence" (208); Miss Nightingale receives it. "It sometimes happens that the plans of Providence are a little difficult to follow, but on this occasion all was plain; there was a perfect co-ordination of events" (135). In Strachey's narrative these events are coordinated so that they induce a transgressional, transformational, and transsexual defamiliarization of the traditional recognition of the life-course. By showing that Florence Nightingale's "true history was far stranger even than the myth" (155) of 'the Lady with the Lamp,' the familiar path her life has usually traced in cultural discourse, *Eminent Victorians* subtly interrogates 'cultural reality,' the pose of the body politic.

Sublimating her "passional" to her "moral" nature (133), Nightingale deviates from the straight line of social and familial duty conventionally associated with her class and gender by pursuing an independent career in nursing, which, before the trajectory of her life-course intersected with it, was a "peculiarly disreputable" profession (131). Refusing to follow the conventional path marked out for a respectable, marriageable woman who wishes to exert her 'moral nature' (for example, a marriage of convenience to a foreign missionary or a domestic maidenhood of good works), she leads a sisterhood of nurses, "a band of amateurs and females" (142), into an alien theater of war. The "popular imagination," Strachey asserts, can recover her only as "the saintly, self-sacrificing woman, the delicate maiden of high degree who threw aside the pleasures of a life of ease to succour the afflicted, the Lady with the Lamp, gliding through the horrors of the hospital at Scutari, and consecrating with the radiance of her goodness the dying soldier's couch" (129). "But," *Eminent Victorians* sets out to demonstrate, "the truth was different" (129). Strachey's narrative demystifies the "popular conception" (129) of "the pattern of a perfect lady" (148), reveals Florence Nightingale to have been (in terms of traditional cultural stereotypes) more masculine than feminine, a "master" of "irresistible authority" (148), a potent force of "indomitable will" (148) possessed by "a Demon" (129). This capacity (indeed, this need, this desire) to transgress and transform conventional class and gender expectations, to displace a disreputable career with an alternative trajectory that interrogates conventional cultural arrangements, prepares her to re-arrange the known world, to restore "the complete breakdown of our medical arrangements at the seat of war" (136), and thus to minister to the deep disease of the body politic.

We can trace this shift within a single paragraph, during which a "ministering angel, a gentle 'lady with a lamp'" becomes "this remarkable woman [who] was in truth performing the function of an administrative chief" (146). Indeed, throughout the narrative, in another more or less direct echo of Waltonian biography, Nightingale is constantly shifting from one kind of 'minister' to another—from a curer of bodies and souls (as nurse, spiritual inspiration, lay preacher, amateur metaphysician) to a procurer and overseer of goods, services, personnel, and policy (as unofficial departmental administrator, cabinet official, and government advisor). This is one of the many traits she shares with the other titular subjects of *Eminent Victorians*. Manning, who in his capacity as priest exercises "the power of administering the Holy Eucharist" (22), "seemed almost to revive in his own person that long line of diplomatic and administrative clerics which, one would have thought, had come to an end with Cardinal Wolsey" (11); "he ruled his diocese with the despotic zeal of a born administrator" (112). Arnold, who rarely sheds the robes of a Doctor of Divinity, is truly comfortable only in the sacred ritual of "the administration of the elements," to which he attends "with glistening eyes, and trembling voice, and looks of paternal solicitude" (203), while his sixth-formers, to whom he has ceded disciplinary authority, "administered a kind of barbaric justice" (215). Gordon, a lay preacher who aspires to be a messiah, is incapable of administering or being administered to: his earlier "administration [in the Sudan] had, by its very vigour, only helped to precipitate the inevitable disaster" (247), the fall of Khartoum, which is also attributed to his ignoring the instructions of the cabinet ministers back home. Similarly, Nightingale, who as a child is "driven . . . to minister to the poor in their cottages" (130), becomes in the Crimea "an administrative chief" (146), "the leading authority on the medical administration of armies" (167), "the adviser of all Europe" (187), the focal point of the clandestine "Nightingale Cabinet" (170, 173), who "work[s] far harder than most Cabinet Ministers" (182), writes a three-volume metaphysical treatise instructing English "artisans upon the nature of Omnipotent Righteousness" (193), and forms an intimate relationship with the foremost theologian of her day, whom she helps "to draw up a special form of daily worship" (185).

Constantly displacing each other, these various modes of 'ministering' describe a trajectory that both reinforces and subverts the traditional Victorian life-course, the conventional path of submissive devotion and familial duty expected of a woman in Nightingale's situation. The familiar myth, of course, powerfully supports this conventional recognition. But "the true history," which "was far stranger even than the myth" (155), forcefully resists it, for in this latter version Florence Nightingale has what Victorian women are not supposed to have, a professional career. Like all the titular subjects of

Eminent Victorians, she displaces and repositions a traditional vocation already situated in cultural discourse, and overcomes great obstacles in doing so. Yet her displacement is more radical, the obstacles she faces more restrictive. Nursing is a disreputable profession when she enters it; wars, medical corps, and cabinet ministries are fought, supplied, and formed by men. Her insistence on participating in all the modes of ministering, especially those from which women were traditionally excluded, is what makes her remarkable and (a word which appears throughout *Eminent Victorians*) "strange." She is not satisfied to be a sick-bed visitant and saintly inspiration; she must also be (if unofficially) an administrative chief, cabinet official, and spiritual leader, all roles commonly enacted only by men. This is her strange truth, her demon, which propels her into a professional career, but (and this is the crucial point) a professional career that cannot, must not, be recognized.

A prisoner of her myth, and the restraining cultural conventions it glorifies, she must disappear from public view, become a virtual invalid who influences policy by establishing an alternative, subversive, clandestine government. This is "her 'Cabinet'" (165), as she calls it, a devoted band of family and friends operating in the interstices of established authority. That Nightingale can fashion a long, successful career out of such unpromising materials suggests that the notion of the career, which (as we have seen) emerges as a dominant, middle-class mode of structuring the life-course only in the nineteenth century, was perhaps not as impermeable and inviolate as the training, accreditation, and organizational structures of the new professional associations were making it seem. Yet Strachey's narrative also calculates the price she has to pay for her success. She must sacrifice her own body to the cure of the body politic. As a motive force, as a figure that moves through the world, her body remains behind in the Crimea, forever enshrined in the popular imagination. To move it about in England would demystify its potent force. She thus becomes and remains an invalid, but, as Strachey (himself a more or less chronic valetudinarian)[41] notes, "an invalid of a curious character—an invalid who was too weak to walk downstairs and who worked far harder than most Cabinet Ministers. . . . Lying on her sofa in the little upper room in South Street, she combined the intense vitality of a dominating woman of the world with the mysterious and romantic quality of a myth. She was a legend in her lifetime, and she knew it. She tasted the joys of power, like those Eastern Emperors whose autocratic rule was based upon invisibility, with the mingled satisfactions of obscurity and fame. And she found the machinery of illness hardly less effective as a barrier against the eyes of men than the ceremonial of a palace" (178).

"In civilization, as in the early altars of a religious culture," Elaine Scarry argues, "the body is turned inside-out and made sharable." Nightingale's inside-out body is just such a shared cultural artifact, "an intermediate object between the inseparable (however conceptually distinguishable) actions of projection and reciprocation"—what Scarry calls "a 'lever' or 'fulcrum' in order to underscore that it is . . . only a midpoint in a total action." Itself a projection of a particular human being (and of human sentience in general), this (dis)embodied body, this intermediate object, recreates the human being by reciprocation, by directly or indirectly referring back to and remaking human sentience.[42] Thus Florence Nightingale takes to her bed, from which she rarely departs. Banking on her body as shared artifact, she uses it as the cultural capital upon which the authority of her (ad)ministration rests. In fact, Strachey describes Nightingale's quite conscious manipulation of her myth in precisely Scarry's terms, that is, as a lever or fulcrum projecting and reciprocating human sentience, and consequently marking the trajectory along which her life-course, restructured now as a career, can move. "In Miss Nightingale's own eyes the adventure of the Crimea was a mere incident— scarcely more than a useful stepping-stone in her career. It was the fulcrum with which she hoped to move the world; but it was only the fulcrum. For more than a generation she was to sit in secret, working her lever; and her real life began at the very moment when, in the popular imagination, it had ended" (155).

That Florence Nightingale's emergence as a shared cultural artifact (ad)ministering to the deep disease of the body politic comes in response to wartime injury is another indication that the events of her life are perfectly coordinated. "The attributes of a particular political philosophy," Scarry argues, as if she were explicating Stracheyan biography, "are most apparent in those places where it intersects with, touches or agrees not to touch, the human body." This intersection, powerful enough in peacetime to authorize medical, legal, and other interpositions by the state in and on the human body, becomes in wartime a "radical self-alteration," because "the human body opens itself and allows 'the nation' to be registered there in the wound." Thus *"the injuring* [of war] not only provides a means of choosing between disputants [the winner commonly has or perceives he has less physical, economic, or other 'injuries'] but also *provides, by its massive opening of human bodies, a way of reconnecting . . . derealized and disembodied beliefs with the force and power of the material world."* That is, "in the dispute that leads to war, . . . 'cultural reality' . . . is exposed as a 'cultural fiction.'" Subsequently, "as the dispute intensifies and endures, the exposed 'cultural fiction' may seem in danger of eroding further into a 'cultural fraud.'" Injury reconnects threatened cultural belief structures to a "radical material base, . . . investing them with the bodily attribute of reality until there is time [after the conflict] . . . to consent to them, enact them, make them real."[43] Published on 9 May 1918, *Eminent Victorians* appears at a critical moment in English cultural history. Greeted (and attacked) at its appearance as the first post-War book (even though the Armistice was six months away), it points both backward and forward, reopening the wounds of the past as it interrogates the fraudulence of traditional values and attempts to defer the future re-imposition of 'cultural reality.'

Florence Nightingale's life-course, which inscribes a true history stranger than the myth nurtured in the Crimean killing fields, is a cautionary tale for those who have lived through the Great War, and who should understand (in a more general, immediate, profound, and unsettling way) the complex relationship between the massive opening of human bodies and the erosion of 'cultural reality.' Indeed, in many respects, as Paul Fussell has shown in *The Great War and Modern Memory,* the genealogy of Scarry's thesis can be traced to the devastating disillusionment of 1914–18 and the pacifist attitudes it engendered.[44] In the popular imagination Nightingale represents the miraculous restoration of antebellum beliefs. Her myth mediates between injury and cultural fraud, restoring faith in traditional, established values—pluck, devotion, fortitude, duty, et al., all features of what Strachey disparages as "the romantic sentimental heroism with which mankind loves to invest its chosen darlings" (147). This is how the Victorians dealt with threats to their cultural reality exposed by wartime conflict. The injuries that reconnected their disembodied beliefs to the material world were 'cured' by reinvesting them in cultural myths (like 'the Lady with the Lamp') drawn from that very structure of beliefs which war had momentarily derealized. But

Strachey will not allow the myth, and the cultural re-synthesis it sponsors, to go unchallenged. Nightingale's "heroism was not of that simple sort so dear to the readers of novels and the compilers of hagiologies . . . : it was made of sterner stuff" (147). Indeed, as we have noted, the "true history" of Nightingale's heroism is "far stranger" than the familiar and reassuring myth with which she has been simplified and softened.

Nightingale's transformation from 'ministering angel' to 'administering demon' is just this kind of defamiliarization, this 'making strange' so characteristic of Strachey's work. Throughout *Eminent Victorians* 'strangeness' is an essential feature, if not a pre-condition, of true history, an articulation of the subtler strategy through which Strachey interposes his body in the recognition of the life-course, through which he, like Lord Henry Wotton in *The Picture of Dorian Gray,* can "convey [his] temperament into another as though it were a subtle fluid or a strange perfume." Moreover, in diagnosing the deep disease of the body politic, he isolates and observes, as does Lord Henry, "maladies so strange that one had to pass through them if one sought to understand their nature."[45] Thus *Eminent Victorians* celebrates the strange, exposes it as the necessary condition of the eminent career. Newman's "strange and weary pilgrimmage of so many years" (88) is contrasted with Manning's "long and strange career" (111), which is itself symbolized by the Cardinal's Hat, "the strange, the incongruous, the almost impossible object" (127). Arnold cannot understand why there is "'so much of sin combined with so little of sorrow'" among his public-school boys—it "struck him as particularly strange" and hence he laid the "strange burden" of discipline upon his sixth-formers (214–15). In Gordon's story "one catches a vision of strange characters, moved by mysterious impulses, interacting in queer complication" (224), including most prominently Gordon himself, who inspires "a strange reverence" (230) as he proceeds through "all his strange and agitated adventures" (237).

Nightingale's strange career is exemplified in her 'Cabinet,' that "little group of devoted disciples. . . . bound body and soul in that strange servitude" (163) which she demands. She establishes this substitute family and unofficial ministry in imitation of and opposition to the more familiar institutions, and in doing so exposes them as unenlightened frauds ineptly promoting "the emptiness of convention" (182). When Sidney Herbert, a member of her inner circle, finally becomes Secretary of War, he is nominally, as she acknowledges, her "'Master'" (175), but, in fact, as Strachey points out, "the roles were reversed" (162). She coaches him in the intricacies of his ministry; he is her "facile instrument" (175) in whose name are implemented the recommendations in her massive report on hospital administration in the British Army. Thus she is actually the 'Master,' running a shadow ministry which, until she destroys Herbert and her other 'family' members by overwork, makes and implements national policy. Where then is a ministry that is not fraudulent: for instance, a duly installed national government that ministers to the body politic knowledgeably and effectively, or an unofficial cabinet that does not mercilessly debilitate its administrators of public health? Our reading of *Eminent Victorians* suggests that such ministries cannot be found; as even the indefatigable Nightingale discovers, the deep disease can only be diagnosed, it cannot be cured. This is the strange truth revealed by Strachey's subtler strategy. In reversing gender roles, displacing the various modes of administration, interposing her body in the generic recognition of the life-course, Strachey's Nightingale exposes a wound in cultural history that is always being opened and closed. A (dis)embodiment of shared beliefs, a cultural artifact functioning as a fulcrum across which the path of a strange career can be traced, Nightingale is symbolically represented, as are all these eminent Victorians, by the Cardinal's Hat, "the strange, the incongruous, the almost impossible object."[46]

In a sense Strachey's story of Nightingale's strange life-course re-enacts the Derridean drama of generic recognition.[47] The "law of genre," Jacques Derrida writes, is a cultural practice that seeks to legislate, articulate, isolate, and demarcate "a type . . . of reading from an infinite series of trajectories or possible courses" (227). "Play[ing] the role of order's principle" (228), generic recognition is instrumentalized by the iterative "re-mark of belonging [that] does not belong," by the "supplementary and distinctive trait . . .[that] does not properly pertain to any genre or class" (212). An "edgeless boundary" (228), a "formless form," the re-mark "remains nearly invisible"; "declass[ing] what it allows to be classed," "it cuts a strange figure" (213). Moreover, Derrida points out, "the motif of the law in general" covers (among other things) "sexual difference between the feminine and masculine genre/gender," the edgeless boundary here being "the hymen between the two," which can be understood as "a

relationless relation" that re-marks "an identity and difference between the feminine and masculine" as between what does and does
not properly pertain to a genre (221). Obscuring sexual difference as
she illuminates it, Strachey's Nightingale also cuts a strange figure.
Mythologized and invalided, she is (after the Crimea) a nearly invisible, formless form that does not properly belong to any gender,
genre, or class but is now a supplementary and distinctive trait, a
fulcrum across which cultural discourse moves, an iterative re-mark
articulating a powerful and recognizable life-course which, in revealing itself to be but one of an infinite series of trajectories or possible
courses, declasses what it allows to be classed.

Thus the body that Florence Nightingale (and through her, Lytton
Strachey) interposes in English biography is a (dis)embodiment, the
projected and reciprocated body of generic recognition—transgressional, transformational, transsexual. As Strachey asks, "who shall
limit the strangeness of the possibilities that lie in wait for the sons
of men?" (309), a strangeness exemplified in this passage from "Gordon" by the homoerotic poet Rimbaud, "a peculiar eminence . . .
fulfilling a destiny more extraordinary than the wildest romance,"
who has "forgotten the subtleties and the frenzies of inspiration, forgotten the agonized embraces of Verlaine" (309) and vanished just as
he is emerging into cultural consciousness. Rimbaud's and Nightingale's bodies, of course, are not the only 'peculiar eminences' arising
in *Eminent Victorians* and unexpectedly redirecting the gaze of biographical recognition. For instance, "the peculiar eminence of his
office" (113) elevates Cardinal Manning (formally addressed as 'Your
Eminence') above all his English co-religionists except Newman, the
"one figure which, by virtue of a peculiar eminence, seemed to challenge the supremacy of his own" (80). Indeed, no eminence emerges
in Strachey's narrative that is not peculiar. The 'subtler strategy' defamiliarizes eminence itself, transforms it into an emblem or pose
of strange possibility from which the (momentarily refocused) vision of 'cultural reality' cannot be averted. As Strachey wrote in *Elizabeth and Essex,* "the path [to the past] seems closed to us" until
we find a means, an "art," through which we can "worm our way
into those strange spirits, those even stranger bodies," and thus, in
a sense, make them our own or discover that they were our own all
along.[48]

Arranged in its well-known aesthetic, pacifist, homoerotic pose, the peculiar eminence of Strachey's strange body also arises in *Eminent Victorians*. Ironically interposed between the German soldier and one of Strachey's sisters, it exposes the unlimited strangeness of generic possibility by participating in a (figur)ative exchange with the bodies of his sister, Nightingale, and, indeed, all his biographical subjects. Nancy Huston explains: religious, anthropological, psychoanalytic, sociological, literary, and other discourses reveal that childbirth and war are metaphorically analogous and reciprocal—violent bodily events that differentiate (as they equate) the sexes, and that are almost invariably compared and contrasted with each other. The ancient Greeks uses the same word for "the pains of labor" and "an interminable labor of war"; virginity is characteristically symbolized as "an invisible armor" which, if lost, "makes women vulnerable" and "deprives them of their capacity to fight"; "combat," writes Ernst Junger in *War, Our Mother* (1934), "is not exclusively destruction, it is also a virile form of regeneration"—to cite but three of the scores of illustrations Huston provides.[49] By renouncing marriage (and the childbearing function associated with it) Strachey's Nightingale remains a 'maiden' (a "delicate maiden of high degree") who thus—in what Huston calls the 'warrior discourse of Western culture'—can go to the scene of battle, where she can be 'manned' and begin to trace (as she does in Strachey's narrative) an aggressive, 'masculine' life-course. Analogously, by renouncing war and avowing pacifism, Strachey foregoes the male initiation ritual of wartime bloodletting, and is 'unmanned,' assuming a submissive 'feminine' posture as he is metaphorically sodomized by the German soldier. Indeed, it is in just such a posture that many of *Eminent Victorians'* contemporary and more recent readers have imagined him: the homosexual shirker of his national duty submitting himself to a rear attack that unmans his social criticism and disqualifies him as a potent cultural force.[50] But such an approach does not take into account the metaphorical reciprocity between war and childbirth that Huston is describing.

To paraphrase Huston, as Strachey chooses not to accomplish his military service, so Nightingale opts not to accomplish her maternal service. In a sense, they exchange places (and poses). Nightingale goes to war and administers the army medical corps. Strachey (who, immediately after Cambridge, failed his civil service interview) stays home, knits mufflers for the lads in the trenches, and keeps a maternal eye on the Cambridge Apostles, the elite secret society which he and

Maynard Keynes transformed into a "homosexual cult" in the first decade of the century and which traditionally denominated prospective members "embryos" and their induction ceremonies "births."[51] As Eve Sedgwick has suggested, English culture characteristically triangulates male homosocial desire in and through the female body, a graphing of cultural empowerment that relies (as Foucault has argued) on the variability of gender identification, a mutability and interchangeability that is nevertheless (as Sedgwick and Huston both demonstrate) not 'arbitrary.'[52] This last point is important because it reaffirms the Derridean premise that contextual variation underscores the edgeless boundary along which the motivated (that is, the non-arbitrary) re-mark of generic recognition plays. In the context through which we have been careering, this endorsement signifies that, by transgressing gender identifications in terms of a powerful, culturally motivated scheme of transformational and transsexual exchange, Nightingale and Strachey interpose their bodies into the recognition of the life-course, into the 'doctrine of pursuits,' in a way that is simultaneously strange and familiar. Consequently, this ongoing exchange designates the scene (if not the play) of a generic re-mark, of a trait that simultaneously classes and declasses as it delineates the variable, intersecting trajectories of all life-courses, including most prominently those of the biographer and biographical subject, whose reciprocity is perhaps the most distinctive and most supplementary trait of biographical recognition—a relationless relation inducing a mutual affection, a 'sympathy of (bodies and) souls' re-marking English biography from Walton to Strachey.

IV

And so, inevitably it seems, we come to . . . relativity, another alternative 'doctrine of pursuits,' which, as a general theory, Einstein published in 1916, the same year Strachey appeared before the Military Tribunal. One of the consequences of the general theory of relativity is what philosophers of science refer to as the 'world-line' thesis, which tries to describe the trajectories in space-time of individual moving bodies. In a sense, the general theory of relativity problematizes the classical understanding of the 'world-line' in much the same way that our post-modern approach (informed by Derridean and Foucauldian perspectives) calls into question the traditional recognition of the 'life-course,' which is concerned with the trajectories in cultural space-time of individual human bodies. In both, the relationship between the straight and the curved is crucial. "The fundamental difference between Newtonian mechanics and the generalized theory of relativity," Milic Capek explains, "is that in the former the world lines of material particles are straight lines [as in Euclidean geometry] . . .; all deviations . . . , that is, all curvatures of the world lines, are due to the action of some material—whether matter or 'force'—present *in* space, but *different* from it." But, "in the general theory of relativity *every* motion, accelerated or not, results naturally from the local structure of time-space," where the geometry is non-Euclidean and 'curvature' is not a metaphorical deviation projected on to a two-dimensional surface but a 'naturally' occurring event, in a four-dimensional 'block' of space-time, indistinguishable from the world-line itself (although it is important to remember that "the term 'curvature' is essentially metaphorical," its privileged relationship to the 'natural' "based on an analogy with curvature of two-dimensional surfaces"). "There is no relation of causality between matter and a local warping of space. The relation is that of identity: matter and local curvature of space are *one and the same reality.*" This local curvature obtains throughout all regions of non-Euclidean space, which "is probably not infinite, though still without limits," and "is indissolubly united with time." Thus "relativistic space-time does not have a rigid structure because its curvature varies not only from place to place, but also from one moment to another. This is an inevitable consequence of the fact that there is a mutual displacement of material bodies, or, in the language of the general theory, a mutual displacement of local deformations of space-time."[53]

We are back again in an entangled country of unlimited strangeness. The straight lines of moral rectitude, careering invariably toward rising eminences of universal assurance, are now 'curvatures'—not deviations, inversions, or eccentricities, but (temporarily privileged) contextualized re-marks of generic recognition which are (now naturalized as) identical with relativistic reality and which trace the mutual displacement of local deformations of space-time. The trajectories of life-courses, like those of four-dimensional world lines, are limitless because their possible contexts are unlimited, but they are not infinitely progressing or regressing beyond our horizon of understanding because we always (and only) recognize them in relation to *some* context, although one which is always being displaced and enjoys at best a temporary privilege.[54] As we have seen, *Eminent Victorians* exposes and (to a certain extent) thematizes the concept and range of these possibilities; but its experimentation is more or less restricted to 'interposition,' to a subtle, ironic strategy of rhetorical defamiliarization. Nevertheless, Strachey's contemporaries saw *Eminent Victorians* as a radical document, as (to quote Cyril Connolly) "a revolutionary text-book on bourgeois society."[55] Other, more 'formally' adventurous experiments in biographical writing during the ensuing decades—which, if not directly influenced by *Eminent Victorians* owed a great deal to the impact of its 'interposition' in cultural discourse—explored the strangeness of unlimited possibility in ways that Strachey did not or could not.

We shall look briefly at two examples. Virginia Woolf's *Orlando* (1928), a mock-biography which Leon Edel has called "a fable for biographers,"[56] presents a local deformation of space-time by tracing a life-course that displaces classical notions of the 'world-line.' Orlando lives for over three hundred years without aging past thirty-six; born and raised a boy, s/he falls asleep for a week and wakes up a woman; simultaneously adapting to and resisting the so-called periods of cultural history through which s/he passes, Orlando moves through a constantly varying "career" as courtier, ambassador, gypsy, blue-stocking, wife, and author. A sexual, generic, and cultural hermaphrodite, Orlando is a "fulfillment of natural desire," whose "thick stream of life" celebrates the trajectory of the human body "in whatever form it comes, and may there be more forms, and stranger."[57] A. J. A. Symons' *The Quest for Corvo* (1934) traces another strange "career," that of Frederick William Rolfe, a/k/a Baron Corvo, a homoerotic artist and writer (author of *Hadrian VII*). An impoverished Roman Catholic convert who wished to become a priest but was expelled from seminary, as well as an enigmatic, alienated figure inspiring passionate friendship and betrayal, Corvo was often accused of being "'a mere poseur'" or "'a man demon'"[58] (the characterization here is D. H. Lawrence's). *The Quest for Corvo* is especially interesting because, until he more or less abandons the effort halfway through, Symons organizes his narrative in terms of the meandering course of his own biographical research rather than his subject's career.

In somewhat different ways both *Orlando* and *The Quest for Corvo* add chapters to *Eminent Victorians'* revolutionary text-book in 'recognizing the life-course.' In reminding us that, until recently, most of the individual human bodies careering through English biography have been male, or else have been positioned in biographical recognition as a consequence of masculinist (generally heterosexual) cultural expectations, Woolf's narrative proposes an alternative doctrine of pursuits informed by a feminist perspective and tradition which only now is emerging from obscurity.[59] Emplotting generic recognition in an unfamiliar mode, the 'local curvature' of Woolf's narrative tells a story about English biography that differs radically from efforts (such as mine) to describe the patriarchal 'mainstream,' although obviously these readings intersect in many ways. Of course, Woolf and Strachey were intimate acquaintances, 'original Bloomsberries' who conversed, corresponded, and competed constantly and who, for one, brief, crazy moment, were engaged to each other.[60] Simultaneously, and in some respects mutually and reciprocally, they were exploring together the unlimited strangeness of biographical possibility. An anecdote which momentarily privileges Strachey's role in this complex relationship suggests one way that his reappropriation of 'bio-power' helped Woolf imagine an alternative sexuality for the alternative body she was to interpose in English biography.

In an autobiographical essay, Woolf remembers a moment about the year 1908 when the discursive environment she and her sister inhabited changed abruptly and irrevocably. "Suddenly the door opened and the long and sinister figure of Mr Lytton Strachey stood on the threshold. He pointed his finger at a stain on Vanessa's white dress. 'Semen?' he said. . . . With that one word all barriers of reticence and reserve went down. A flood of the sacred fluid seemed to overwhelm us. Sex permeated our conversation. The word bugger was never far from our lips. We discussed copulation with the same excitement and openness that we had discussed the nature of good. It is strange to think how reticent, how reserved we had been and for how long."[61] 'Strangeness' is now associated with the residual Victorian reticence and reserve of the sisters' youth; 'buggery,' a term the long and sinister Strachey used to denote any unconventional relationship (or any feeling or physical act denoting it),[62] is the transgressional expression that transforms the stain of semen into a sacred fluid permeating conversation and, indeed, all modes of Bloomsbury discourse. Of course, we should not attach too much significance to this one incident; there were many others like it in the early days of

Bloomsbury and Strachey was not their only inseminator. Nevertheless, for Woolf at least, it had tremendous symbolic value; in retro-
spect, if in no other way, Strachey's strategic manipulation of
sexuality broke down barriers, displaced discussions of the nature of
good, and demonstrated that, as Foucault has written, "sexuality is
not the most intractable element in power relations, but rather one
of those endowed with the greatest instrumentality: useful for the
greatest number of maneuvers and capable of serving as a point of
support, as a linchpin, for the most varied strategies."[63]

The Quest for Corvo makes explicit what is always implicit in biographical recognition: a narrative of the biographer's course of research is competing with (as it is complementing) a narrative of the
biographical subject's life-course. The biographer is also tracing paths
in relativistic space-time, his moving body (and its attributes) a fulcrum across which human sentience is being projected and reciprocated in and through cultural discourse. By refusing (or at least
deferring, until the second half of his book) to privilege a narrative of
his subject's life-course (as is customary in biographical recognition),
Symons depicts the constantly varying variance between these two
modes of emplotment, although (because it is unfamiliar) this strategy may appear to be privileging a narrative of his course of research,
which is usually displaced to the margins of biographical writing (in
prefaces, notes, appendices, etc.). In interposing his body between
Corvo's body and its trajectories in cultural discourse, Symons deforms biographical recognition by projecting, as does Boswell, the
labor of his body, whereas Strachey (more inclined toward Freudian
than Marxist articulation) ironically 'curves' the straight world-line
of Victorian biography by projecting the *desire* of his body.[64] Thus he
could write of Macaulay: "the absence from his make-up of intense
physical emotion brought a barrenness upon his style. His sentences
have no warmth and no curves; the embracing fluidity of love is lacking."[65] In this respect Strachey is more like Corvo, who assumed a
bogus Italian title and felt most comfortable in the medieval world of
his historical researches. Strachey too was more at ease with an older,
(more or less imaginary) aristocratic world view, one in which the
labor of composition is the effortless expression and gratification of
desire, one in which the 'labored' narcissism of Symons' compositional
reflexivity has been forestalled and ennobled by the pervasive structuring force of sovereign desire.[66]

For Strachey, as for Corvo, homoeroticism is (as Symons writes) "the starting point" of a "twisted [and twisting] career," symbolized by "the crab, which beneath its hard crust has a very tender core, which approaches its objective by oblique movements, and, when roused, pinches and rends with its enormous claws."[67] Moving obliquely through the world, the twisted career of the crab delineates the trajectories of all life-courses, which emerge, in the work of Strachey, Woolf and Symons, as local curvatures of generic space-time mutually displaced by biographer and biographical subject, whose reciprocal (dis)embodiments in biographical narrative enable (as they disable) *The Desire and Pursuit of the Whole*. This was the hopelessly hopeful title of Corvo's last unpublished and mislaid work. It names as well a doctrine of pursuits, motivated by a desire for eternal, inseparable union, which emplots not only the life-course but all generic frames. What *Eminent Victorians* suggests, and this chapter has tried to articulate, is that, in a post-Einsteinian universe, the desire and pursuit of the whole can be recognized only in the mutual deformations of local curvatures. We seem to inhabit simultaneously a land beyond and a world lost, an entangled country in which a succession of rising and falling eminences re-marks a limitless diversity of obscure paths. This is the human, the *very* human, situation that we are exploring and trying to understand whenever and however we are recognizing the life-course.

Notes

CHAPTER I

1. For the ongoing relationship between biographical and historical recognition see, e.g., Maurice Mandelbaum, *The Anatomy of Historical Knowledge*
(Baltimore and London: Johns Hopkins, 1977), pp. 13–14, and 207–08n12,
where Mandelbaum argues "that in order for an individual to be of concern to a
historian his character and actions must be viewed in relation to the place that
he occupied and the role that he played in the life of a society or in relation to
some facet of culture." Hence "Biographies constitute a special form of historical
account, in which the interest is focused on the person who is the subject of the
biography." Mandelbaum's attempt to privilege the historical subject and to
appropriate the biographical subject as one of its special cases is a conventional
maneuver in the study of historical recognition, as is the attempt to privilege
the opposing view (which Mandelbaum acknowledges and summarizes) that
"the subject matter of all historical accounts" is "human actions." Indeed, these
and similar efforts to privilege and appropriate have long characterized the
relationship between historical and biographical recognition. Compare these
oft-cited, contemporaneous, nineteenth-century statements: biography is "only
a branch of history"—attributed by Richard Altick to the 1835 *Penny Cyclopae-
dia* (in *Lives and Letters: a history of literary biography in England and America* [New
York: Knopf, 1965], p. 79); and "'History,' it has been said, 'is the essence of
innumerable Biographies,'" an opinion which Thomas Carlyle endorses in an
1832 review of an edition of Boswell's *Johnson* (reprinted in *Biography as an Art:
selected criticism 1560–1960,* ed. James L. Clifford [New York: Oxford, 1962],
p. 80).

2. Mass-media observations on the popularity of biography range from the
typical comment that "The art, or at least the enterprise of literary biography
. . . flourishes so prodigiously these days" (Hilton Kramer, "Writing Writers'
Lives," *New York Times Book Review,* 8 May 1977, p. 3), to *Time*'s stories on Leon
Edel's inaugurating the Vernon Visiting Professorship of Biography at Dart-
mouth, and on the current popularity of imaginative, well-written biographies
by non-academics ("The Lesson of the Master," 22 Aug. 1977, p. 47; and "Raw
Bones, Fire and Patience," 21 Feb. 1983, pp. 76, 78). See also Angus Paul's

"'Biography' Is One Sign of What May Be New Life in the Art of Recounting Lives," *Chronicle of Higher Education*, 24 March 1982, pp. 19, 21, which reviews for the general academic community the recent "resurgence" of interest in the writing and study of biography.

3. This is essentially the approach taken in recent efforts to posit a poetics of history. See, e.g., Hayden White, *Metahistory: the historical imagination in nineteenth-century Europe* (Baltimore and London: Johns Hopkins, 1973), esp. "Introduction: the poetics of history," pp. 1–42; and Louis O. Mink, "Narrative Form as a Cognitive Instrument," in *The Writing of History: literary form and historical understanding*, ed. Robert H. Canary and Henry Kozicki (Madison and London: Wisconsin, 1978), pp. 129–49. The Canary and Kozicki volume also contains relevant articles by White, "The Historical Text as Literary Artifact," pp. 41–62, and Lionel Gossman, "History and Literature: reproduction or signification," pp. 3–39. Also instructive is the exchange between White, Mink, and Marilyn Robinson Waldman (occasioned by White's "The Value of Narrativity in the Representation of Reality," *Critical Inquiry*, 7[Autumn 1980], 5–27) in *Critical Inquiry*, 7(Summer 1981), 777–98.

These and other recent efforts to explore the poetics of history pursue two often conflicting aims: (1) to present historical recognition as enmeshed in cultural discourse, and (2) to represent it, in terms of this approach, as, nevertheless, a distinct way of understanding the world. For instance, Gossman treats "historical discourse" as "a language constructed out of material that is itself already language," as "a secondary system of signs" which presents "the relation between signifier and concept" as "in some way natural" (pp. 29, 33); and White treats the "historical work" as "a verbal structure in the form of a narrative prose discourse" employing "generic plot-structures conventionally used in our culture to endow familiar events and situations with meanings" (*Metahistory*, p. 2; and "Historical Text as Literary Artifact," p. 52). Yet, generally, this approach also entails a reluctance to abandon the notion of historical understanding as a distinct cognitive activity. White bases *Metahistory* on the two-part question, "What does it mean to *think historically*, and what are the unique characteristics of a specifically *historical method* of inquiry?" (p. 1); and Mink ends his essay with the admonition that "It would be disastrous . . . if common sense were to be routed from its last stronghold on this point ['that history is true in a sense in which fiction is not']. . . . If the distinction were to disappear, fiction and history would both collapse back into myth and be indistinguishable from it as from each other" (pp. 148–49). The tenacity with which even these 'poeticians' hold on to historical understanding as a distinct cognitive activity is an indication of the power and perseverance of generic recognition.

4. Jean-Jacques Chartin, Philippe Lacoue-Labarthe, Jean-Luc Nancy, and Samuel Weber, "Appendix: situating the colloquium 'Genre,'" *Glyph*, 7(1980), 236.

5. The term "recognition" is a commonplace in cognitive science—see, e.g., Benjamin J. Kuipers, "A Frame for Frames: representing knowledge for recognition," in *Representation and Understanding: studies in cognitive science,* ed. Daniel G. Bobrow and A. M. Collins (New York: Academic Press, 1975), pp. 151–83. But its exploration as a term supporting various meanings is not so common; nevertheless, see William Ray, "Recognizing Recognition," *Diacritics,* 7:4(1977), 20–33; Richard H. Brown, *A Poetic for Sociology* (1977; Cambridge, London, New York, and Melbourne: Cambridge, 1978), pp. 35–36; and, from a different perspective, Roman Ingarden, *The Cognition of the Literary Work of Art,* trans. Ruth Ann Crowley and Kenneth R. Olson (1968; 1973; Evanston, IL: Northwestern, 1979), pp. 335 ff. and passim, for "preaesthetic reflective cognition" as "reconstruction."

6. For various approaches to "common frames" see Marvin Minsky, "A Framework for Representing Knowledge," in *The Psychology of Computer Vision,* ed. Patrick Henry Winston (New York: McGraw-Hill, 1975), pp. 211–77; Eugene Charniak, "Inference and Knowledge 2," in *Computational Semantics: an introduction to artificial intelligence and natural language comprehension,* ed. Charniak and Yorick Wilks (Amsterdam, New York, and Oxford: North Holland, 1976), pp. 147–54; Roger C. Schank and Robert P. Abelson, *Scripts, Plans, Goals and Understanding: an inquiry into human knowledge structures* (Hillsdale, NJ: Lawrence Erlbaum, 1977), passim, but esp. pp. 10, 17–19, 36–68; David E. Rumelhart, "Notes on a Schema for Stories," in Bobrow and Collins, pp. 211–36; Teun A. van Dijk, *Text and Context: explorations in the semantics and pragmatics of discourse* (London and New York: Longman, 1977), pp. 99–108, 135–42, 159–61; Wallace L. Chafe, "Creativity in Verbalizations for the Nature of Stored Knowledge," in *Discourse Production and Comprehension,* ed. Roy O. Freedle (Norwood, NJ: Ablex, 1977), pp. 41–55; Gregory Bateson, *Steps to an Ecology of Mind* (1972; New York: Ballantine, 1978), pp. 184–92; Erving Goffman, *Frame Analysis: an essay on the organization of experience* (New York: Harper and Row, 1974); Janos Petöfi, "A Frame for FRAMES (A Few Remarks on the Methodology of Semantically Guided Text Processing)," *Proceedings of the Second Annual Meeting of the Berkeley Linguistics Society,* ed. Henry Thompson et al. (Berkeley, CA: Berkeley Ling. Soc., 1976), pp. 319–29; Victor Raskin, "Literal Meanings in Speech Acts," *Journal of Pragmatics,* 3(1979), 489–95; Wolfgang Iser, *The Act of Reading: a theory of aesthetic response* (1973; Baltimore and London: Johns Hopkins, 1980), pp. 90–93, 141–46, 183–89; and Umberto Eco, *The Role of the Reader: explorations in the semiotics of texts* (Bloomington, IN, and London: Indiana, 1979), pp. 17–27.

Useful overviews, which associate "frames" (and the cognate terms "scripts" and "schemata") with Piaget, Gombrich, Hume, Kant, and others can be found in Bobrow and Collins, esp. Terry Winograd, "Frame Representations and the Declarative/Procedural Controversy," pp. 185–210; Freedle, esp. Winograd, "A Framework for Understanding Discourse," pp. 63–87; Brown, "Chapter 2—

Cognitive Aesthetics: symbolic realism and perspectival knowledge," *A Poetic for Sociology,* pp. 24—48; John D. Bransford, *Human Cognition: learning, understanding, and remembering* (Belmont, CA: Wadsworth, 1979), pp. 181—89; Daniel C. Dennett, "Chapter 7—Artificial Intelligence as Philosophy and as Psychology," *Brainstorms: philosophical essays on mind and psychology* (Montgomery, VT: Bradford, 1978), pp. 109—26; and *The Handbook of Artificial Intelligence,* ed. Avron Barr and Edward A. Feigenbaum, vol. 1 (Los Altos, CA: William Kaufmann, 1981), pp. 216—22. "Framing" as a metaphor in post-modern critical theory is discussed in Jacques Derrida, "The Parergon," *October,* 9(Summer 1979), 3—41, and in Floyd Merrell, *Deconstruction Reframed* (West Lafayette, IN: Purdue, 1985).

7. See Jacques Derrida, "La Loi Du Genre/The Law of Genre," trans. Avital Ronell, *Glyph,* 7(1980), 176—232.

8. Chartin et al., p. 237.

9. Roger North, *General Preface & Life of Dr John North,* ed. Peter Millard (Toronto: Toronto, 1984), p. 79. The manuscripts discussed below are in the library of St. John's College, Cambridge, Add. Mss. 32,514—17, which I have seen.

10. James L. Clifford, *From Puzzles to Portraits: problems of a literary biographer* (Chapel Hill: North Carolina, 1970), pp. 100—02. See also *Biography as an Art,* ed. Clifford.

11. David Novarr, *The Lines of Life: theories of biography, 1880—1970* (West Lafayette, IN: Purdue, 1986).

12. North, p. 79.

13. Saintsbury's comments are in an essay entitled "Some Great Biographies," *Macmillan's Magazine,* 66(June 1892), 97—107; Gosse's can be found in "The Custom of Biography," *Anglo-Saxon Review,* 8(March 1901), 195—208; for Dunn, see *English Biography* (London: Dent, 1916); for Stewart, see "Biography," in *The Craft of Letters in England,* ed. John Lehmann (London: Cresset Press). All these works are cited, quoted, and summarized in Novarr: see, esp., pp. 6, 17, 26, 110, and 171n26.

14. Harold Nicolson, "The Practice of Biography," *American Scholar,* 23(Spring 1954), 153—61, excerpted in *Biography as an Art,* ed. Clifford, pp. 197—205. I quote from pp. 197—98, 202. See also Nicolson's *The Development of English Biography* (1928; rpt. London: Hogarth, 1968), pp. 9—13, where Nicolson first differentiated 'pure' and 'impure' biography. Novarr summarizes Nicolson's arguments in both the book and essay (the latter from its appearance a year earlier in *Cornhill Magazine,* 166[Summer 1953], 471—80), pp. 45—51, 103—5.

15. *Sewanee Review,* 85:2(Spring 1977); *Georgia Review,* 35:2(Summer 1981); and *Yale Review,* 73:1(Autumn 1983) and 73:2(Winter 1984).

16. *Telling Lives: the biographer's art,* ed. Marc Pachter (Washington, DC:

New Republic, 1979; Philadelphia: Pennsylvania, 1981); *New Directions in Biography*, ed. Anthony M. Friedson (Honolulu: Hawaii, 1981); *The Biographer's Gift: life histories and humanism*, ed. James F. Veninga (College Station, TX: Texas A & M, 1983); *Studies in Biography*, ed. Daniel Aaron, Harvard English Studies 8 (Cambridge and London: Harvard, 1978); *Biography and Society: the life history approach in the social sciences*, ed. Daniel Berraux, Sage Studies in International Sociology 23 (Beverly Hills, CA, and London: Sage, 1981); and *The Craft of Literary Biography*, ed. Jeffrey Meyers (London and Basingstoke: Macmillan, 1985).

17. Ira Bruce Nadel, *Biography: fiction, fact and form* (New York: St. Martin's, 1984); Leon Edel, *Writing Lives: principia biographica* (New York and London: W. W. Norton, 1984); Robert Gittings, *The Nature of Biography* (Seattle: Washington, 1978); Alan Shelston, *Biography*, The Critical Idiom Series 34 (London: Methuen, 1977); Paul Murray Kendall, *The Art of Biography* (London: George Allen & Unwin, 1965); John A. Garraty, *The Nature of Biography* (New York: Knopf, 1957).

18. Leon Edel, *Literary Biography* (Toronto: Toronto, 1957; rpt. Bloomington and London: Indiana, 1973); Altick, *Lives and Letters: a history of literary biography in England and America*—cited earlier; James L. Clifford, *From Puzzles to Portraits: problems of a literary biographer*—cited earlier; Dennis Petrie, *Ultimately Fiction: design in modern American literary biography* (West Lafayette, IN: Purdue, 1981); Peter Nagourney, "The Basic Assumptions of Literary Biography," *Biography*, 1:2 (1978), 86–104; and Katherine Frank, "Writing Lives: Theory and Practice in Literary Biography," *Genre*, 13:4 (1980), 499–516.

19. Arnaldo Momigliano, *The Development of Greek Biography* (Cambridge: Harvard, 1971); Patricia Cox, *Biography in Late Antiquity: a quest for the holy man* (Berkeley, Los Angeles, London: California, 1983); Michael Rewa, *Reborn as Meaning: panegyrical biography from Isocrates to Walton* (Washington, DC: University Press of America, 1983).

20. A. O. J. Cockshut, *Truth to Life: the art of biography in the nineteenth century* (London: Collins, 1974); Francis R. Hart, *Lockhart as Romantic Biographer* (Edinburgh: Edinburgh, 1971); Judith H. Anderson, *Biographical Truth: the representation of historical persons in Tudor-Stuart Writing* (New Haven and London: Yale, 1984). For a somewhat earlier example, see Joseph W. Reed, Jr., *English Biography in the Early Nineteenth Century, 1801–38*, Yale Studies in English 160 (New Haven: Yale, 1966).

21. Donald J. Winslow, *Life-Writing: a glossary of terms in biography, autobiography, and related forms* (Honolulu: Hawaii, 1980).

22. Norman Mailer, *Marilyn: a biography* (New York: Grosset & Dunlap, 1973), and *The Executioner's Song* (Boston and Toronto: Little, Brown, 1979); Vladimir Nabokov, *The Real Life of Sebastian Knight* (1941; Norfolk, CT: New Directions, 1959); Bernard Malamud, *Dubin's Lives* (New York: Farrar, Straus,

Giroux, 1979); Julian Barnes, *Flaubert's Parrot* (New York: Alfred A. Knopf, 1985); Richard Holmes, *Footsteps: adventures of a romantic biographer* (London: Hodder and Stoughton, 1985); Steven Millhauser, *Edwin Mullhouse: the life and death of an American writer 1943–1954* (New York: Alfred A. Knopf, 1972).

CHAPTER 2

1. Notable discussions of traditional narrative, generic, and symbolic structures in Walton's *Donne* can be found in David Novarr, *The Making of Walton's Lives* (Ithaca: Cornell, 1958); R. C. Bald, *John Donne: A Life* (Oxford: Clarendon, 1970); Francisque Costa, *L'Oeuvre D'Izaak Walton (1593–1683),* Etudes Anglaises, no. 48 (Montreal, Paris, Bruxelles: Didier, 1973); John Butt, "Izaak Walton's Methods in Biography," *Essays and Studies (English Association),* 19(1934), 67–84, and *Biography in the Hands of Walton, Johnson, and Boswell* (Los Angeles: California, 1966), pp. 1–18; Richard Wendorf, "'Visible Rhetorick': Izaak Walton and Iconic Biography," *Modern Philology,* 82:3(1985), 269–91; and Judith H. Anderson, "Walton: Likeness and Truth," in *Biographical Truth: the representation of historical persons in Tudor-Stuart writing* (New Haven and London: Yale, 1984), pp. 52–71.

2. Izaak Walton, *The Lives of John Donne, Sir Henry Wotton, Richard Hooker, George Herbert, and Robert Sanderson,* World's Classics (London: Humphrey Milford and Oxford, 1927), p. 37. Subsequent references will be cited parenthetically by page number only. Until the publication of the new Oxford edition, the World's Classic version, based on the 1675 second collected edition of Walton's *Lives,* will remain the most frequently cited and readily available text in scholarly discourse. The details of many of the textual differences among the 1640, 1658, 1670, and 1675 editions of the *Life of Donne* are discussed in Novarr, pp. 19–126. Novarr's basic points can be summarized briefly. Walton's "Elegy" (first printed in the 1633 edition of Donne's *Poems*) and Walton's presumed editing of the 1635 *Poems* can be approached as a kind of proto-biography upon which Walton drew in putting together his hastily composed "prefatory memoir" of 1640. The many minor stylistic changes of 1658, which was the first of Walton's *Lives* to be printed independently, heightened Donne's dignity and religiosity and "made the *Life* into a work of art." The 1670 first collected edition, to which Walton's "Elegy" was first appended, continued this "process of taking nothing for granted" by seeking "precise impression" through "double expression." By the 1675 second collected edition the original narrative "had doubled in length" through the accretion of many minor changes and the addition, in 1675, of "three apocryphal stories about Donne." "With every revision Donne approached closer to sainthood," so that what had begun in 1640 as "not a typical hagiography" because "its detail was too particularized" became, by 1675, "Walton's closest approach to hagiography."

3. The crucial narrative functioning of this "letter" is adumbrated by R. E. Bennett's demonstration in "Walton's Use of Donne's Letters," *Philological Quarterly,* 16(Jan. 1937), 30–34, that what I have been calling a "letter" is "a composite of eight passages from five letters, all of which had been printed in 1651," a composite which Walton introduced with the phrase "And thus in other letters" but presented as if they formed one continuous epistolary narrative. Bennett considers that Walton's alterations and paraphrases do not conceal an "intention to deceive" but reveal a "purpose to put in relief Donne's gloom" and "may be essentially true regardless of the sources of the details." Especially relevant are the alterations Bennett notes in the passage beginning *"but to be no part of any body"*: by dropping the first part of the second sentence, substituting "I" for "they," and making several other minor changes, "Walton has caused Donne to seem to talk directly about himself instead of about himself by means of a general truth." Nevertheless, for our purposes at least, the key words "incorporated" and "body" are retained. See also Novarr, pp. 98–99, and 99n17.

4. "Walton's account [of this 'Vision' episode] is riddled with inaccuracies. . . . The seventeenth century cherished such tales of apparitions and supernatural appearances. Even so, it is not inconceivable that some such hallucination occurred. . . . In the course of telling and retelling, the story, no doubt, became more and more circumstantial and therefore less accurate, but the substratum of truth may well be there" (Bald, *Life,* pp. 252–53). This is one of the many instances in which Bald and other modern scholars examine Walton's factual reliability. The key articles in this examination are by Butt, Bennett, I. A. Shapiro, John Sparrow, and Evelyn M. Simpson. Of course, Bald is the major mid-twentieth-century authority on this issue; even before his biography of Donne appeared, he summarized this ongoing evaluative project in "Historical Doubts Respecting Walton's *Life of Donne,*" in *Essays in English Literature from the Renaissance to the Victorian Age,* ed. Millar MacLure and F. W. Watt (Toronto: Toronto, 1964), pp. 69–84.

Although finding fault with Walton's documentary integrity, twentieth-century scholarship has generally adhered to Bald's opinion that Walton's narrative "has traced the main outlines of Donne's life: even if the pattern has since had to be modified here and there, the essential impression remains" (*Life,* p. 11). Other scholars make the same point with the same metaphor or use a "portrait" metaphor in a similar context. See, e.g., Butt, "Walton's Methods," p. 81; Bennett, "Walton's Use of Donne's Letters," p. 34; H. C. Beeching, "Izaak Walton's *Life of Donne:* an apology," *Cornhill Magazine,* n.s. 8 (Jan.–June 1900), 255; and *The English Works of George Herbert,* ed. George Herbert Palmer, 6 vols. (Boston and New York: Houghton Mifflin, 1905), I, 46. Two commonly held notions influence this acceptance of Walton's 'impression' or 'portrait' of Donne: (1) "Walton's ideals were not those of present-day historical scholarship" (Bald, "Historical Doubts," p. 69), and (2) "Walton's contemporaries seem to have recognized the fundamental truth of the *Life*" (Bald, *Life,* p. 13). But I do not wish to become involved in evaluating documentary evidence or deciding vexing problems of biographical interpretation. I am only peripherally interested in approaching Walton's biography as a nominally factual narrative to be evaluated in terms of its conformity to standards of scholarly research developed and enshrined (for the most part) well after the mid-seventeenth century. Primarily, I wish to approach Walton's narrative as an aesthetic object revealing and concealing language-structures through which biography can be distinguished from and contextualized with other (nominally) literary and non-literary genres. A recent article which generally adopts this approach is Clayton D. Lein, "Art and Structure in Walton's *Life of Mr. George Herbert*," *University of Toronto Quarterly,* 46(Winter 1976/77), 162–76.

5. "Perhaps [Walton] was not the first biographer to recognize the potential value of such material: but certainly he is the first biographer to employ it so extensively," Butt, *Biography in the Hands,* p. 9.

6. In discussing the "Vision" section as "the major addition to the *Life* of 1675," Novarr asserts that it is "a kind of double dream" linked to Monica and her son, St. Augustine, as well as to "the doctrine of sympathy of souls" as inscribed in "A Valediction, forbidding to Mourn," a title which is, as Novarr incidentally reports, "unique" for this poem (pp. 111–13).

7. All these senses of "undertaker" were current sometime in the seventeenth century, although, according to the *OED,* two of them (one who prepares a literary work and one who arranges funerals) did not enter written language until after 1675. Of course, the pre-dating of various senses of words listed in the *OED* has long been a small, scholarly industry, and the *OED* only claimed to list the earliest written use of a word which its researchers could find, not the *ur*-written usage or the moment of the word's assuming a particular nuance of meaning in spoken language (and thus becoming available for puns in a literature which was, after all, frequently and at times exclusively circulated in oral subcultures). One alternative is to accept the premise of much twentieth-century revisionist literary study, that is, that all meanings of all words are entangled in the net of language and hence are always already present. Another seventeenth-century sense of "undertaker" is an investor in a joint-stock company, certainly a familiar usage to a merchant like Walton. In this respect, we could say that Walton (and his friends) invest cultural and literary stock in Donne, an economic approach to biographical recognition explored in detail in Chapter 6 ("Recognizing the Biographer: Boswell's *Life of Johnson*"). See also Chapter 1 ("Introduction: Recognizing Biography").

8. Actually, the narrative explicitly attributes "an unwilling-willingness" to the attitude with which Donne's wife gives her "faint Consent to the Journey" (39), but the term also describes well the attitude of the "I" of the introductory materials and the Donne of the "Vision" section. Moreover, the term echoes the

claim of "The Epistle to the Reader" that, unlike the writing of the lives of Donne and Hooker, which were "*accidental*" and/or "*injoin'd,*" the life of Herbert is "a Free-will offering, . . . *writ, chiefly to please my self*" (5–6). As we shall see, "*Free-will offering*" is also the phrase with which Walton's elegy on Donne describes itself (89).

9. Situating Walton's *Donne* at the intersection of medieval hagiography and seventeenth-century ecclesiastical biography is a conventional trope of biographical study and Walton criticism, to which we shall attend only in passing. Donald A. Stauffer, for example, sees all Walton's *Lives* as marking both a "culmination" and a "development" of the ongoing "biographical tradition" as they "raised to perfection the saint's life in English" and revealed their author's "belief in biography as an art." See *English Biography Before 1700* (Cambridge: Harvard, 1930), pp. 91, 109, 115, 117. See also, e.g., Richard D. Altick, *Lives and Letters: a history of literary biography in England and America* (New York: Knopf, 1965), p. 20; *English Biography in the Seventeenth Century,* ed. Vivian De Sola Pinto (1951; rpt. Freeport, NY: Books for Libraries Press, 1969), p. 35; Harold Nicolson, *The Development of English Biography* (London: Hogarth, 1928), p. 69; Paul Murray Kendall, *The Art of Biography* (London: George Allen and Unwin, 1965), pp. 97–98; Robert Gittings, *The Nature of Biography* (Seattle: Washington, 1978), p. 26; and, for a summary of a related tradition, Michael P. Rewa, *Reborn as Meaning: panegyrical biography from Isocrates to Walton* (Washington, DC: University Press of America, 1983).

10. Novarr, pp. 28–51.

11. Donne's intimate friendships were literally and figuratively sealed by his sending his closest friends a copy of his seal of the Cross upon an anchor. Among others, copies were sent to Henry King, George Herbert, and Sir Henry Wotton, all of whom figure prominently in either the prefatory materials or interior narrative of Walton's *Life of Donne*. See Walton, p. 63, Bald, *Life,* p. 487, and Novarr, p. 74. King, whose letter to him praising the *Lives* Walton inserts before his own introduction, was also one of the executors of Donne's will (Walton, p. 68, and Bald, p. 488). George Morley, Bishop of Winchester, to whom Walton dedicated the *Lives* and "with whom Walton lived for many years in the episcopal palace at Farnham, . . . was a younger contemporary of King at Westminster School and Christ Church" (Butt, "Walton's Methods," p. 68). Donne and Richard Corbet, Bishop of Oxford, whose epitaph on Donne Walton inserts just after his narrative, were linked by a contemporary in 1621 as "'pleasant poeticall deanes'"; moreover, in 1646 Donne's son presented Corbet with a copy of his father's *Biathanatos* and also "apparently edited Corbet's *Poems*" (Bald, pp. 408, 550). All these associations run deep. As Butt remarks, this pattern of friendship "was part of the acquaintance that prepared Walton for his biographical work, and allowed him to take advantage of the opportunity when it was offered" ("Walton's Methods," p. 68). Indeed, the intricacy of the friend-

ships upon which Walton bases his biographies is one of the major themes of a
forthcoming, full-length, scholarly biography of Walton by Clayton D. Lein,
portions of which I have been privileged to read in manuscript.

12. Novarr describes Donne, at 53, as "the most eminent preacher in England" (p. 24); Bald discusses "his later reputation as one of the great preachers
of his age" (*Life*, p. 315).

13. Bald's description (*Life*, p. 322) of Donne as the Reader at Lincoln's Inn
(drawn from various sources) reinforces Walton's general presentation of the
impact of Donne as preacher.

14. "The death of his wife marked a turning point in Donne's life; it deep-
ened his sense of religious vocation, and produced something much closer to a
conversion than the feelings which had prompted him to enter the Church,"
Bald, *Life*, p. 328. This is a common observation about Donne's life.

15. In remarking that Donne "was doubtless well read in the literature of
penitence and conversion from the *Confessions* of St. Augustine down to his own
time," Bald cites language from Donne's sermons which implicitly and explicitly links the recovery from illness with conversion (*Life*, pp. 235–36). The
conversion motif has been noted before in Walton studies. For a recent example,
see Costa (p. 426): "Cette *Vie* [*Donne*] reste, en effet, un récit dramatique fondé
sur le thème augustinien de la conversion." Bald, who characterizes the *Devotions*
as "unique in the annals of literature," quotes the book's description of the onset
of the illness: "'I was surpriz'd with a sodaine change, and alteration to worse
. . . '" (*Life*, p. 451).

Here we can observe that the term "alteration" was embedded in Walton's
cultural context, as were many of the other key terms we have been tracing in
Walton's narrative. Several examples (among many) from Bald's biography
should indicate the contemporary pervasiveness of such terms as incorporate,
employment, fitness, and undertake. Bald quotes a 1653 history describing
Doncaster (with whom Donne travelled to Germany) as "very fit for his imployment" (p. 348); quotes a letter from Carlisle to Donne (1622) describing the
printing of one of Donne's sermons as "the onely employment it needs" and its
dedication as "fittest to my Lord of *Buckingham*" (p. 435); quotes a letter from
Donne (1608) noting "I have had occasion to imploy all my friends" and citing
one especially who "performed what ever he undertook, (and my requests were
the measures of his undertakings)" (p. 161); quotes another letter from Donne
(1614) describing "certain men (whom they call undertakers)," who try to
influence parliamentary elections (p. 285); and reminds us that a seventeenth-
century use of the phrase "to be incorporated" was to be admitted into a university through the awarding of an honorary degree (p. 227).

16. It is possible to see this alternation between diachronic and synchronic
narrative strategies as an ancient biographical tradition. A. J. Gossage summarizes the argument of the early twentieth-century German scholar F. Leo,

who "distinguished two main elements in Greek and Roman biography": "*Chronologie*, broadly speaking, is the narrative account of a man's career, containing his accomplishments in peace and war, in a chronological sequence, while *Eidologie* is the classified account of deeds, incidents, habits, and sayings illustrative of his character without any chronological relation to each other." See "Plutarch," in *Latin Biography*, ed. T. A. Dorey (New York: Basic Books, 1967), p. 57. Leo and other classicists associate these narrative modes with Plutarchan and Suetonian biography respectively, although there continues to be much scholarly debate about how rigorously and how broadly to apply these categories. See, e.g., Arnaldo Momigliano, *The Development of Greek Biography* (Cambridge: Harvard, 1971), pp. 18–20, 86–87, and Patricia Cox, *Biography in Late Antiquity: a quest for the holy man* (Berkeley, Los Angeles, London: California, 1983), pp. 51–55. All narratives can be said to deploy the diachronic (chronological) and the synchronic (eidological); indeed, these strategies are constantly displacing each other, although we may wish to characterize particular narratives as generally or at specific points privileging one of them. What is especially interesting about Walton's narratives is the biographer's reflexive gesture of calling attention to certain instances when he is shifting from one to another of these constantly alternating narrative strategies. Contemporary critical practice often ascribes to such a gesture a degree of 'conscious artistry' with which we do not usually credit Plutarchan or Suetonian biography.

17. *The Works of George Herbert*, ed. F. E. Hutchinson (Oxford: Clarendon, 1941), p. 26.

18. "To symbolize his new life [as an Anglican priest], Donne had a new seal made," Bald, *Life*, p. 305. For a judicious treatment of "Walton and the Poems about Donne's Seal," see Novarr, Appendix B, pp. 503–6. This tracing of a sympathetic relationship is characteristic of mature Waltonian biography: see Lein, pp. 165–68.

19. But Bald notes: "Miraculously, Donne's monument suffered less damage than any other, and survived almost intact." Bald also notes that "from the first the monument attracted a great deal of attention" and served as a model for many other similar monuments of shrouded figures. "It seems to have been Donne's intention to represent the resurrection of the body; the shrouded figure is rising from the funeral urn," and the last line of the epitaph can be translated as "Whose name is the Rising." "It must have faced the altar" (*Life*, pp. 533–36). See also Novarr, p. 72n17, and 110.

20. To the mid-seventeenth century "artificial" could signify not only contrived, unnatural, fictitious, or deceitful but also artful, workmanlike, or scholarly (*OED*).

21. As Novarr points out, Walton mistranslates the Spanish motto ("*Antes muerto que mudado*"), which probably ought to read "Sooner dead than changed." I agree with Novarr that this mistranslation is "ingenious and artful," and that

its elaboration transforms "the comparison of two pictures into a recapitulation of Donne's life, . . . into a testimonial of Donne's inherent religiosity and even into a meditation on man's journey through life" (pp. 118–19).

22. Butt asserts that Walton's *Donne* was "frankly commemorative. . . . a somewhat hastily produced preface to a great volume of sermons. . . . a memorial tribute to the man who had preached the eighty sermons that followed" (*Biography in the Hands,* pp. 3–4).

23. *The Sermons of John Donne,* ed. Evelyn M. Simpson and George R. Potter, 10 vols. (Berkeley and Los Angeles: California, 1962), X, 239. Novarr also traces "reanimate" to Donne's final sermon (pp. 62–63).

24. Simpson, Novarr, and Bald all point out that the end of Walton's narrative, especially the death-bed scene, echoes Donne's funeral sermon for Magdalen Herbert, *A Sermon of Commemoration for the Lady Danvers.* Bald notes that Walton heard the sermon preached and later bought a published copy of it (*Life,* p. 497n1). Simpson claims that "Walton's indebtedness . . . is not merely verbal, it is seen also in his arrangement of his material" ("The Biographical Value of Donne's Sermons," *RES,* n.s. 2[1951], 350). Novarr also catalogues similar narrative and verbal details as he argues that Walton "does not turn the *Life* into a sermon of commemoration; he writes a sermon of commemoration at the end of the *Life* as a summary of the life" (pp. 65–67). Among the verbal parallels noted is that between Walton's last sentence and the section of Donne's sermon describing "That *body* which now, whilst I speake, is mouldring, and crumbling into lesse and lesse dust. . . . That *body* which was the *Tabernacle* of a *holy Soule,* and a *Temple* of the *holy Ghost*" (*Sermons,* VIII, 92–93; see also Bald, *Life,* pp. 496–97, and Novarr, pp. 62–63).

25. For the various senses of "valediction" and "interdiction" see the appropriate *OED* headings.

26. *Boswell: the ominous years 1774–1776,* ed. Charles Ryskamp and Frederick A. Pottle, The Yale Editions of the Private Papers of James Boswell (New York, Toronto, London: McGraw-Hill, 1963), pp. 55, 175.

27. Walton's impact on Johnson and Boswell, the major biographers of the next century, was profound. Johnson considered the *Lives* "one of his favourite books," and the *Life of Donne* "the most perfect of them." He once contemplated both editing the *Lives* and writing Walton's life, and later encouraged and assisted attempts at both projects. See *Boswell's Life of Johnson,* ed. George Birkbeck Hill and L. F. Powell, 6 vols. (Oxford: Clarendon, 1934–50), II, 279–80, 283–85, 363–64, 445–46, 530, III, 107. Boswell, introduced to the *Lives* by Johnson, admired their "simplicity and pious spirit," and planned both an annotated edition of the *Lives* and "a new life" of their author. See *Boswell's Life,* III, 107; *The Correspondence and Other Papers of James Boswell Relating to the Making of the "Life of Johnson,"* ed. Marshall Waingrow, The Yale Editions of the Private Papers of James Boswell, Research Edition, Boswell's Correspondence: vol. 2

(New York and Toronto: McGraw-Hill, 1969), pp. 567, 572; *Boswell for the Defense 1769–1774,* ed. William K. Wimsatt, Jr., and Frederick A. Pottle, The Yale Editions of the Private Papers of James Boswell (New York, Toronto, London: McGraw-Hill, 1959), pp. 228, 236–37, 269; and *Boswell: the ominous years,* pp. 55, 74, 150, 175, 215–16, 280.

Walton's *Lives* were much edited and read in the nineteenth century. He was "a favorite of the Coleridge-Wordsworth group," as evidenced by Wordsworth's sonnet, "Walton's Books of Lives," and James Gillman's *Life of Coleridge* (1838), which began "with an eloquent tribute to Izaak Walton's art as a biographer" and which tried to present its subject "as a saint of the Waltonian pattern." See Bald, *Life,* pp. 14–15, and B. R. McElderry, Jr., "Walton's *Lives* and Gillman's *Life of Coleridge,*" *PMLA,* 52(June 1937), 412–22. Novarr summarizes "The Walton Tradition" (pp. 3–16), and also suggests parallels between Walton and Strachey (pp. 493–96). Despite his key role in championing the revival of interest in Donne's poetry, Strachey nowhere explicitly reveals a close reading of Walton's *Life of Donne.* The only Stracheyan reference to Walton which I can find is in a review of early-twentieth-century biography of Wotton, to which Strachey briefly compares Walton's biography of Wotton (*Spectatorial Essays* [London: Chatto and Windus, 1964], pp. 18–23).

28. Jacques Derrida associates the term "fold" (*pli*) with the edgeless bounding of genre theory ("The Law of Genre," *Glyph,* 7[1980], 216, 221, 228). My notion of unobtrusively "folding" the pre-text into the text relies on *texere,* to weave. Hence pre-text as a "weaving before or in front" and consequently as a "covering" or "cloaking" which acts as a "disguise" or an "excuse"; and therefore "fold" as a "wrapping or covering," a "layer (of cloth)," which bends, envelops, or entangles as it yields or swerves (from truth). Additional senses of "fold" are also pertinent here, especially "to roll up, as a scroll," and "a leaf of a book" or "a sheaf of paper," as well as the spiritual sense of an enclosure for sheep, that is, a congregrtion, church, or sect as "the fold of Christ." Walton's *Life of Donne* implicitly invokes the "fold" in many of these senses as it envelops, entangles, enwraps, enscrolls, and encloses biographical narrative in the covering, yielding, textualizing and spiritualizing of Donne's life.

29. See Umberto Eco, *A Theory of Semiotics* (Bloomington: Indiana, 1976; rpt. London: Macmillan, 1977), pp. 66, 71, 200–01.

CHAPTER 3

1. Umberto Eco, *A Theory of Semiotics* (Bloomington: Indiana, 1976; rpt. London: Macmillan, 1977), p. 71.

2. Eco, *Theory,* p. 66.

3. Thomas S. Kuhn, *The Structures of Scientific Revolutions,* 2nd ed.,

International Encyclopedia of Unified Science, gen. ed. Otto Neurath, 2:2(1962; Chicago and London: Chicago, 1970), p. 206.

4. Elizabeth W. Bruss, *Beautiful Theories: the spectacle of discourse in contemporary criticism* (Baltimore and London: Johns Hopkins, 1982), p. 15.

5. Jonathan Culler, *Structuralist Poetics: structuralism, linguistics and the study of literature* (Ithaca, NY: Cornell, 1975), pp. 140–41; Culler cites Stephen Heath (pseu. "Cleanth Peters"), "Structuration of the Novel-Text," *Signs of the Times* (Cambridge: Granta, 1971), p. 74. See also Roman Ingarden, *The Cognition of the Literary Work of Art*, trans. Ruth Ann Crowley and Kenneth R. Olson (1968; 1973; Evanston, IL: Northwestern, 1979), p. 195: "Normally, all our cognitive or practical activities are performed on the basis of a general belief, held by us constantly in the natural attitude, in the existence of the real world in which we ourselves also exist."

6. Paul Feyerabend, *Against Method: outline of an anarchistic theory of knowledge* (1975; London: Verso, 1978), p. 73.

7. Roland Barthes, *Elements of Semiology*, trans. Annette Lavers and Colin Smith (1964; 1967; rpt. Boston: Beacon, 1970), p. 51.

8. Robert R. Magliola, *Phenomenology and Literature: an introduction* (W. Lafayette, IN: Purdue, 1977), p. 194n19.

9. The use of the term "trace" here and elsewhere in this chapter invokes, somewhat reductively, the meaning and authority attached to the term after Derrida. In *Of Grammatology*, trans. Gayatri Chakravorty Spivak (1967; 1974; Baltimore and London: Johns Hopkins, 1976), pp. 46–71, the "trace/track" emerges as "the origin of the origin," and hence as "difference" itself because "it does not depend on any sensible plentitude, audible or visible, phonic or graphic," but "is, on the contrary, the condition of such a plentitude." Consequently, "this differance . . . permits the articulation of speech and writing." Ultimately, the "trace" becomes *the absolute origin of sense in general. Which amounts to saying once again that there is no absolute origin of sense in general.* Therefore Derrida's deconstruction of the "trace/track" comes to signify "the undermining of an ontology which, in its innermost course, has determined the meaning of being as presence and the meaning of language as the full continuity of speech"—a deconstruction presented as "my final intention in this book." The notion of the biographical "fact" as an imprint, vestige, or remnant is then, like the Derridean "trace" as "track," an invocation of presence; and the notion of the biographical "fact" as a sign within discourse of discourse is, like the Derridean "trace" as the untraceable "origin of the origin," an invocation of absence. The Derridean presentation of "the presence-absence of the trace, which one should not even call its ambiguity but rather its play," provides then an analogue and an authority for treating the biographical "fact" as a trace of a 'natural' "event" trying to become a 'cultural' sign. Derrida's warning that "the trace whereof I speak is not more *natural* . . . than *cultural*" is especially relevant

here, as is his ongoing effort to disrupt and de-authorize an attempt such as this one to endow and enshrine a term (even an apparently crucial term like "trace") with the power of analogy and authority.

10. Culler, pp. 140, 142, 143; Culler cites Heath, p. 75.

11. As photographically reproduced in S[amuel] Schoenbaum, *William Shakespeare: a compact documentary life* (1977; Oxford, London, and New York: Oxford, 1978), p. 25.

12. See Michel Foucault, "What is an Author?", in *Textual Strategies: perspectives in post-structuralist criticism,* ed. Josué V. Harari (Ithaca, NY: Cornell, 1979), p. 146.

13. Roland Barthes, *Mythologies,* trans. Annette Lavers (1957; 1972; New York: Hill and Wang, 1978), pp. 109–59, but esp. pp. 114–15, 127, 131.

14. *Texere*—to weave, hence "pretext" as a "weaving before or in front," and consequently as a "covering" or "cloaking" which acts as a "disguise" or an "excuse" (*OED*).

15. Jurij Lotman, *The Structure of the Artistic Text,* trans. Ronald Vroon, Michigan Slavic Contributions, gen. ed. Ladislav Matejka, 7(1971; Ann Arbor: Michigan, 1977), p. 27.

16. Edwin Paxton Hood, *The Uses of Biography: romantic, philosophic, and didactic* (London: Partridge and Oakey, 1852), pp. 11–12. The museum metaphor of 'exhibiting' is also often associated with biographical narrative and with 'preservation,' as it is in this letter from James Boswell about his *Life of Johnson:* "My Life of that illustrious Man. . . . will exhibit him more completely than any person ancient or modern has yet been preserved." See *The Correspondence and Other Papers of James Boswell Relating to the Making of the "Life of Johnson,"* ed. Marshall Waingrow, The Yale Editions of the Private Papers of James Boswell, Research Edition, Boswell's Correspondence: vol. 2 (New York and Toronto: McGraw-Hill, 1969), p. 279.

17. Eco, *Theory,* p. 200.

18. Paul Murray Kendall, *The Art of Biography* (London: George Allen and Unwin, 1965), pp. 17, 28.

19. Ferdinand de Saussure, *Course in General Linguistics,* ed. Charles Bally, Albert Sechehaye, and Albert Riedlinger, trans. Wade Baskin (1915; 1959; New York, Toronto, and London: McGraw-Hill, 1966), pp. 131–34; Barthes, *Elements of Semiology,* pp. 50–54; and Eco, *Theory,* pp. 200–01.

20. Derrida, *Of Grammatology,* p. 69.

21. Louis O. Mink, "Narrative Form as a Cognitive Instrument," in *The Writing of History: literary form and historical understanding,* ed. Robert H. Canary and Henry Kozicki (Madison and London: Wisconsin, 1978), pp. 146–48.

22. Mink, p. 133; Hayden White, "The Historical Text as Literary Artifact," in Canary and Kozicki, p. 52.

23. Derrida, "The Law of Genre," trans. Avital Ronell, *Glyph,* 7(1980),

216. Derrida associates the "fold" (*pli*) with the hymen, with the "relationless relation" between "the feminine and masculine genre/gender," and consequently with the edgeless bounding of genre theory (pp. 221, 228).

24. Seymour Chatman, *Story and Discourse: narrative structure in fiction and film* (Ithaca, NY, and London: Cornell, 1978), pp. 22, 27–28, 31–32; Gerald Prince, "Narrativity," in *Narratology: the form and functioning of narrative,* Janua Linguarum, series maior 108 (Berlin, New York, Amsterdam: Mouton, 1982), pp. 145–61. See also, passim, Mieke Bal, *Narratology: introduction to the theory of narrative,* trans. Christine van Boheemen (Toronto, Buffalo, London: Toronto, 1985), and Gérard Genette, *Narrative Discourse: an essay in method,* trans. Jane E. Lewin (1972; Ithaca, NY: Cornell, 1980).

25. See Schoenbaum, *William Shakespeare,* pp. 97–109, and *Shakespeare's Lives* (New York and Oxford: Oxford, 1970), pp. 108–14.

26. Schoenbaum, *Shakespeare's Lives,* p. 114, and *William Shakespeare,* pp. 108–09.

27. James L. Clifford, *From Puzzles to Portraits: problems of a literary biographer* (Chapel Hill: North Carolina, 1970), pp. 84–89. Of the many formal studies of biographical facthood which cite and amend Clifford, Ina Schabert's "Fictional Biography, Factual Biography, and their Contaminations," *Biography,* 5:1(Winter 1982), 1–16, and Ira Bruce Nadel, *Biography: fiction, fact and form* (New York: St. Martin's Press, 1984) are two of the most current and can serve as summary reviews of an ongoing effort to typologize the generic space where biographical and literary recognition overlap.

28. Derrida, "The Law of Genre," pp. 212, 228. See also Derrida's "The Parergon," *October,* 9(Summer 1979), 3–41, which, pursuing an architectonic metaphor from Kant, explores the frame as *parergon,* as that which borders, grounds, ornaments, locates, limits, and warps the work (*ergon*). The frame as *parergon* is "neither simply interior nor simply exterior," but is "the limit between the work and the absence of the work" and "simultaneously constitutes and destroys" both itself and the work. Thus "there is no natural frame. . . . the frame itself *does not exist.*" There is only "framing. . . . only a particular application of the therotetical fiction," the *parergon.*

29. Daniel C. Dennett, *Brainstorms: philosophical essays on mind and psychology* (Montgomery, VT: Bradford, 1978), p. 125. Dennett cites several sources, including Terry Winograd, "Frame Representations and the Declarative/Procedural Controversy," in *Representation and Understanding: studies in cognitive science,* ed. Daniel G. Bobrow and A. M. Collins (New York: Academic Press, 1975), pp. 185–210, and Marvin Minsky, "A Framework for Representing Knowledge," in *The Psychology of Computer Vision,* ed. Patrick Henry Winston (New York: McGraw-Hill, 1975), pp. 211–77. See also *The Handbook of Artificial Intelligence,* ed. Avron Barr and Edward A. Feigenbaum, vol. 1 (Los Altos, CA: William Kaufmann, 1981), p. 177, where the "frame problem" is described as

a "difficulty, common to all representation formalisms," distinguished from "the *frame* as a representation formalism," and traced to J. McCarthy and P. J. Hayes, "Some Philosophical Problems from the Standpoint of Artificial Intelligence," in *Machine Intelligence 4*, ed. D. Michie and B. Meltzer (Edinburgh: Edinburgh, 1969), pp. 463–502.

CHAPTER 4

1. Michel Foucault, "Afterword: The Subject and Power," in *Michel Foucault: beyond structuralism and hermeneutics*, ed. Hubert L. Dreyfus and Paul Rabinow, 2nd ed. (1982; Chicago: Chicago, 1983), pp. 213–15.

2. Foucault, pp. 214–15.

3. Paul Fussell, *Samuel Johnson and the Life of Writing* (New York: Harcourt Brace Jovanovich, 1971), p. 264. The scholarship on Johnson's *Life of Savage* is too vast and diverse to be summarized here. Among the many studies which I have found particularly instructive, I will mention only a few: Robert Folkenflik, *Samuel Johnson, Biographer* (Ithaca and London: Cornell, 1978), esp. pp. 195–213; Patrick Parrinder, "Samuel Johnson: the Academy and the Marketplace," in *Authors and Authority: a study of English literary criticism and its relation to culture 1750–1900* (London, Henley, and Boston: Routledge and Kegan Paul, 1977), pp. 5–31; and John Dussinger, "Style and Intention in Johnson's *Life of Savage*," *ELH*, 37(December 1970), 564–80, revised as "Johnson's *Life of Savage*: the Displacement of Authority," in Dussinger's *The Discourse of the Mind in Eighteenth-Century Fiction*, Studies in English Literature 80 (The Hague and Paris: Mouton, 1974), pp. 127–47. Of course, Johnsonian scholarship owes a huge debt to Clarence Tracy for his edition of the *Life of Savage* (Oxford: Clarendon, 1971) and *The Artificial Bastard: a biography of Richard Savage* (Cambridge: Harvard, 1953).

4. Johnson, *Life of Savage*, ed. Tracy, pp. 72–73. Subsequent references cited parenthetically in the text by page number only.

5. Peter J. Lucas, "The Growth and Development of English Literary Patronage in the Later Middle Ages and Early Renaissance," *The Library*, Sixth ser., 4(September 1982), 237. Lucas is quoting here from J. Capgrave, *Ye Solace of Pilgrimes*, ed. C. A. Mills (London and New York: H. Frowde, 1911), p. 1. Lucas' omnibus article is a gold mine of information and sources, enhanced by an extensive bibliography.

6. Defining patronage as a formal, theoretical operation has been dominated in recent years by anthropologists, sociologists, and political scientists. For a survey of the scholarship in this area see S. N. Eisenstadt and Louis Roniger, "Patron-Client Relations as a Model of Structuring Social Exchange," *Comparative Studies in Society and History* (Cambridge), 22(1980), 42–77, which also enumerates the "core analytical characteristics" of patron-client relations

and posits a "'clientistic' model of structuring the relations between generalized and specific exchange" as an explanation of these characteristics. Eisenstadt and Roniger lack an historical perspective and tend to stress Mediterranean and Third World societies in their analysis.

7. See Elizabeth Eisenstein, *The Printing Press as an Agent of Change: communications and cultural transformations in early-modern Europe,* 2 vols. (Cambridge, London, New York, and Melbourne: Cambridge, 1979), which complements and supersedes such older studies as Marjorie Plant, *The English Book Trade: an economic history of the making and sale of books,* 2nd ed. 1939; London: Allen and Unwin, 1965); David T. Pottinger, *The French Book Trade in the Ancien Regime 1500–1791* (Cambridge: Harvard, 1958); and Frank Arthur Mumby, *Publishing and Bookselling: a history from the earliest times to the present day,* 4th ed. (1930; London: Jonathan Cape, 1956).

8. See Phoebe Sheavyn, *The Literary Profession in the Elizabethan Age,* 2nd ed., rev. J. W. Saunders (1909; Manchester: Manchester, 1967; New York: Barnes and Noble, 1967), as well as Edwin Haviland Miller, *The Professional Writer in Elizabethan England: a study of nondramatic literature* (Cambridge: Harvard, 1959); J. W. Saunders, *The Profession of English Letters* (London: Routledge, 1964; Toronto: Toronto, 1964); and Gerald Eades Bentley, *The Profession of Dramatist in Shakespeare's Time 1590–1642* (Princeton: Princeton, 1971). To these should be added such recent historical and critical studies as *Patronage in the Renaissance,* ed. Guy Fitch Lytle and Stephen Orgel (Princeton: Princeton, 1981), French R. Fogle and Louis A. Knafla, *Patronage in Late Renaissance England* (Los Angeles: Clark Library, 1983), Richard Helgerson, *Self-Crowned Laureates: Spenser, Jonson, Milton, and the literary system* (Berkeley, Los Angeles, and London: California, 1983), and Stephen Greenblatt, *Renaissance Self-Fashioning: from More to Shakespeare* (Chicago and London: Chicago, 1980).

9. A. S. Collins, *Authorship in the Days of Johnson; being a study of the relation between author, patron, publisher and public 1726–1780* (1927; rpt. Clifton, NJ: Augustus M. Kelley, 1973), and *The Profession of Letters: a study of the relation of author to patron, publisher, and public, 1780–1832* (London: Routledge, 1928); Paul Korshin, "Types of Eighteenth-Century Literary Patronage," *Eighteenth-Century Studies,* 7(Summer 1974), 453–73. Also of interest here are Alexandre Beljame, *Men of Letters and the English Public in the Eighteenth Century, 1660–1744, Dryden, Addison, Pope,* ed. Bonamy Dobrée, trans. E. O. Lorimer, International Library of Sociology and Social Reconstruction, ed. Karl Mannheim (1881; 1897; London: Kegan Paul, Trench, Trubner, 1948); Michael Foss, *The Age of Patronage: the arts in society 1660–1750* (London: Hamish Hamilton, 1971); *Books and their Readers in Eighteenth-Century England,* ed. Isabel Rivers (Leicester: Leicester, 1982; New York: St. Martin's, 1982), esp. Terry Belanger, "Publishers and writers in eighteenth-century England," pp. 5–25, and W. A. Speck, "Politicians, peers, and publication by subscription 1700–50," pp. 47–

68; and a recent special issue of *Eighteenth-Century Studies,* 17(Summer 1984), "The Printed Word in the Eighteenth Century," ed. Raymond Birn, esp. John Feather, "The Commerce of Letters: the Study of the Eighteenth-Century Book Trade," pp. 405–24, and Martha Woodmansee, "The Genius and the Copyright: Economic and Legal Conditions of the Emergence of the 'Author,'" pp. 425–48. In addition, the work of contemporary historians and critics like Robert Darnton, Lawrence Lipking, and Jerome Christensen has altered our notions of the conditions for producing literature in and around the eighteenth century. For Darnton, see *The Business of the Enlightenment: a publishing history of the Encyclopédie, 1775–1800* (Cambridge and London: Harvard, 1979), and *The Literary Underground of the Old Regime* (Cambridge and London: Harvard, 1982). For Lipking, see *The Life of the Poet: beginning and ending poetic careers* (Chicago and London: Chicago, 1981). For Christensen, see *Practicing Enlightenment: Hume and the formation of a literary career* (Madison: Wisconsin, 1987).

10. Korshin, pp. 457, 459, and passim.

11. Korshin, pp. 464, 467.

12. Samuel Johnson, *Poems,* ed. E. L. McAdam, Jr., and George Milne, Yale Edition of the Works of Samuel Johnson, vol. 6 (New Haven and London: Yale, 1964), p. 99, l. 160. See also *The Poems of Samuel Johnson,* ed. David Nichol Smith and Edward L. McAdam, 2nd ed. (1941; Oxford: Clarendon, 1974), p. 122, l. 160.

13. The phrase is from Johnson's famous letter to Chesterfield, 7 February 1755, *The Letters of Samuel Johnson with Mrs. Thrale's Genuine Letters to Him,* ed. R. W. Chapman, 3 vols. (Oxford: Clarendon, 1952), I, 64, no. 61.

14. See Howard Weinbrot, "Johnson's *Dictionary* and *The World:* the Papers of Lord Chesterfield and Richard Owen Cambridge," *Philological Quarterly,* 50(October 1971), 663–69. There has always been intense interest in the Johnson-Chesterfield relationship and the scholarship continues to grow; see, for instance, the exchange between Paul Korshin and Jacob Leed in *Studies in Burke and His Time,* 12(1970), 1676–90, 12(1970–71), 1804–11, and 13(1971), 2011–15.

15. *Letters of Johnson,* ed. Chapman, I, 64–65, no. 61.

16. Gae Holladay and O. M. Brack, Jr., "Johnson as Patron," in *Greene Centennial Studies,* ed. Paul J. Korshin and Robert R. Allen (Charlottesville: Virginia, 1984), pp. 177, 199–200.

17. *Boswell's Life of Johnson,* ed. George Birkbeck Hill, rev. L. F. Powell, 6 vols. (Oxford: Clarendon, 1934–50), I, 443.

18. "To the Visiter," *The Universal Visiter and Monthly Memorialist,* 4(April 1756), 159–66. The new title emerges in *The Works of Samuel Johnson, LL.D.,* ed. F. P. Walesby, 11 vols. (London: William Pickering, 1825; Oxford: Talboys and Wheeler, 1825), V, 355–62. For a discussion of this essay in the context of Johnson's satiric writing see Carey McIntosh, *The Choice of Life: Samuel Johnson*

and the world of fiction (New Haven and London: Yale, 1973), pp. 73–75. It is also worth noting that Johnson considered the 99-year contract which Smart and Rolt, the *Universal Visiter*'s editors, signed with their publisher Gardner "'an excellent instance . . . of the oppression of booksellers towards their poor authours'" (Boswell's *Johnson*, II, 344–45).

19. Lucas, pp. 223–24, also explores the connection between patron and *pater*, which, he claims, implies an "imbalanced relationship" that "comes about in a society where wealth is unevenly distributed."

20. *Poems of SJ*, ed. Smith and McAdam, p. 56; *Poems*, ed. McAdam and Milne, p. 44, concurs and adds that the epigram should be read as "part of a campaign for recognition in the pages of the *Gentleman's Magazine*, if not employment."

21. "Ad Ricardum Savage," *Gentleman's Magazine*, 8(April 1738), 210; see also *Poems of SJ*, ed. Smith and McAdam, pp. 56–57, and *Poems*, ed. McAdam and Milne, pp. 43–44.

22. *Savage*, ed. Tracy, pp. xvii–xviii.

23. See the *Oxford Latin Dictionary* (Oxford: Clarendon, 1971), fasc. 3, p. 729.

24. See Laurence Sterne, *A Sentimental Journey Through France and Italy by Mr. Yorick*, ed. Gardner D. Stout, Jr. (Berkeley and Los Angeles: California, 1967), pp. 197–206, and W. B. Carnochan, "'Like Birds i' th' Cage': The Poet and the Happy Man," in *Confinement and Flight: an essay on English literature of the eighteenth century* (Berkeley, Los Angeles, London: California, 1977), pp. 171–92.

25. *Collected Works of Oliver Goldsmith*, ed. Arthur Friedman, 5 vols. (Oxford: Clarendon, 1966), I, 315. See also Dussinger, "Style and Intention," p. 570, where Johnson's narrative shows Savage's attempt "to translate his quest for a legitimate filial relationship to the poet's role as 'the child of the public.'"

26. Neil McKendrick, John Brewer, and J. H. Plumb, *The Birth of a Consumer Society: the commercialization of eighteenth-century England* (Bloomington: Indiana, 1982), pp. 13, 33, 50, 197–200, 202.

27. McKendrick, pp. 43–45.

28. Josiah Wedgwood and Richard Bentley, *A Catalogue of Cameos, Intaglios, Medals, Busts, Small Statues, and Bas-Reliefs: with a general account of vases and other ornaments after the antique*, 5th ed. (London: Cadel, Robson, and Johnson, 1779), p. 30.

29. Boswell, *Life of Johnson*, 11, 389.

30. Izaak Walton, *The Lives of John Donne, Sir Henry Wotton, Richard Hooker, George Herbert, and Robert Sanderson*, World's Classics (London: Humphrey Milford and Oxford, 1927), pp. 21–22.

31. Walton, p. 85.

CHAPTER 5

1. See Roger North, *General Preface & Life of Dr John North,* ed. Peter Millard (Toronto: Toronto, 1984), pp. 14, 17, 40; and *Biography as an Art: selected criticism 1560–1960,* ed. James L. Clifford (New York: Oxford, 1962), pp. xi–xiii. Subsequent references to North cited parenthetically in text by page number only.

2. North, p. 11, where Millard quotes and cites *Tatler* no. 69.

3. Samuel Johnson, *Life of Savage,* ed. Clarence Tracy (Oxford: Clarendon, 1971), p. 98.

4. *The Oxford Dictionary of English Etymology,* ed. C. T. Onions, with the assistance of G. W. S. Friedrichsen and R. W. Burchfield (Oxford: Clarendon, 1966), p. 658.

5. The argument that I shall make below—that the relationship between biographer and biographical subject depicted in North's *General Preface* is an ongoing feature of biographical recognition and not merely an outgrowth of specific historical circumstances—applies as well to the notion of biography as 'profitable.' For instance, in his note to the reader, dated 24 January 1579, Sir Thomas North, Roger North's family relation, describes Plutarch's *Lives* as "the profitablest story of all authors"; indeed, he opens his remarks with an observation on "the profit of stories" and closes them by "wish[ing] you all the profit of the book." See *Plutarch's Lives of the Noble Grecians and Romans,* Fr. trans. James Amyot, Engl. trans. Thomas North, ed. Roland Baughman, 2 vols. (New York: Heritage, 1941), I, xxvii.

6. See, in general, Jacques Derrida, *Of Grammatology,* trans. Gayatri Chakravorty Spivak (1967; Baltimore and London: Johns Hopkins, 1976), esp. II:2, "'. . . That Dangerous Supplement . . . ,'" and II:4, "From/Of the Supplement to the Source: The Theory of Writing," and Michel Serres, *Le Parasite* (Paris: Grasset, 1980).

7. This is a feature of generic recognition that eighteenth-century biography shares with (or perhaps bestows on) eighteenth-century fiction. For example, one of the congratulatory letters with which Richardson's *Pamela* is prefaced describes it as "This little Book [that] will infallibly be looked upon as the hitherto much-wanted Standard or Pattern for this Kind of Writing," Samuel Richardson, *Pamela or, Virtue Rewarded,* ed. T. C. Duncan Eaves and Ben D. Kimpel, Riverside pb. (Boston: Houghton Mifflin, 1971), p. 4. Note how the term "pattern" is used here in the sense of a generic model. The term's applicability to both biographical subject and biographer can be found in Fielding's *Joseph Andrews,* which more or less consistently (re)presents itself as a biography. In Book I, chapter i, *"Of writing Lives in general, and particularly of* Pamela," the narrator associates himself with "those Biographers who have recorded the

Actions of great and worthy Persons of both Sexes" and notes how, "by communicating such valuable Patterns to the World, [such a writer] may perhaps do a more extensive Service to Mankind than the Person whose Life originally afforded the Pattern." Later he ironically adopts "the Language of a late Apologist [Colley Cibber], a Pattern to all Biographers," Henry Fielding, *Joseph Andrews,* ed. Martin C. Battestin, The Wesleyan Edition of the Works of Henry Fielding (Middletown, CT: Wesleyan, 1967), pp. 17, 273. Here, and also in *Tom Jones,* where the narrator distinguishes "those Historians who relate publick Transactions" from "we who deal in private Character," Fielding echoes the language of North's *General Preface,* which, of course, it is unlikely he could have seen. See Henry Fielding, *The History of Tom Jones, a Foundling,* ed. Martin C. Battestin and Fredson Bowers, The Wesleyan Edition of the Works of Henry Fielding, 2 vols. (Middletown, CT: Wesleyan, 1975), I, 402. All these examples suggest the cultural currency of the term "pattern," its use in formal and informal generic criticism, and the tangled relationships (often acknowledged) between eighteenth-century biography, fiction, and history.

8. Derrida, *Of Grammatology,* p. 51.

9. Arnaldo Momigliano, *The Development of Greek Biography* (Cambridge: Harvard, 1971), pp. 48, 96, 99–100.

10. Mikhail Bakhtin, *Problemy poetiki Dostoevskogo,* 2nd ed. (Moscow, 1963), as in Tzvetan Todorov, *Mikhail Bakhtin: the dialogical principle,* trans. Wlad Godzich, Theory and History of Literature 13 (Minneapolis: Minnesota, 1984), p. 84.

11. Derrida, *Of Grammatology,* pp. 51, 65.

12. Another way of saying this is to describe the biographical subject, *pace* Roland Barthes, as a supplemented sum of semes, that is, as a "*figure* (an impersonal network of symbols combined under the proper name)" to which "a precious remainder" has been added to produce a "*person* (a moral freedom endowed with motives and an overdetermination of meanings)." The problem with this approach, as Barthes acknowledges, is that it indulges "the vulgar bookkeeping of compositional characters," as if a narrative accounting of discursive traces can (mystically and mechanically) compose "something like *individuality.*" See *S/Z,* trans. Richard Miller (1970; New York: Hill and Wang, 1974), pp. 94, 191. The advantage of the term "extra-discursive" is that it characterizes individuality or personhood as that which resists semiotic encoding, and thus draws attention to the radical discontinuity of the discursive and the non-discursive— a gap in generic recognition that no modification of presence or intersection of discursive traces can bridge or fill. It should also be noted that my use of the term "trans-discursive" differs from that of Michel Foucault in "What Is an Author?", in *Textual Strategies: perspectives in post-structuralist criticism,* ed. Josué V. Harari (Ithaca: Cornell, 1979), p. 153.

13. Boulton is quoted in a letter to his wife, dated 18 November 1765, cited in E. Robinson, "Eighteenth-Century Commerce and Fashion: Matthew Boulton's Marketing Techniques," *Economic History Review,* 2nd ser., 16(1963–64), 41n5. For Wedgwood see *Letters of Josiah Wedgwood 1771 to 1780* (Manchester: E. J. Morten, 1903), p. 6, *Letters of Josiah Wedgwood 1762 to 1770* (Manchester: E. J. Morten, 1903), pp. 290–91, and *A Catalogue of Cameos, Intaglios, Medals, Busts, Small Statues, and Bas-Reliefs; with a general account of vases and other ornaments after the antique, made by Wedgwood and Bentley, and sold at their rooms in Greek-Street, Soho, London,* 5th ed. (London: Cadel, Robson, and Johnson, 1779), pp. 22–23.

For general observations on the pattern books of Boulton, Wedgwood, and their contemporaries, see Neil McKendrick, John Brewer, and J. H. Plumb, *The Birth of a Consumer Society: the commercialization of eighteenth-century England* (Bloomington: Indiana, 1982), pp. 66–71, 74–75, 118–19. For the furniture designers, see Thomas Chippendale, *The Gentleman and Cabinet-Maker's Director* (London: Chippendale, 1754), rpt. in *The Furniture Designs of Thomas Chippendale,* ed. J. Munro Bell (London: Gibbings, 1910), esp. pp. xix–xxi; George Heppelwhite, *The Cabinet-Maker and Upholsterer's Guide,* 3rd ed. (London: I. and J. Taylor, 1794), rpt. in *The Furniture Designs of George Heppelwhite,* ed. J. Munro Bell (London: Gibbings, 1910), esp. p. xvii, where Heppelwhite discusses choosing "three hundred different patterns" that "were most likely to be of general use"; Thomas Sheraton, *The Cabinet-Maker and Upholsterer's Drawing-Book,* 3rd ed. (London: T. Bensley for W. Baynes, 1802), rpt. in *The Furniture Designs of Thomas Sheraton,* ed. J. Munro Bell (London: Gibbings, 1910), esp. pp. xix–xxiii, where Sheraton mentions the need for "accurate patterns . . . to copy from" and reviews Chippendale's, Sheraton's, and other influential pattern books of the late eighteenth century; and, for an historical overview of "The Pre-'Director' Period (1740–1754)," when furniture pattern books were introduced in England, and also of "The Post-'Director' Period," see Ralph Fastnedge, *English Furniture Styles from 1500 to 1830* (1955; rpt. 1961; rpt. London: Herbert Jenkins, 1962). For architecture, see *The Works in Architecture of Robert and James Adam,* ed. Robert Oresko (London: Academy Editions; New York: St. Martin's Press, 1975), in which are included the two-volume 1779 edition of the Adams' plans of various houses and public buildings. See also Rupert Gentle and Rachael Feild, "Patterns and Pattern Books," in their *English Domestic Brass 1680–1810 and the History of its Origins* (London: Paul Elek, 1975), pp. 59–66; Eric Delieb and Michael Roberts, *The Great Silver Manufactory: Matthew Boulton and the Birmingham silversmiths 1760–1790* (London: November Books, 1971), esp. "Appendix VI: The Soho Pattern Books"; and W. C. Aitken, "Brass and Brass Manufactures," in *The Resources, Products, and Industrial History of Birmingham and the Midland Hardware District,* ed. Samuel Timmins

(London: Robert Hardwicke, 1866; rpt. London: Frank Cass, 1967), pp. 225–80, esp. p. 241, where Aitken discusses the commercial traveller's use of pattern cards and pattern books.

The *OED* cites the emergence of such terms as pattern-drawer, pattern-suit, pattern-shirt, and pattern-hat in the early- and mid-eighteenth century. Wedgwood's letters (cited here by date and page only) reveal how often the term 'pattern' and such usages as 'pattern cards' (predating the earliest *OED* citation) and 'pattern room' (not mentioned in the *OED*) occurred in eighteenth-century commerce: see, e.g., 6 July 1765 (pp. 47–48), 2 Aug. 1765 (p. 51), 7 Oct. 1765 (p. 60), [?] July 1766 (p. 94), 17 Nov. 1766 (p. 107—"pattern room"), 18 Feb. 1767 (p. 119), [?] March 1767 (p. 132—"Pattern Room"), 21 Nov. 1767 (p. 189), 24 March 1768 (p. 211), [?] Dec. 1768 (pp. 236–37—instructions on how to paste up a pattern book for vases, although the term itself is not used), 17 Feb. 1769 (p. 247), 27 Sept. 1769 (pp. 290–91), 30 Sept. 1769 (p. 296—"the pattern room at Etruria," that is, in the factory showroom), 23 Jan. 1771 (p. 6), 9 Sept. 1771 (p. 43), 21 Nov. 1771 (p. 51), 30 Dec. 1773 (p. 173—"Pattern cards," and p. 174), 2 March 1774 (p. 175), 15 Dec. 1776 (p. 356), 13 Feb. 1778 (p. 404), 6 April 1778 (p. 418), 16 April 1778 (p. 422), 18 April 1778 (p. 425), 28 Oct. 1780 (p. 603).

14. *Catalogue of Wedgwood and Bentley,* p. 30.

15. Thomas E. Lewis, "Notes toward a Theory of the Referent," *PMLA,* 94(May 1979), 466, 472–73.

16. Although it should be pointed out that Walton's "Epistle to the Reader" claims that his *Life of Herbert* is *"so far a* Free-will-offering, *that it was writ, chiefly to please my self," The Lives of John Donne, Sir Henry Wotton, Richard Hooker, George Herbert, & Robert Sanderson* (London: Oxford, 1927), p. 6. Perhaps it is significant that Walton refers to Herbert, in the general dedication, as "that *pattern of primitive Piety"* (p. 3).

17. *Boswell's Life of Johnson,* ed. George Birkbeck Hill and L. F. Powell, 6 vols. (Oxford: Clarendon, 1934–50), I, 30.

18. Michel Foucault, *The Archaeology of Human Knowledge,* trans. A. M. Sheridan Smith (1969; 1972; London: Tavistock, 1974), p. 12.

19. Barthes, *S/Z,* pp. 129–30.

20. See *Los Angeles: biography of a city,* ed. John and LaRee Caughey (Berkeley: California, 1976); James Sledd and Gwin Kolb, *Dr. Johnson's Dictionary: essays in the biography of a book* (Chicago: Chicago, 1955); Sherman Paul, *The Music of Survival: a biography of a poem by William Carlos Williams* (Urbana, Chicago, and London: Illinois, 1968); Broadus Mitchell and Louise Pearson Mitchell, *A Biography of the Constitution of the United States: its origin, formation, adoption, interpretation,* 2nd. ed. (1964; New York: Oxford, 1975); *The Twentieth-Century Sciences: studies in the biography of ideas,* ed. Gerald Holton (New York: Norton, 1972); John W. Dodds, *The Age of Paradox: a biography of England, 1841–1851*

(New York: Rinehart, 1952); Elvin Hatch, *Biography of a Small Town* (New York: Columbia, 1979); Helen Huntington Howe, *The Gentle Americans, 1864–1960: biography of a breed* (New York: Harper and Row, 1965); Donald Sutherland, *Gertrude Stein: a biography of her work* (New Haven: Yale, 1951); Homer O. Brown, *James Joyce's Early Fiction: the biography of a form* (Cleveland: Case Western Reserve, 1972); David Ayerst, *The Manchester "Guardian": biography of a newspaper* (Ithaca: Cornell, 1971); A. Eustace Haydon, *Biography of the Gods* (1941; New York: Ungar, 1967); Madelon Bedell, *The Alcotts: biography of a family* (New York: C. N. Potter, 1980); Ruth P. Randall, *Mary Lincoln: biography of a marriage* (Boston: Little, Brown, 1953); Polly Redford, *Billion-Dollar Sandbar: a biography of Miami Beach* (New York: E. P. Dutton, 1970); James P. Jackson, *The Biography of a Tree* (Middle Village, NY: Jonathan David; London: W. H. Allen, 1979); R. A. Weale, *A Biography of the Eye: development, growth, age* (London: H. K. Lewis, 1982); *The Biography of a Victorian Village: Richard Cobbold's account of Wortham, Suffolk, 1860,* ed. Ronald Fletcher (London: Batsford, 1977); David Duff, *Eugenie and Napoleon III: a dual biography* (New York: Morrow, 1978).

21. Pierre Bourdieu, *Outline of a Theory of Practice,* trans. Richard Nice, Cambridge Studies in Social Anthropology 16, gen. ed. Jack Goody (1972; Cambridge: Cambridge, 1977), pp. 164, 166.

22. Bourdieu, p. 133.

23. Bourdieu, p. 123.

24. Bourdieu, p. 8.

25. Bourdieu, p. 86.

26. One effort to reify the notion of the biographical subject as a metaphysical presence, that is, as a 'real' coin involved in 'real' circulation, occurs at the end of Boswell's *Life of Johnson:* "Let me add, as a proof of the popularity of his character, that there are copper pieces struck at Birmingham, with his head impressed on them, which pass current as half-pence there, and in the neighbouring parts of the country" (IV, 422n). As Boswell's editors point out, "no less than seven different varieties of copper token impressed with the bust of Johnson" have been found; "they were all struck at Birmingham, from about 1792 to 1800" (IV, 555), that is, following the publication of Boswell's *Life,* which, in Boswell's opinion (and that of most of the English-speaking world), permanently fixed Johnson's "character" as a biographical subject. Note how Boswell uses the coin as "proof" of the "popularity" of this "character." It is as if Boswell is reversing (or obliterating) the customary distinction between a 'pattern' (a 'proof') and a 'real' coin: the copper half-pence coin 'proves' the 'pattern' (the "character") already minted and circulated by Boswell's *Life.*

Note also the intersection here of 'pattern' and 'character,' two words that share not only a variety of meanings but also a reciprocal deployment in the recognition of the biographical subject. A stamp or "distinctive mark impressed, engraved, or otherwise formed," "a graphic symbol" used in writing or printing, "the sum of the moral and mental qualities which distinguish an individual," a person's reputation, and "a personality invested with distinctive attributes and qualities" in fiction or drama (*OED*), 'character' is also the descriptive term for both an ancient Greek biographical genre (offering "generalized portraits of character types" which were "only occasionally based on actual lives") and an eighteenth-century lifewriting convention ("the summarizing character sketch at the end of a biography"). See Donald Winslow, "Glossary of Terms in Life-Writing, Part I," *Biography*, 1:1(Winter 1978), 68—69.

27. M. M. Bakhtin, *The Dialogic Imagination*, ed. Michael Holquist, trans. Caryl Emerson and Michael Holquist (Austin: Texas, 1981), pp. 131—32.

28. Momigliano, pp. 12—13.

29. Jacques Derrida, "Limited Inc abc . . . ," *Glyph*, 2(1977), 251.

30. Derrida, "Limited Inc," p. 251.

31. Harold Nicolson, "The Practice of Biography," *American Scholar*, 23(Spring 1954), 153—61, excerpted in *Biography as an Art*, ed. Clifford, pp. 197—205. I quote from pp. 197—98, 202. See also Nicolson's *The Development of English Biography* (1928; rpt. London: Hogarth, 1968), pp. 9—13, where Nicolson first differentiated "pure" and "impure" biography.

32. Jacques Derrida, "The Law of Genre," trans. Avital Ronell, *Glyph*, 7(1980), 202—32.

33. Momigliano, pp. 13—14.

CHAPTER 6

1. James Boswell, *Life of Johnson*, ed. R. W. Chapman, corr. J. D. Fleeman, 3rd ed. (1904; 1953; London, Oxford, and New York: Oxford, 1970), p. 1363. Subsequent references cited parenthetically in the text by page number only. In this chapter (unlike in the other chapters) I have decided to use the Chapman-Fleeman, the standard reading edition of the *Life*, rather than the Hill-Powell, the standard scholarly edition. There are several reasons for this somewhat unorthodox choice. First, this chapter presents the *Life* as a text which is read rather than consulted. Second, the Hill-Powell includes the *Tour*, which was originally published separately in 1785, six years earlier than the *Life*, and to which I refer only peripherally. Third, quoting from the Chapman-Fleeman is a convenience for those who teach and study the *Life*, for it is the overwhelming choice as a classroom text. Fourth, the Chapman-Fleeman, prepared by two of this century's outstanding Johnson scholars and textual editors, is thoroughly reliable for its text (based on the 3rd edition of the *Life*) and has actually received more recent editorial attention than the Hill-Powell.

2. I wish to acknowledge some general debts; subsequent notes cite scholarship dealing with specific issues. Frederick A. Pottle's work has long domi-

nated Boswell scholarship: *The Literary Career of James Boswell* (Oxford: Clarendon, 1929); *James Boswell: the earlier years 1740–1769* (New York, Toronto, and London: McGraw-Hill, 1966); and, of course, his general editorship of The Yale Editions of the Private Papers of James Boswell, which since 1950 has been publishing trade and research editions of Boswell's journals, correspondence, and other manuscript materials. Pottle also shared the editorial duties with Geoffrey Scott on *The Private Papers of James Boswell from Malahide Castle,* 18 vols. (Mt. Vernon, NY: privately printed, 1928–34). Frank Brady has assisted and supplemented Pottle's editorial and biographical research, most notably in *James Boswell: the later years 1769–1795* (New York, Toronto, and London: McGraw-Hill, 1984). Without their efforts, as well as those of Marion Pottle, Irma Lustig, and Marshall Waingrow, projects like mine would not be possible.

Influential criticism exploring Boswell's methods, themes, and style can also be found in Scott's *The Making of the "Life of Johnson,"* vol. 6 of the *Private Papers* (1929); Paul K. Alkon, "Boswell's Control of Aesthetic Distance," *University of Toronto Quarterly,* 38(1969), 174–91, and "Boswellian Time," *Studies in Burke and His Time,* 14(1973), 239–56; David L. Passler, *Time, Form, and Style in Boswell's "Life of Johnson"* (New Haven and London: Yale, 1971); William R. Siebenschuh, *Form and Purpose in Boswell's Biographical Works* (Berkeley, Los Angeles, and London: California, 1972); Elizabeth W. Bruss, "James Boswell: Genius and Stenography," *Autobiographical Acts: the changing situation of a literary genre* (Baltimore and London: Johns Hopkins, 1976), pp. 61–92; Robert H. Bell, "Boswell's Notes Toward a Supreme Fiction from *London Journal* to *Life of Johnson,"* *Modern Language Quarterly,* 38(1977), 132–48; Richard B. Schwartz, *Boswell's Johnson: a preface to the "Life"* (Madison and London: Wisconsin, 1978); William C. Dowling, *The Boswellian Hero* (Athens, GA: Georgia, 1979); Hugo M. Reichard, "Boswell's Johnson, the Hero Made by a Committee," *PMLA,* 95(1980), 225–33; and Allen Ingram, *Boswell's Creative Gloom: a study of imagery and melancholy in the writings of James Boswell* (Totowa, NJ: Barnes and Noble; London and Basingstoke: Macmillan, 1982).

A continuing debate about the *Life* as factual and/or fictional narrative can be traced in Francis R. Hart, "Boswell and the Romantics: a Chapter in the History of Biographical Theory," *ELH,* 27(1960), 44–65; William K. Wimsatt, Jr., "The Fact Imagined: James Boswell," in *Hateful Contraries* (Lexington: Kentucky, 1965), pp. 150–83; Ralph W. Rader, "Literary Form in Fictional Narrative: the Example of Boswell's *Johnson,"* in *Essays in Eighteenth-Century Biography,* ed. Philip B. Daghlian (Bloomington: Indiana, 1968), pp. 3–42; Leopold Damrosch, Jr., "The *Life of Johnson:* an Anti-Theory," *Eighteenth-Century Studies,* 6(1973), 486–505; Donald Greene, "'Tis a Pretty Book, Mr. Boswell, But—," *Georgia Review,* 32(1978), 17–43; Irma Lustig, "Fact into Art: James Boswell's Notes, Journals, and the *Life of Johnson,"* in *Biography in the 18th*

Century, ed. John D. Browning, Publications of the McMaster University Association for 18th-Century Studies 8 (New York and London: Garland, 1980), pp. 112–46; Frank Brady, "Boswell's *London Journal:* the Question of Memorial and Imaginative Modes," in *Literature and Society: the Lawrence Henry Gipson Symposium, 1978,* ed. Jan Fergus (Bethlehem, PA: Lawrence Henry Gipson Institute, 1981), pp. 33–47; and Dowling, *Language and Logos in Boswell's "Life of Johnson"* (Princeton: Princeton, 1981).

Overviews on these and other significant issues are provided by *Twentieth Century Interpretations of Boswell's "Life of Johnson,"* ed. James L. Clifford (Englewood Cliffs, NJ: Prentice-Hall, 1970), especially valuable for the introductory survey and reprinted essays by Scott, Alkon, and Green, and by *Boswell's "Life of Johnson": new questions, new answers,* ed. John A. Vance (Athens, GA: Georgia, 1985), particularly for the introductory survey and reprinted articles by Rader, Greene, and Pottle. The tangled relationship between Boswellian studies, eighteenth-century studies, and contemporary theory is discussed in Frederic V. Bogel, "'Did you once see Johnson plain?': Reflections on Boswell's *Life* and the State of Eighteenth-Century Studies," in Vance, pp. 73–93, and William H. Epstein, "*Bios* and *Logos:* Boswell's *Life of Johnson* and Recent Literary Theory," *South Atlantic Quarterly,* 82(1983), 246–55.

3. See H. W. Dickinson, *Matthew Boulton* (Cambridge: Cambridge, 1937); John Lord, *Capital and Steam-Power 1750–1800* (London: P. S. King and Son, 1923), esp. pp. 88–135; E. Robinson, "Eighteenth-Century Commerce and Fashion: Matthew Boulton's Marketing Techniques," *Economic History Review,* 2nd ser., 16(1963–64), 39–60; Neil McKendrick, John Brewer, and J. H. Plumb, *The Birth of a Consumer Society: the commercialization of eighteenth-century England* (Bloomington: Indiana, 1982), pp. 69–77; Fernand Braudel, *The Wheels of Commerce,* trans. Sian Reynolds, vol. 2 of *Civilization and Capitalism: 15th–18th century* (1979; New York: Harper and Row, 1982), pp. 300–02, 329–35, where Braudel discusses distinctions between manufactories and factories in the eighteenth century.

4. See P. G. M. Dickson, *The Financial Revolution in England: a study in the development of public credit, 1688–1756* (London: Macmillan, 1967); Braudel, pp. 385–95, 521–28; and J. G. A. Pocock, "Neo-Machiavellian Political Economy: the Augustan Debate over Land, Trade, and Credit," in *The Machiavellian Moment: Florentine political thought and the Atlantic republican tradition* (Princeton and London: Princeton, 1975), pp. 423–61. Subsequent references to Pocock in this paragraph are cited parenthetically by page number only.

5. For a summary of and response to this criticism see Frank Brady, "Boswell's Self-Presentation and His Critics," *Studies in English Literature,* 12(1972), 545–55.

6. Pierre Bourdieu, *Outline of a Theory of Practice,* trans. Richard Nice, Cambridge Studies in Social Anthropology 16, gen. ed. Jack Goody (1972; Cambridge: Cambridge, 1977), p. 181.

7. For Boswell's "whole conception of Johnson as the hero of a drama of almost national proportions," see Chauncey Brewster Tinker, *Young Boswell* (Boston: Atlantic Monthly Press, 1922), p. 225.

8. Collected in *The Correspondence and Other Papers of James Boswell Relating to the Making of the "Life of Johnson,"* ed. Marshall Waingrow, The Yale Editions of the Private Papers of James Boswell, Research Edition, Correspondence: vol. 2 (New York and Toronto: McGraw-Hill, 1969), an invaluable resource for Boswellian studies. Unless otherwise noted, all subsequent references to Boswell's journals and correspondence will be to Waingrow's "Chronology of the Making of the *Life*," pp. li–lxxviii, or to the letters printed, excerpted, or summarized throughout his volume. Journal entries will be cited parenthetically by date, letters by date and correspondent.

9. John Locke, *An Essay Concerning the True Original, Extent, and End of Civil Government,* in *Two Treatises of Government,* ed. Peter Laslett (Cambridge: Cambridge, 1964), pp. 303–20. This is chapter v, "Of Property."

10. Kurt Heinzelman, *The Economics of the Imagination* (Amherst: Massachusetts, 1980), pp. 166–67, 169. See also Crawford Brough Macpherson, *The Political Theory of Possessive Individualism: Hobbes to Locke* (Oxford: Clarendon, 1962).

11. Heinzelman, p. 169.

12. Pottle, *Earlier Years,* pp. 42–43.

13. Pottle, *Earlier Years,* p. 42; *Boswell's Life of Johnson,* ed. George Birkbeck Hill and L. F. Powell, 6 vols. (Oxford: Clarendon, 1934–50), V, 30–31n3.

14. Heinzelman, pp. 169, 172–73.

15. The term 'work' (in these and other senses) appears hundreds of times in the *Life* and the materials relating to its production. The most common word that Boswell employs to refer to a 'literary composition,' its use in this respect was and is conventional. Indeed, it is this commonality that I wish to stress here. A deeply embedded discursive practice that is seldom examined, referring to the result of literary activity as a 'work' continually and tacitly acknowledges the relationship between literary and other modes of production. This is hardly an original or profound observation, but, in the context of the argument of this chapter, it can bear repetition. On this subject, as on so many others, Carlyle's 1832 essay (which first appeared in *Fraser's Magazine*) anticipates and guides later criticism. Johnson, he writes, "is animated by the spirit of a true *workman,* resolute to do his work well; and he *does* his work well; all his work, that of writing, that of living." See "Boswell's Life of Johnson," in *The Works of Thomas Carlyle,* ed. H. D. Traill, Centenary Edition, 30 vols. (London: Chapman and Hall, 1898–1907), XXVIII, 116.

16. The notion of 'intrinsic value,' which emerges here and elsewhere in Boswell's correspondence (see, e.g., the letters from Holt and Abercrombie quoted above), is, of course, a vexing one. For Locke, the invention of money "altered the intrinsic value of things, which depends only on their usefulness to

the Life of Man" (*Of Civil Government*, p. 312). Thus, as a foundational economic concept, 'intrinsic value' is an epistemological contention already stripped of the ontological possibility of inherent worth, "fixed in the nature of the thing" (Johnson's *Dictionary* s.v. "Intrinsick"). As Locke acknowledges in *Further Considerations Concerning Raising the Value of Money* (1692), "The intrinsick Value of Silver consider'd as Money, is that estimate which common Consent has placed on it" (in *The Works of John Locke Esq.*, 3 vols. [London: Bettesworth, Pemberton, and Symon, 1727], II, 67). This diathesis persisted in the writings of economists throughout the eighteenth century, even if the nostalgic habit of employing 'intrinsic value' to mean something like 'inherent, original, or true worth' remained in common usage (as with Boswell and his correspondents). See, e.g., *An Essay on Money and Bullion* (London: B. Lintot, 1718), pp. 1–5, a response to Locke that distinguishes between "Value Instrinsick" ("the Affection we have for any Thing" and which thus "changes with our Circumstances") and "Value Extrinsick" ("the Value we put upon any Thing" according to its "Use" and which thus "alters with the Opinion People generally have" of such an object). Smith more or less preserves this distinction in the difference between "value in use" and "value in exchange"; see *An Inquiry into the Nature and Causes of the Wealth of Nations*, gen. ed. R. H. Campbell and A. S. Skinner, text. ed. W. B. Todd, The Glasgow Edition of the Works and Correspondence of Adam Smith, 6 vols. in 7 (1976; rpt. Oxford: Clarendon, 1979), II, 44–45.

17. See, e.g., Ian Ross, "Boswell in Search of a Father? or a Subject?" *Review of English Literature*, 5(1964), 19–34, and Felicity A. Nussbaum, "Father and Son in Boswell's *London Journal*," *Philological Quarterly*, 57(1978), 383–97.

18. *Boswell: the applause of the jury, 1782–1785*, ed. Irma S. Lustig and Frederick A. Pottle (New York, Toronto, and London: McGraw-Hill, 1981), p. 274, 28 December 1784.

19. Brady, *Later Years*, pp. 115–21, 135–36.

20. Brady, *Later Years*, p. 88.

21. Johnson's position in the Literary Property Cause is revealed by two somewhat elaborate statements in the *Life* (309–10, 546–47). A creature if not a creation of 'the Trade,' who considered booksellers "the patrons of literature" (217), Johnson "was zealous against a perpetuity" (310), although, logically, he felt, there was a strong case to be made that authors were entitled to a perpetual metaphysical right. Recognizing that "'the consent of nations is against'" such a right, he concurred in the eventual legislative and legal compromise which prescribed a limited copyright (fourteen years), although "he thought that the term of the exclusive right of authours should be considerably enlarged" (310).

22. *The Decision of the Court of Session, upon the Question of Literary Property* (Edinburgh: A. Donaldson, 1774), p. 35. The title page reads "Published by James Boswell, Esq; Advocate, One of the COUNSEL in the Cause." The pamphlet has been reprinted in photo-facsimile in *The Literary Property Debate:*

Six Tracts 1764–1774, The English Book Trade 1660–1853, ed. Stephen Parks (New York and London: Garland, 1975).

23. Sir David Rae, Lord Eskgrove, *Information for Mess. John Hinton of London, Bookseller, and Alexander MacKonochie, Writer in Edinburgh, his Attorney, Pursuers; against Mess. Alexander Donaldson, and John Wood, Booksellers in Edinburgh, and James Meurose, Bookseller in Kilmarnock, Defenders*, in *Literary Property Debate*, ed. Parks. The document is dated 2 January 1773. Subsequent references in this paragraph are cited parenthetically by page number only.

24. Ilay Campbell, *Information for Alexander Donaldson and John Wood, Booksellers in Edinburgh, and James Meurose, Bookseller in Kilmarnock, Defenders: against John Hinton, Bookseller in London, and Alexander McConoghie, Writer in Edinburgh, his Attorney, Pursuers*, in *Literary Property Debate*, ed. Parks. Dated 2 January 1773. Subsequent references in this paragraph are cited parenthetically by page number only. Parks mistakes Campbell's first name as "Hay."

25. Jacques Derrida, "Otobiographies: the Teaching of Nietzsche and the Politics of the Proper Name," trans. Avital Ronell, in *The Ear of the Other: otobiography, transference, translation*, ed. Christie V. McDonald, trans. Peggy Kamuf (New York: Schocken, 1985), pp. 7–9.

26. Or in which he urges his readers to engage: see, e.g., p. 994, "My readers will decide upon this dispute."

27. Heinzelman, pp. 175–76.

28. Donald A. Stauffer, *The Art of Biography in Eighteenth Century England* (Princeton: Princeton, 1941), p. 249. See also Richard D. Altick, *Lives and Letters: a history of literary biography in England and America* (New York: Knopf, 1965), p. 19, where it emerges as one of "the chief repositories of biographical knowledge concerning virtually all English authors who lived before 1700."

29. Bruss concurs: "He places continuing emphasis on his act as one of 'preservation'" (p. 24). See also Ira Bruce Nadel, *Biography: fiction, fact and form* (New York: St. Martin's Press, 1984), p. 165.

30. This notion is everywhere in Derrida's work, most succinctly perhaps in "Signature Event Context," trans. Samuel Weber and Jeffrey Mehlman, *Glyph*, 1(1977), 172–97.

31. See, e.g., Frederick A. Pottle, "The Power of Memory in Boswell and Scott," in *Essays on the Eighteenth Century Presented to David Nichol Smith* (Oxford: Clarendon, 1945), pp. 168–89; and William R. Siebenschuh, "Boswell's Second Crop of Memory: a New Look at the Role of Memory in the Making of the *Life*," in Vance, pp. 94–109.

32. Heinzelman, quoting Marx, pp. 178, 181.

33. The metaphors of 'monument' and 'embalming' are also noted by Schwartz, p. 15; Passler, "Johnson and Form: a Monument for Posterity," pp. 31–63; and Alkon, "Boswellian Time," p. 244.

34. Jerome Christensen, *Practicing Enlightenment: Hume and the formation of a*

literary career (Madison: Wisconsin, 1987). I quote from the chapter "The Commerce of Letters," which I was graciously allowed to read in galley proofs.

35. Donald A. Stauffer, *English Biography Before 1700* (Cambridge: Harvard, 1930), pp. 217–19, shows how "shortly after 1660 the word *biography* and its allies appeared in more than isolated instances, and appeared suddenly."

36. John Dryden, "The Life of Plutarch," in vol. 1 of *Plutarch's Lives, Translated from the Greek by Several Hands* (1683–86), as in *Biography as an Art: selected criticism 1560–1960,* ed. James L. Clifford (New York: Oxford, 1962), pp. 17–18. Emphasis added.

37. Dryden, as in *Biography as an Art,* ed. Clifford, p. 18.

38. Waingrow, pp. lxvii–iii, newspaper advertisements listed under 11 July 1793 and 18 May 1799.

39. Michel Foucault, *Discipline and Punish: the birth of the prison,* trans. Alan Sheridan (1975; New York: Vintage, 1979), pp. 200, 208, 249, 317n2, and passim.

40. Boswell's technique of 'scenifying' is also discussed in Schwartz, p. 52, and Sven Eric Molin, "Boswell's Account of the Johnson-Wilkes Meeting," *Studies in English Literature,* 3(1963), 307–22. Brady notes that "Boswell's habit of perceiving his own life, in part, as a series of scenes . . . was an eighteenth-century commonplace" (*Later Years,* p. 565).

41. Foucault, p. 252.

42. Foucault, p. 319n4.

43. See John Richetti, *Popular Fiction Before Richardson: narrative patterns 1700–1739* (Oxford: Clarendon, 1969), pp. 23–59, and Benjamin Boyce, "Johnson's *Life of Savage* and its Literary Background," *Studies in Philology,* 53(1956), 576–98.

44. It must be said that, in answering Boswell's request, Johnson is arguing for victory, and that, moreover, in so doing, is restricted by juridical precedents and the cause he must defend. The cultural myopia his argument evinces here is not, as we know, characteristic of his discerning mind. All discursive events are context-bound. Perhaps we can say that, on this occasion, Johnson (constrained by circumstances) reproduces an embedded belief structure which, in other contexts, he may 'see through.' My point is that, in this particular situation, Johnson's articulation is constrained in a particular way, and that his treatment of 'correction' determines and is determined by this constraint.

45. Bourdieu, p. 167.

46. Waingrow, p. lix.

47. Strachey's remarks were made in the *Spectator,* 2 January 1909. They are quoted here as in Michael Holroyd, *Lytton Strachey: a critical biography,* 2 vols. (New York, Chicago, and San Francisco: Holt, Rinehart and Winston, 1968), II, 262. See also David Novarr, *The Lines of Life: theories of biography, 1880–1970* (West Lafayette, IN: Purdue, 1986), p. 28.

48. See Edward Gibson, *The History of the Decline and Fall of the Roman Empire*, ed. J. B. Bury, 7 vols. (London: Methuen, 1896–1900), II, 170.

49. Smith, II, 148, 330–31.

CHAPTER 7

1. Laurence Sterne, *The Life and Opinions of Tristram Shandy, Gentleman*, ed. Melvyn New and Joan New, The Florida Edition of the Works of Laurence Sterne, 3 vols. (Gainesville: Florida, 1978), II, 570–72. This is from bk. 6, ch. 40. I have eliminated paragraph breaks and some dashes in the long quoted passage.

2. Laurence Sterne, *The Life and Opinions of Tristram Shandy, Gentleman*, ed. Ian Watt, Riverside Editions (Boston: Houghton Mifflin, 1965), p. 360n2. See also vol. 3 of the Florida Edition, ed. Melvyn New with Richard A. Davies and W. G. Day (1984), pp. 442–43, which also points out the sexual innuendo of 'planting cabbage,' a pun suggesting that 'interposing the body' in order to ironically 'curve' the straight line of moral rectitude (the 'subtler strategy' with which we shall credit Strachey) was a trope already available in English cultural discourse.

3. See David Novarr, *The Lines of Life: theories of biography, 1880–1970* (West Lafayette, IN: Purdue, 1986).

4. *The Divine Comedy of Dante Alighieri,* trans. John D. Sinclair, vol. 1: *Inferno* (1939; 1948; New York: Oxford, 1961), p. 23. Dante's Italian for 'the straight way' is "la diritta via." The anonymous 1658 work is listed in the *NUC*. *Lavengro* is cited from *The Works of George Borrow*, ed. Clement Shorter, Norwich Edition, 16 vols. (1923; rpt. New York: AMS, 1967), III, 225. Maccall's lines are from the poem "Duty."

5. Magali Sarfatti Larson, *The Rise of Professionalism: a sociological analysis* (Berkeley, Los Angeles, London: California, 1977), pp. 10–11, stress added. Subsequent references in this paragraph cited parenthetically by page number.

6. Burton J. Bledstein, *The Culture of Professionalism: the middle class and the development of higher education in America* (New York: W. W. Norton, 1976), pp. 111–12, 171–72.

7. Arnold to W. A. Greenhill, 31 October 1836, in Arthur P. Stanley, *The Life and Correspondence of Thomas Arnold, D. D.,* 12th ed., 2 vols. (London: John Murray, 1881), II, 48.

8. *Lytton Strachey by Himself: a self-portrait,* ed. Michael Holroyd (New York, Chicago, San Francisco: Holt, Rinehart and Winston, 1971), p. 25. Strachey also notes that these "solid bourgeois qualities were interpenetrated by intellectualism and eccentricity" (25), as if the distinguishing features of his rebellion had already 'penetrated' Victorian middle-class professionalism.

9. The publishing history of *Eminent Victorians* is somewhat complicated

and affects our choice of text. The first English edition was published by Chatto and Windus (London, 1918); the first American edition by G. P. Putnam's Knickerbocker Press (New York and London, 1918). Both contain illustrations of the four principal subjects and of Newman and Gladstone, but they are paginated differently. The next important edition is in The Collected Works of Lytton Strachey, a Uniform Edition published in six separately issued volumes by Chatto and Windus (London, 1948), which is paginated differently from either of the first editions and does not contain the illustrations. The most readily available present-day edition, at least in America, is the Harcourt, Brace, & World paperback (New York, n.d.), which is based on the first American edition and also lacks the illustrations. Following Michael Holroyd, I cite the volume in the Uniform Edition of the Collected Works (rpt. 1957), but I also refer readers to the illustrations in the first edition, upon which Strachey drew in arranging his subects in the 'poses' I discuss later. Details of these and other editions can be found in Michael Edmonds, *Lytton Strachey: a bibliography* (New York and London: Garland, 1981). Subsequent references to *Eminent Victorians* are cited parenthetically by page number.

10. Bledstein, pp. 171–72, also looks at some definitions of the term 'career.'

11. William Wordsworth, *The Prelude or Growth of a Poet's Mind*, ed. Ernest De Selincourt, rev. Helen Darbishire, 2nd ed. (1926; Oxford: Clarendon, 1959), pp. 487, 489, 491, 493, 505, bk. 14, ll. 130–38, 193–202, 430–32; *The Poems of Matthew Arnold*, ed. Kenneth Allott and Miriam Allott, 2nd ed. (1965; London and New York: Longman, 1979), p. 288, ll. 39–40.

12. As we shall see, Strachey 'inverts' this premise by deploying a 'line of beauty' that refuses to be compliant. The beauty of Strachey's prose style has long been a critical commonplace. See, e.g., Max Beerbohm, *Lytton Strachey*, The Rede Lecture (Cambridge: Cambridge, 1943), p. 25: "If I were asked what seemed to me the paramount quality of Lytton Strachey's prose, I should reply, in one word, Beauty."

13. James Field Stanfield, *An Essay on the Study and Composition of Biography* (Sunderland: George Garbutt, 1813), pp. 311–12. Subsequent references in this paragraph cited parenthetically by page number.

14. *Eclectic Review*, ser. 2 , 1(February 1814), 113–27; I quote from p. 125.

15. It has been rediscovered to some extent by recent scholarship. See, e.g., *Biography as an Art: selected criticism 1560–1960*, ed. James L. Clifford (New York: Oxford, 1962), pp. 60–71, where excerpts are reprinted; Richard D. Altick, *Lives and Letters: a history of literary biography in England and America* (New York: Alfred A. Knopf, 1965), pp. 184–85 and passim, where Stanfield's own career is traced and his book summarized and quoted; and Francis R. Hart, *Lockhart as Romantic Biographer* (Edinburgh: Edinburgh, 1971), pp. vi, 3, and passim, where Stanfield is characterized as "the most voluminous of biographi-

cal theorists" and cited and quoted frequently for his "pervasively Romantic principles."

16. Walter E. Houghton, *The Victorian Frame of Mind 1830–1870* (New Haven and London: Yale, 1957), p. 318.

17. James Anthony Froude, "Representative Men," in *Short Studies on Great Subjects* (New York: Charles Scribner, 1869), pp. 465–85. Subsequent references in this paragraph cited parenthetically by page number.

18. Froude, p. 472.

19. Charles Babbage, *A Comparative View of the Various Institutions for the Assurance of Lives* (London: J. Mawman, 1826; rpt. New York: Augustus M. Kelley, 1967), p. 105.

20. *Popular View of Life Assurance* (London: Jones and Causton, 1840), p. iv.

21. Besides Babbage and *Popular View,* see Algernon Frampton, *An Account of the Mutual Life Assurance Society: with remarks on the subject of life assurance generally* (London: Smith, Elder, 1830); and Lewis Pocock, *A Familiar Explanation of the Nature, Advantages, and Importance of Assurances Upon Lives* (London: Smith, Elder, 1842).

22. John Addington Symonds, *Essays Speculative and Suggestive* (London, 1890), I, II, cited and quoted in Philip Appleman, "Darwin: On Changing the Mind," in *Darwin,* ed. Philip Appleman, 2nd ed., Norton Critical Edition (1970; New York: W. W. Norton, 1979), p. 548.

23. "'This is an age of biography!' Never was a cliche more faithful to fact than this one, which echoed all the way down the long corridors of the nineteenth century," Altick, p. 77. See also Houghton, "Hero Worship," *Victorian Frame of Mind,* pp. 305–40; and, passim, Hart, *Lockhart,* and A. O. J. Cockshut, *Truth to Life: the art of biography in the nineteenth century* (London: Collins, 1974).

24. Thomas Carlyle, *Critical and Miscellaneous Essays,* in *The Works of Thomas Carlyle,* ed. H. D. Traill, Centenary Edition, 30 vols. (London: Chapman and Hall, 1898–1907), XXVIII, 80, 90. This is from "Boswell's Life of Johnson," pp. 62–135, a review for *Fraser's Magazine;* see also pp. 44–61, an influential essay published the same year in the same magazine, entitled "Biography."

25. Samuel Smiles, *Duty: with illustrations of courage, patience, and endurance* (London: John Murray, 1880), p. 21; *Character* (1872; New York: A. L. Burt, 188-?), p. 271; and *Self-Help: with illustrations of conduct and perseverance,* intro. Asa Briggs (1859; London: John Murray, 1958).

26. Edwin Paxton Hood, *The Uses of Biography: romantic, philosophic, and didactic* (London: Partridge and Oakley, 1852), pp. 11–12, 195.

27. Michael Foucault, *The History of Sexuality,* vol. 1: *An Introduction,* trans. Robert Hurley (1976; 1978; New York: Vintage, 1980), pp. 125–26, 139–43.

28. Foucault, p. 151. Subsequent references to Foucault in this paragraph are cited parenthetically by page number.

29. All biographical information in the preceding three paragraphs is from Michael Holroyd, *Lytton Strachey: a critical biography,* 2 vols. (New York, Chicago, San Francisco: Holt, Rinehart and Winston, 1967–68), II, 176–79, and passim. I have eliminated the paragraph break in Holroyd's narrative between the examiner's question and Strachey's response. In *Lytton Strachey: a biography* (Harmondsworth: Penguin, 1971), a revised one-volume edition of Holroyd's two-volume critical biography, Strachey's famous remark to the Board, uttered now with "ambiguous gravity," becomes "'I should try and come between them'" (p. 629). The specific reason for this change is not explained; in any event, the new wording more or less stresses the senses of 'interposition' explored in my narrative, and expresses the sexual pun even more clearly. Adopting Holroyd's stated preference in his "Preface to the Revised Edition" that the "original version" continue to serve "as a work of reference" (p. 24), I cite the two-volume edition throughout this chapter; in only one other instance among the materials I quote do the two versions differ significantly (see n. 62 below).

Based on masses of previously unpublished materials, Holroyd's biography is the most crucial event in Strachey scholarship. All the books and articles which appeared before it avoided what is now generally acknowledged to have been a powerful factor in Strachey's life and work, his homosexuality, although his sexual preferences were well known and at least some of those scholars had been allowed to inspect James Strachey's archive of letters and other documents. See Michael Holroyd, "Biographer's Progress," *Twentieth Century,* 1036(1968), 9–14. Martin Kallich provides a bibliography of reviews and criticism covering most of this earlier period in *English Fiction in Transition,* 5:3(1962), 1–77. Of this group the most frequently cited books or pamphlets are Guy Boas, *Lytton Strachey,* The English Association 93 (London: Oxford, 1935); K. R. Srinivasa Iyengar, *Lytton Strachey: a critical study* (1938; rpt. Port Washington, NY: Kennikat Press, 1967); Beerbohm, *Lytton Strachey* (1943)—cited earlier; J. K. Johnstone, *The Bloomsbury Group: a study of E. M. Forster, Lytton Strachey, Virginia Woolf, and their circle* (London: Secker and Warburg, 1954); R. A. Scott-James, *Lytton Strachey,* Writers and Their Work 65 (London, New York, Toronto: Longman, Green, 1955); Charles Richard Sanders, *Lytton Strachey: his mind and art* (New Haven: Yale; London: Oxford, 1957); and Martin Kallich, *The Psychological Milieu of Lytton Strachey* (New York: Bookman, 1961). Johnstone and Sanders are the most detailed and most useful. Holroyd also published the critical materials from his biography in a separate volume, *Lytton Strachey and the Bloomsbury Group: his work, their influence* (Harmondsworth: Penguin, 1971).

Holroyd is nearly the only person working intensely on Strachey: in the last twenty years only two articles of note on *Eminent Victorians* have appeared, in addition to chapters or sections on Strachey in various books on Bloomsbury and in general studies on biography. See John Halperin, "*Eminent Victorians* and History," *Virginia Quarterly Review,* 56:3(1980), 433–54, which follows a long tradition of treating Strachey as a minor artist who distorted historical fact; Ira Bruce Nadel, "'Lytton Strachey's 'Subtler Strategy': Metaphor in *Eminent Victorians*," *Prose Studies,* 4:2(1981), 146–52, which discusses military, animal, and other metaphors; see also, passim, Quentin Bell, *Virginia Woolf: a biography* (New York: Harcourt Brace Jovanovich, 1972), and *Bloomsbury* (New York: Basic Books, 1968), David Gadd, *The Loving Friends: a portrait of Bloomsbury* (New York and London: Harcourt Brace Jovanovich, 1974), *The Bloomsbury Group: a collection of memoirs, commentary and criticism,* ed. S. P. Rosenbaum (Toronto and Buffalo: Toronto, 1975), and Leon Edel, *Bloomsbury: a house of lions* (Philadelphia and New York: J. B. Lippincott, 1979); see also (this is only a partial list), Altick, "The Stracheyan Revolution," *Lives and Letters,* pp. 281–300, Novarr, *Lines of Life,* esp. pp. 27–31, Ira Bruce Nadel, *Biography: fiction, fact and form* (New York: St. Martin's, 1984), passim, and Leon Edel, *Writing Lives: principia biographica* (New York and London: W. W. Norton, 1984), passim.

An instructive review of Holroyd's biography is Goronwy Rees, "A Case for Treatment," *Encounter,* 30:3 (1968), 71–83, which, while inaccurate in some details, recognizes how "Mr. Holroyd's book has now made it impossible to write again about Strachey and his circle without accepting the fact, and its importance, of the part which homosexuality played in their lives" (80). Rees also writes perceptively about the pervasiveness throughout the twentieth century of homosexuality at Oxford and Cambridge and consequently in the British ruling classes, a point elaborated by George Steiner's 1975 essay "Eros and Idiom," later collected in *George Steiner: a reader* (New York: Oxford, 1984), pp. 314–44. Steiner discusses how "since about 1890 homosexuality has played a vital part in western culture and, perhaps even more significantly, in the myths and emblematic gestures which that culture has used in order to arrive at self-consciousness" (329).

30. Holroyd, II, 177.

31. Describing *Eminent Victorians* as, in one way or another, exhibiting a 'subtler strategy' is a traditional convention of Strachey scholarship, induced by the Preface and popularized by H. H. Asquith, the former prime minister, who, in the Romanes Lecture at Oxford in June 1918, praised "'Mr Strachey's subtle and suggestive art'" (Holroyd, II, 330–31). For a recent example, see Nadel, "Strachey's 'Subtler Strategy': Metaphor in *Eminent Victorians.*"

32. The relaxation of censorship over the last quarter century, the decriminalization of private, adult homosexual activities by parliamentary act in 1967, as well as the emergence of the gay-rights movement in general and gay studies in particular, have begun to produce a scholarship which examines Steiner's claim (referred to in a note above) that homosexuality has exerted a significant influence on contemporary life. This scholarship traces an emerging genealogy of homoeroticism in English culture, which reaches backward from Wilde and

his contemporaries (e.g., John Addington Symonds, Edward Carpenter, Walt Whitman, an honorary Englishman in this respect) through such literary figures as Byron, Beckford, Marlowe, and Shakespeare to the Greek philosophers, and which extends forward through the work of many of the most important twentieth-century British writers. Combined with Holroyd's biography, which details Strachey's sexual preferences and emotional relationships, this scholarship (enhanced by the work of Michel Foucault, Elaine Scarry, and Nancy Huston) has provided a context for my approach.

Among the works which I have found most useful are K. J. Dover, *Greek Homosexuality* (Cambridge: Harvard, 1978); Louis Crompton, *Byron and Greek Love: homophobia in 19th-century England* (Berkeley and Los Angeles: California, 1985); Timothy d'Arch Smith, *Love in Earnest: some notes on the lives and writings of English 'Uranian' poets from 1889 to 1930* (London: Routledge and Kegan Paul, 1970); Rictor Norton, *The Homosexual Literary Tradition: an interpretation* (New York: Revisionist Press, 1974); Jeffrey Meyers, *Homosexuality and Literature 1890–1930* (Montreal: McGill-Queen's, 1977); A. L. Rowse, *Homosexuals in History: a study of ambivalence in society, literature and the arts* (London: Weidenfeld and Nicolson, 1977); Eve Kosofsky Sedgwick, *Between Men: English literature and male homosocial desire* (New York: Columbia, 1985); H. Montgomery Hyde, *The Love That Dared Not Speak Its Name: a candid history of homosexuality in Britain* (Boston and Toronto: Little, Brown, 1970); D. J. West, *Homosexuality* (Chicago: Aldine, 1967); and Jeffrey Weeks, *Coming Out: homosexual politics in Britain, from the nineteenth century to the present* (London, Melbourne, New York: Quartet, 1977).

33. H. Montgomery Hyde, *Oscar Wilde: a biography* (London: Eyre Methuen, 1975), p. 185.

34. Oscar Wilde, *The Picture of Dorian Gray,* ed. Isobel Murray (London, New York, Toronto: Oxford, 1974), pp. 91–92. *Dorian Gray* was originally published in a magazine in 1890, then revised and expanded as a book for publication in 1891. Murray uses the 1891 first edition as her text.

35. See Havelock Ellis, *Sexual Inversion,* vol. 2 in *Studies in the Psychology of Sex,* 5 vols. (Philadelphia: F. A. Davis, 1904). The book was first published, in translation, in Germany in 1896. "An English edition, under the names of both Ellis and Symonds, appeared in 1897," but was bought up and Symonds' name "expunged from future editions" in the aftermath of Wilde's trials. See "Havelock Ellis and *Sexual Inversion,*" in Weeks, *Coming Out,* pp. 57–67. Weeks, Foucault, and others see works like *Sexual Inversion* as part of a general nineteenth-century discursive phenomenon: the creation of a medical model or *scientia sexualis,* which coined the term 'homosexual' (as well as others, like 'sexual invert' or 'ulrich') and identified the homosexual not as "a temporary aberration" but as "a species," characterized by a psychological and physiological pathology, "a certain way of inverting the masculine and feminine in oneself,

. . . a kind of interior androgyny, a hermaphrodism of the soul" (Foucault, p. 43).

36. *Dorian Gray,* p. 130. References to Wilde's novel in the next paragraph are cited parenthetically by page number.

37. Hyde, *Oscar Wilde,* p. 222. See also, passim, H. Montgomery Hyde, *The Trials of Oscar Wilde* (New York: Dover, 1962).

38. Hyde, *Oscar Wilde,* pp. 210–11, 214, 271n1.

39. An unsigned notice in the *Scots Observer,* 4(5 July 1890), 181, reprinted in *Oscar Wilde: the critical heritage,* ed. Karl Beckson (New York: Barnes and Noble, 1970), pp. 74–75. See also Hyde, *Oscar Wilde,* pp. 117–18. Hyde and others claim the review is by Charles Whibley, but Beckson disagrees.

40. The impact of Wilde's life and work on Strachey has been noted previously, most forcefully by Holroyd, who suggests parallels in their literary themes and styles as well as in their university careers, their manners of dress and talk, their personalities and reputations, their capacities to form intimate relationships and engender bitter enmity. "In both cases their homosexuality was tied to an exaggerated self-preoccupation which, with its accompanying passion for the applause of others, acted as the limiting factor in their creative output" (I, 201). Strachey maintained a lifelong interest in Wilde: reading books by and about him, befriending his acquaintances (like Max Beerbohm), starting a petition to reimburse the sculptor (Jacob Epstein) of Wilde's desecrated cemetery monument in Paris, and referring to him familiarly as 'Oscar' (thus incorporating him retrospectively in Bloomsbury's attack on last-name British formality).

41. Strachey's chronic invalidism and hypochondria is discussed throughout Holroyd's biography. "His resistance to illness was certainly weak, and he was plagued by a constant and unremitting succession of disorders throughout his life. But no one ever seemed to know what, fundamentally, was the cause of these maladies. . . . But, perhaps because his bad health was partly self-induced and not the result of a purely physical indisposition, no remedy, however far-fetched, was to secure his lasting improvement" (I, 43).

42. Elaine Scarry, *The Body in Pain: the making and unmaking of the world* (New York and Oxford: Oxford, 1985), pp. 252, 307–10.

43. Scarry, pp. 111–12, 128, 132.

44. Paul Fussell, *The Great War and Modern Memory* (New York and London: Oxford, 1975).

45. *Dorian Gray,* pp. 35, 57.

46. Early in their marriage, Queen Victoria and Prince Albert also reverse roles in Strachey's *Queen Victoria* (New York: Harcourt, Brace and World, 1921). "Albert very soon perceived that he was not master in his own house" (108); "was he the wife and she the husband?" (112).

47. Jacques Derrida, "The Law of Genre," trans. Avital Ronell, *Glyph,*

7(1980), 203–32. References in this paragraph cited parenthetically by page number.

48. Lytton Strachey, *Elizabeth and Essex: a tragic history* (New York: Harcourt, Brace & World, 1928), p. 8. The 'strangeness' exposed by historical or biographical inquiry is a constant theme in Strachey's work. As he wrote in his essay on "Voltaire," originally published in 1919: "The world is full of strange contradictions; and, on the whole, it is more interesting, and also wiser, to face them than to hush them up" (*Biographical Essays* [New York: Harcourt, Brace and World, 1949], p. 55). See also *Landmarks in French Literature* (1912; London: Chatto and Windus, 1948), p. 37: "as we look back upon it [the age of Louis XIV], we may still feel something of the old enchantment, and feel it, perhaps, the more keenly for its strangeness."

49. Nancy Huston, "The Matrix of War: Mothers and Heroes," in *The Female Body in Western Culture: contemporary perspectives,* ed. Susan Rubin Suleiman (Cambridge and London: Harvard, 1986), pp. 119–36.

50. For a somewhat recent example, see Rowse, *Homosexuals in History,* p. 271.

51. For the various biographical details cited here, see Holroyd, I, 155, II, 135, and (for the Apostles) passim, but esp. I, 157–239. See also Richard Deacon, *The Cambridge Apostles: a history of Cambridge University's elite intellectual secret society* (London: Robert Royce, 1985), esp. pp. 6, 38. The role that Strachey played in the Apostles, the impact it had on his life and on the Bloomsbury Group, and the continuing interest he maintained in it have been well documented. The society's current notoriety stems from spy scandals involving men who were undergraduates in the '30s, after Strachey's death, but its traditions of secrecy and homosexuality have brought even the earlier periods under a general, retrospective charge of subversiveness.

52. Sedgwick, "Gender Asymmetry and Erotic Triangles," *Between Men,* pp. 21–27, and Foucault, *History of Sexuality,* p. 99 and passim. Strachey characteristically formed triangular relationships, some of which included Dora Carrington, with whom he lived for the last fifteen years of his life in a relationship of deep emotional attachment that (apparently) did not involve sexual relations. Holroyd writes: "If she could attract the boy-friends whom he liked, then, she felt, her place with him was reasonably secure, her influence more indispensable" (II, 377). Although this triangular relationship seems to describe one of the traditional patterns by which (Sedgwick claims) male homosocial desire exploits the female body, the situation is much more complex. Carrington also exploited Strachey, triangulating her relationships with men and women through her attachment to him, which she used as an elaborate cover for her frigidity and promiscuity. A literary indication of Strachey's interest in the mutability of gender and the variation of sexuality is *Ermyntrude and Esmeralda* (New York: Stein and Day, 1969), written in 1913, a brief, fictional tale de-

scribing the sexual awakening of two young girls, in which gender roles and sexual preferences are constantly varying. It should also be pointed out that Strachey was an occasional transvestite (usually for costume balls and informal dramatic evenings), identified closely with the powerful female figures he wrote about (such as Queen Elizabeth, Queen Victoria, Florence Nightingale, Madame du Deffand), and was constantly trying out new roles (both passive and dominant) in his physical relationships.

53. Milic Capek, *The Philosophical Impact of Contemporary Physics* (Princeton, NJ, Toronto, New York, London: D. Van Nostrand, 1961), pp. 177–83. See also Floyd Merrell, *Deconstruction Reframed* (West Lafayette, IN: Purdue, 1985), pp. 103–05.

54. See Jacques Derrida, "Signature Event Context," *Glyph,* 1(1977), 172–97. See also Jonathan Culler, *On Deconstruction: theory and criticism after structuralism* (Ithaca, NY: Cornell, 1982), p. 123, who summarizes the Derridean postmodern position in what is now a familiar formulation: "Total context is unmasterable, both in principle and practice. Meaning is context-bound, but context is boundless."

55. Cyril Connolly, *Enemies of Promise,* rev. ed. (New York: Macmillan, 1948), p. 47.

56. Leon Edel, *Literary Biography* (1959; Bloomington and London: Indiana, 1973), p. 139. The term with which I describe *Orlando* here, 'mock-biography,' can be defined as a narrative that (re)presents itself as a biography yet has a conventionally misrecognized biographical subject (that is, one which, in ordinary cultural terms, is not recognized as one or more of the following—individual, human, extra-discursive). See Chapter 5, "Recognizing the Biographical Subject."

57. Virginia Woolf, *Orlando: a biography* (1928; New York: Harcourt Brace Jovanovich, n.d.), pp. 119, 294–95.

58. A. J. A. Symons, *The Quest for Corvo: an experiment in biography* (London, Toronto, Melbourne, Sydney: Cassell, 1934), pp. 14, 136, 165.

59. See William H. Epstein, "Milford's *Zelda* and the Poetics of the New Feminist Biography," *Georgia Review,* 36:2(1982), 335–50.

60. Holroyd, I, 425–36.

61. Quoted from the manuscript and dated in Quentin Bell, *Virginia Woolf: a biography,* 2 vols. (New York: Harcourt Brace Jovanovich, 1972), I, 124.

62. For instance, Holroyd (I, 212) describes "a special glossary" for deciphering the homosexual language of Strachey's Cambridge circle: "To 'propose' would seem to indicate little more than the slight ambiguous pressure of one hand upon another [or, "little more than an invitation to use Christian names," in the revised version of Holroyd's biography, p. 244]; to 'rape' or even to 'bugger' usually means a peck on the cheek, or a dubious embrace."

63. Foucault, p. 103.

64. The distinctions here between the labor and the desire of the body are Scarry's, p. 284. See also Kallich, *The Psychological Milieu of Lytton Strachey,* who explores Strachey's interest in Freudian approaches but never discusses Strachey's homosexuality.

65. Lytton Strachey, "Macaulay," *Literary Essays* (New York: Harcourt Brace and World, 1949), p. 199. The essay was first published in 1928.

66. Sedgwick (pp. 206–08) and others have distinguished two dominant 'styles' of male homosexuality in late nineteenth- and early twentieth-century England. The traditional aristocratic mode, associated with Beckford and Byron and applied retrospectively to Wilde, was leisured, affluent, cosmopolitan, 'feminine,' 'tragic,' decadent, and aesthetic; the emerging middle-class mode, more or less actively promoted by Edward Carpenter (*Homogenic Love* and *The Intermediate Sex*) and J. A. Symonds (co-author of *Sexual Inversion*), was democratized, domesticated, virile, idealistic, and socialistic. Such categorizations are always facile, but to the extent that they can be applied to Strachey he could be described as exhibiting the public 'pose' of the aristocratic style, mixed occasionally with the radical politics of the middle-class style (although even his pacifism and feminism could be construed as the assertion or gratification of upper-class privilege). In any event, as Holroyd's biography demonstrates over and over again, such formal distinctions are soon obscured by the constant variance of individual human behavior.

67. Symons, *Quest for Corvo,* pp. 236, 249. Strachey dubbed one symptom of his last illness "the Strachey twist," a convulsive spasm which Holroyd reads symbolically as "the literal, premature straining of his spirit to wriggle free from the dying carcass in which it was incarcerated" (II, 688–89), and which we can also interpret as yet another 'twist' or 'curve' with which his body interposes itself in the recognition of the life-course.

Index

prison reform, 133; project of, 79; province of, 137; referential space, 79; rupture in, 103; strai(gh)tened, 146; supplementary trait, 166; and textualization, 41–42; threatened, 81; and transfer of authority, 74–75; and truth, 43; underwritten, 81. *See also* Cognitive activity; Generic recognition; Historical recognition; Literary recognition; Misrecognition; Poetics; Recognition

Biographical subject, 33; anthropomorphized, 82–83; authorizes conversion, 19–20; and biographer, 20–21, 23–25, 29–30, 32, 53, 67–70, 74, 80–81, 102, 108, 115, 128, 166, 170–71, 193 n.5; biography as commission of, 16; before 1700, 79–80; and class hierarchy, 69; commercialized, 79; commodified, 114; and consumerism, 66–67; course of career, 168; as cultural outlaw, 75, 85, 88; decentered, 75, 85–88; demand for, 66; democratized, 78; as discursive specimen, 76; exploited, 103; as fashion doll, 66; and fictional subject, 77; as figure and person, 194 n.12; in flux, 65, 72; force of, 54; and historical subject, 173 n.1; master-sign and generative model, 74, 76, 84, 88; as material figure, 76; as metaphysical presence, 197 n.26; misrecognized, 84–88, 213 n.56; as monument, 27–30, 91, 124–25; original sameness, 88; patronizing of, 52–70, 74, 77–80, 84–85; and pattern, 72–77, 84–85; pattern and character, 197–98 n.26; poly-functional, 41; as producer, 74; professional reputation of, 143; as property, 121; and reader, 73, 87; recognition of, 71–89; as remembered patron/pattern, 76, 80, 82; Savage as eminently apposite, 69; Shakespeare as, 41; space-time configurations of, 37; submits, 82; supply of, 65; underwrites English biography, 80; value of, 102; virtually materialized 80. *See also* Subject.

Biographical subjection, 54

Biography, age of, 207 n.23; ally of authority, 41; as altar, 19–23; altering life and text, 32; American, 4; "applied" or "mixed," 7–8; as an art, 43, 136, 181 n.9; aspires to literary status, 64; and autobiography, 81, 114–20; as axiological project, 129; before Johnson and Boswell, 71; best plan of, 124; Bible as, 145–47; 'biographia,' 127; and bio-power, 146–48; as *bios.* 86; capital of, 123; chairman of, 106; character, 198 n.26; charm of, 145; classical Greek and Roman, 10, 75, 85–86, 124, 198 n.26; client of dominant authority, 68; as commerce, 74, 79; conditions that produce, 70; as conversion, 17–20; as converting vision, 30; corruption of blood, 8–9; criminal, 65, 133; debunking, 32; ecclesiastical, 19, 31, 68, 79, 151, 181 n.19; economy of, 5–6, 67, 70, 72–75, 94, 96; as employment, 18, 26–27, 32–33; and eighteenth-century fiction, 193 n.7; and eighteenth-century history, 194 n.7; English, 3–5, 7, 10, 14, 19–20, 27, 31–33, 40, 53, 55, 67, 70, 75, 79–80, 92, 131, 136–37, 143, 148, 150, 164, 166, 169; as errand or commission, 16; as a genre, 1–2; Greek, 10, 85–86, 198 n. 26; hagiography, 19, 31, 41, 53, 55, 138, 144, 151, 162, 181 n.9; hierarchical, 65; and history, 45–46, 173 n.1; as house of correction, 132–37; as implement, 16; as individualizing tactic, 54, 71–72; ironic, 50; Johnson as father/patron of, 69; law of, 3, 8; as 'life,' 21; limits of, 123; literary, 9–10; a looking backward, 140; magazine, 65; manufacturing of, 91, 126; mock, 67, 168, 213 n.56; as monument, 27–30, 33, 124–25; as museum of life, 43; narrow compass of, 129; new species of, 91–92, 118; panegyric, 10; and panopticism, 132; and pastoral power, 53–54, 67, 69–70, 71–73; and patronage, 54, 64–70; perfection of, 128; and philology, 88; poetics of, 6, 9, 43, 49; popularity of, 1, 173 n.2; and portrait paint-

Person, 194 n.12
"Peters, Cleanth" (Stephen Heath), 186
    n.5
Petöfi, Jenos, 175 n.6
Petrie, Dennis, 10, 177 n.18
Piaget, Jean, 175 n.6
Piozzi, Hester Lynch Thrale, 94, 135;
    Anecdotes, 135
Plant, Marjorie, 190 n.7
Plumb, J.H., 65, 192 n.26, 195 n.13,
    200 n.3
Plutarch, 49, 75, 91, 124, 183 n.16,
    193 n.5
Pocock, J.G.A., 93, 200 n.4
Pocock, Lewis, 207 n.21
Poetics, of biography, 6, 9, 43, 49; of
    history, 174 n.3; post-modern, 1–2,
    4, 11. *See also* Biographical recogni-
    tion; Generic recognition; Genre;
    Historical recognition; Misrecogni-
    tion; Recognition
Polanyi, Michael, 35
Pompey, 17, 30
Pope, Alexander, 63
Popper, Karl, 35
Pose, of body politic, 157; homoerotic,
    164; homosexual, 214 n.66; motif of,
    152–55, 206 n.9; of the sodomite,
    164. *See also* Interposition
Potter, George R., 184 n.23
Pottinger, David T., 190 n.7
Pottle, Frederick A., 184 n.26, 185
    n.27, 198–99 n.2, 201 nn.12–13,
    202 n.18, 203 n.31
Pottle, Marion, 199 n.2
Powell, L.F., 184 n.27, 191 n.17, 196
    n.17, 198 n.1, 201 n.13
Preservation, 120–25, 132; in Boswell's
    Life, 203 n.29; defined, 121; em-
    balming, 203 n.33; of facts, 42–43
Pre-text, 45–46, 48, 50, 187 n.17
Prince, Gerald, 47, 188 n.24
Professional careerism, 139–41, 144–
    45, 158–59, 204 n.8. *See also* Career;
    Doctrine of pursuits; Life-course; Pur-
    suit
Property, and copyright, 107–8, 110–
    15; interest of, 107; and labor, 110–
    11; literary and hereditary, 107–14;
    Lockean, 100–101, 111. *See also*
    Copyright

Prose Studies, 1, 9
Proto-biography, Walton's elegy on
    Donne as, 19–20
Pursuit, curve of, 142; as the doctrine of
    the life-course, 143–48, 166; mean-
    ings of, 142–43. *See also* Career; Doc-
    trine of pursuits; Life-course;
    Professional careerism

Rabinow, Paul, 189 n.1
Rader, Ralph W., 199 n.2
Rae, David, Lord Eskgrove, 111–13,
    203 n.23
Randall, Ruth P., 197 n.20
Rashleigh, John Colman, 100
Raskin, Victor, 175 n.6
Ray, William, 175 n.5
Reality, sense of (Bourdieu), 83
Recognition, of the biographer, 4–5,
    90–137; biographical, compared to
    literary and historical, 1–2, 188 n.27;
    biographical and historical, 1–2, 45,
    173 n.1, 174 n.3; of the biographical
    subject, 3–4, 71–89; generic, 174
    n.3; historical, 174 n.3; of the life-
    course, 4, 138–71; of the life-text,
    34–51; meanings of, 2, 174–75 n.5;
    and misrecognition, 83. *See also* Bio-
    graphical recognition; Cognitive ac-
    tivity; Frame; Generic frame; Generic
    recognition; Historical recognition;
    Literary recognition; Misrecognition
Recollection, 123–25. *See also* Memory
Redford, Polly, 197 n.20
Reed, Joseph W., 177 n.20
Rees, Goronwy, 209 n.29
Reichard, Hugo M., 199, n.2
Relativity, theory of (Einstein), 166–67
Rewa, Michael P., 10, 177 n.19, 181
    n.9
Reynolds, Joshua, 94, 99, 107
Reynolds, Sian, 200 n.3
Richardson, Samuel, 193 n.7
Richetti, John, 204 n.43
Reidlinger, Albert, 187 n.19
Rimbaud, Jean-Nicholas-Arthur, 164
Rivers, Richard Savage, 4th Earl, 60
Rivers, Isabel, 190 n.9
Roberts, Michael, 195 n.13
Robinson, E., 195 n.13, 200 n.3